JUDAISM in COLD WAR AMERICA 1945-1990

edited
with introductions by

Jacob Neusner
UNIVERSITY OF SOUTH FLORIDA

KANSAS SCHOOL OF RELIGION
UNIVERSITY OF KANSAS
1300 OREAD AVENUE
LAWRENCE, KANSAS 66044

A Garland Series

Contents of Series

Volume 1
The Challenge of America: Can Judaism Survive in Freedom?

Volume 2
In the Aftermath of the Holocaust

Volume 3
Israel and Zion in American Judaism: The Zionist Fulfillment

Volume 4
Judaism and Christianity: The New Relationship

Volume 5
The Religious Renewal of Jewry

Volume 6
The Reformation of Reform Judaism

Volume 7
Conserving Conservative Judaism: Reconstructionist Judaism

Volume 8
The Alteration of Orthodoxy

Volume 9
The Academy and Traditions of Jewish Learning

Volume 10
The Rabbinate in America: Reshaping an Ancient Calling

VOLUME 10

The Rabbinate in America: Reshaping an Ancient Calling

edited with introduction by
Jacob Neusner

Garland Publishing, Inc.
New York and London 1993

Introduction copyright © 1993 by Jacob Neusner
All rights reserved

Library of Congress Cataloging-in-Publication Data

The Rabbinate in America : reshaping an ancient calling / edited by Jacob Neusner.
    p. cm. — (Judaism in Cold War America, 1945–1990 ; v. 10)
  ISBN 0-8153-0082-4
  1. Rabbis—United States—Office. 2. Judaism—United States—History—20th century. I. Neusner, Jacob, 1932–   . II. Series.
BM652.R335   1993
296.6'1—dc20   92-37068
                                                                                CIP

Printed on acid-free, 250-year-life paper
Manufactured in the United States of America

Contents

Volume Introduction vii

Inner Dynamics of the Rabbinate
Jack H. Bloom 2

The Seminary and the Modern Rabbi
Arthur Cohen 9

The Function of the Rabbi
Nathan Glazer 22

The Role of the Rabbi Today
Robert Gordis 36

The Rabbinate—A Restless Body of Men
Ephraim Greenberg 45

The Rabbinate and the Jewish Community Structure
Simon Greenberg 58

The Changing American Rabbinate
Arthur Hertzberg 66

The Intellectual and the Rabbi
Milton Himmelfarb 80

The Synagogue in America
Wolfe Kelman 95

The End Is Where We Start From...
Theodore I. Lenn 116

The Changing Rabbinate: A Search for Definition
Stanley Rabinowitz; Arthur Hertzberg, The Changing Rabbinate 141

The Inner Life of the Rabbi
Victor E. Reichert, Marcus Kramer and Ephraim F. Einhorn 161

The American Rabbi in Transition
Max J. Routtenberg 167

A Rabbi Dies
Richard L. Rubenstein 180

Studying at Hebrew Union College, 1942–1945
Richard Rubenstein 194

The Future of Rabbinic Training in America
A Symposium: Arnold Jacob Wolf, Daniel Jeremy Silver,
   Sheldon Zimmerman, Mark Loeb, Ira Eisenstein,
   Emanuel Rackman, Eugene Weiner, Eugene B. Borowitz,
   Arthur Green, Seymour Siegel, Charles S. Liebman 201

The Conservative Rabbinate—In Quest of Professionalism
Viviana A. Zelizer and Gerald L. Zelizer 236

Acknowledgements 243

Introduction

The rabbi, the principal religious leader of the Judaism that appeals to the Torah, written and oral, as God's will for Israel and humanity, has been defined in a variety of ways. In the first and second immigrant generations, the rabbi was the spokesman for Jewry, the educated and articulate Jew, who could speak English well (thus the first generation could appeal to his leadership) and who also knew the Jewish tradition (which made a difference to the second generation). Rabbis founded major organizations; for example, Stephen Wise founded the American Jewish Congress and the World Jewish Congress. They held principal offices in important movements; for instance, Abba Hillel Silver was a leading figure in American Zionism, and in general rabbis formed the principal cadre of American Jewish leadership. Riches as such did not qualify. In Cold War America, the rabbi was understood to be the religious authority of a particular synagogue. He (after the early 1970s, he or she) was not assumed to be a candidate for important positions of community leadership or to serve as an authority for the Jews beyond the walls of his or her synagogue.

Two other types of leadership competed with the rabbi for priority in Jewish community affairs, the rich, qualified by wealth to direct affairs (so they thought), and the secular but bureaucratically well-trained. The latter were products not of a religious education in the Torah, but of a university education in social work and community administration. Rabbis' leadership may be classified as charismatic, administrators' as routine; the former led by reason of personal gifts of knowledge and character. The latter appealed to their know-how in getting things done. While the rich exercised influence episodically, the real contest for long-term influence and power in Jewry was between the rabbis and the bureaucrats, and Jewry in the corporate model prevailed—and passed the community over into the hands of the rich.

These "professional Jews" who run the Jewish institutions and organizations that constitute for the ordinary folk the "holy way" are anonymous, faceless, wholly secular. People relate to them no differently than they do to other bureaucrats, in government offices, public schools, and department stores. One Jewish functionary, however, the common people continue to regard as quintessentially "Jewish," important and formative of values. The least powerful and least effective figure is the rabbi. For nearly twenty centuries the rabbi was the holy man of Judaic tradition. He became a rabbi through study of Torah, which comprehended not only the Hebrew Scriptures, but also the Oral Torah, believed to have been handed on in Mosaic revelation and eventually recorded in the pages of the Babylonian Talmud and related literature. The rabbi was a holy man consecrated not by prayer, though he prayed, nor by asceticism, though he assumed taxing disciplines, but by study and knowledge of Torah. That knowledge made him not merely learned or wise, but a saint, and endowed him with not only information, but also insight into the workings of the universe. Consequently, in former times rabbis were believed to have more than commonplace merits, therefore more than ordinary power over the world, and some of them, especially qualified by learning and piety, were seen as being able to pray more effectively than common people and to accomplish miracles.

Today the rabbi (now both women and men) will be an essentially peripheral figure in organized Jewish life, outside of the framework of the synagogue. Dropping the rabbi out of the decision-making circles of the Jewish community merely took account of the rabbi's profoundly different role. Formerly judge, administrator, holy man, scholar, and saint, in American Judaism the rabbi at first served as a rather secular leader of a rather secular community, spokesman for Jews to Gentiles, representative of his synagogue to the larger Jewish group, agent of Zionist propaganda, and certifier of the values of the upper-class Jews who employed him. But as time passed these roles and tasks passed into the hands of others, better equipped for them because of community position, economic power, and public acceptance. By the 1950s a truly professional Jewish civil service was in control in the more enlightened communities. The rabbi was left to preside at circumcisions, weddings and funerals, to "conduct" religious worship, which, in traditional synagogues, meant to announce pages and tell people when to stand up and sit down, to counsel the troubled, and to teach the children, in all a slightly anachronistic figure, a medicine man made obsolete by penicillin.

But that is not the whole story. With the decline of the effectiveness of education enterprises, the rabbi, who normally was nearly the only Jew in town who could read Hebrew and intelligently comprehend a Jewish book, stood apart for the same reason as in classical times. He was distinguished because of his learning. So far as access to Judaic tradition and capacity to comprehend Judaic thinking proved important, the rabbi continued to hold the key to the mind and intellect of Judaism. Second, and still more important, while the rabbi could be made into a pathetic remnant of ancient glories of his office, he remained the rabbi. The title and the role persisted in setting the rabbi apart from others, in making him a kind of holy man. In psychological terms, he continued to function as a surrogate father and God. Secularity did not, could

Introduction

not in the end, deprive him of his role as a religious figure, even leader. The holy man remained just that, even to the most secular people.

Today, the rabbi serves primarily his or her congregation. In a sense the rabbi has become a more religious figure than earlier. That means, to be sure, rabbis have less power in Jewish communal affairs, but it is likely that they now enjoy more influence than before, and influence in shaping the ideas and purposes of others represents significant power to achieve concrete ends. The rabbi does not stand at the head of organizations, of community bureaus. But the rabbi stands behind those who do, for Jewish leaders nearly universally belong to synagogues and rely upon religious rites at least at the time of life crises—birth, puberty, marriage, death. They are accessible to the rabbi's words.

Above all, community leaders are under the spell of the rabbi as a holy person, in a way in which the passing generation was not. To be sure, lay people are as well educated as the rabbi in many ways. But in respect to the knowledge of Judaism, standards of literacy have fallen so much that the rabbi now predominates in precisely the one area appropriate to his calling. So far as people remain Jews, they depend more than ever upon rabbis to explain to them why and what they should mean. It is the rabbi who retains the prestige and the learning to fill that empty commitment of Jews to being Jewish with purpose and meaning. The real foundations for the rabbinical position are the convictions people retain from archaic times about holy men, set aside for God and sanctified by sacred disciplines. In archaic times the rabbi was a holy man because of his mastery of Torah. Today the rabbi remains a holy man for that very reason. Thus far we have seen the sociological side of that holiness: The rabbi continues functionally to dominate because of his knowledge of Torah. With women now included, the rabbi has new opportunities for effective contemporary service.

The advent of women to the Reform and Conservative and Reconstructionist rabbinates has already given the Reform sector of the Jewish community access to talent formerly excluded from the pulpit. With the ordination of women in the Conservative and Reconstructionist rabbinates, the vast majority of American Jews—certainly 80 percent of the whole—now turn to women, as much as to men, as authority figures in Judaism. The renewed energy flowing from the formerly excluded half of the Jewish people already has made its mark. Women in synagogues find themselves more normal, more at home, than they could when only men occupied liturgical and other positions of symbolic importance and real power. Highly talented young women, who formerly would have chosen other callings or professions, now aspire to the rabbinate. In these and other obvious ways, the advent of women to the rabbinate has redefined the profession and renewed its promise.

The Rabbinate in America: Reshaping an Ancient Calling

Inner Dynamics of the Rabbinate

Rabbi Jack H. Bloom
Fairfield, Connecticut

I want to share some of my personal history which brought me to the work I ended up doing for my dissertation at Columbia. I began very much adoring and loving the pulpit, to some extent being seduced by those years, but by the time the sixth or seventh or eighth year came along I found myself isolated and alone, living behind a glass wall. That feeling became intolerable for me and I left the pulpit. On the way out, I got a Ph.D. To get a Ph.D., a student needs a lot of energy. While wandering around the first couple of years trying to think of a topic for my dissertation, what finally hit me was one which could mobilize most of my energy.

What I tried to do with my dissertation was to figure out what had happened during the ten years of my pulpit existence, because in many ways I enjoyed being a rabbi and it would have been a worthwhile carrer to continue. What I came to realize was that probably the most distinguishing factor of the pulpit rabbi, and the pulpit clergyman in general, is that he is, most of all, a symbolic exemplar. The rabbi is the symbol of something other than himself and the pulpit rabbi is a symbolic leader who is set apart to function within his community as a symbol of that community and as an exemplar of that community's desire for moral perfection. The rabbi is a walking, talking, living symbol and stands for something other than himself. In order to function effectively he must be seen and perceived in that way so he can have the power to change the future of the American Jewish community. In order to be effectual the rabbi must not act in such a way as to destroy that symbol.

It is crucial for the rabbi to fulfill the symbolic aspects of the role. The major expectation is that the rabbi in some crucial way is expected to be a different kind of human being. He is the embodiment of what people ought to do but have no intention of doing. He is expected to be different in his morality, in how he cares for people and thus different as a husband and as a father.

The pulpit rabbi must truly care and must fully believe, or at least he must be seen as fully believing, in what he is doing. Who he is is much more important than what he does. In my own work I've measured what laymen expect of rabbis vis-à-vis other professions. The crucial factor in terms of their expectation of the rabbi always has to do not with the rabbi's skills, not with how he functions, but who the man is and, most importantly, the authenticity of the rabbi.

Other people are hired or fired or valued in terms of what they do. The rabbi is valued in terms of who he is perceived to be. For the symbol to exist the rabbi must have special attributes. He is expected to be a different kind of person and that expectation makes functioning as a clergyman a hazardous job. A doctor may have his bedside manner, a teacher his classroom presence, an executive may be a tiger on the job and a pussycat at home, but a rabbi is expected to be the same person on and off the job. If he is not, then how do you measure real caring and true believing?

What was intiguing to me was how rabbis and laymen work together at maintaining the symbol because the symbolic exemplar is the essence of a rabbi and to break the symbol is to lose efficacy. You may have an objection, you may say that rabbis are not the only walking, talking symbols. There are celebrities in royalty and presidents of countries and it is true that all of these people are public property and are symbols. That's not an illusion. The public has adopted as celebrity the queen of England and our President as a certain kind of symbol, and they expect them to fill the role of that symbol. President Carter recently held a news conference and his face was somber concerning Iran, but one of the newscasters at a local station pointed out that when the President was off-stage talking to his press officer, he didn't look solemn any more. He was pleased with how things had gone and the solemnity about Iran was part of his public image. Having the private image and the public image contradict becomes risky because the newscaster asked, "Did he really mean it?" If he didn't mean it, "Can you trust him?"

Let me tell you a story about a man who played at being a symbol. Some of you may remember the TV serial, Ben Casey, starring Vince Edwards. Listen to Vince Edwards' description of himself after he had been Ben Casey for a while. Vince Edwards had become uncomfortably aware of the discrepancies between his own life, which happened to include a devotion to betting on horses, and the god-like image that he had come to represent to the public. "I won't do anything to destroy the image," he said, and he tried to keep his private life subdued and separate, yet it was not easy because magazines published pictures of his horseplaying and the public watched him every possible moment and even his close friends began to be affected. Vince Edwards stated, "Some of my old friends begin to weigh their words when we get together now. They don't see me as plain old Vince Edwards. What they see now is the image. They see Ben Casey. And it makes a

3

difference, believe me. Their attitude changes, they stiffen and I can't say I like it, and I'm not sure I like losing a little privacy. I wish it were different in some ways, the whole success thing, but that's how it is. How do you fight it?"

That happens when a man is only a role on T.V. He is playing at being a doctor. He is not a doctor, and not only not a doctor, but not even a rabbi. You can imagine what happens to a rabbi, who is so visible and so unprotected, because the rabbi is expected to be a symbol without this physical distance, and is expected to be a unique and moral person.

Rabbis maintain the symbol. There is variation, of course. Not all rabbis are the same. Some accept the exemplarhood of being a rabbi, work hard at it and try hard to be consistent, fair, sensitive, pious and moral models. Virtually all of us do some editing; we act the role. We try to keep the private private and relish anonymity when we can get it. We channel our anger only in what we consider to be appropriate places, keep some distance, act circumspect. It is true that prudence, politeness and restraint help to maintain the symbolic image. Each of us has the inner sense that there is a limit to the symbol, and we act in such a way so as not to break those limits.

The layman does a great deal to create a symbolic exemplar of the rabbi. If you ask a layman, "Is the rabbi human," he says, "Yes, he is human, but...." And he always attributes special attributes to the rabbi. The rabbi is supposed to be more moral, more learned.

Let me tell you a story which is a superb example of this. Back in 1973 my wife Meryl was about to go to Israel, and she was going for the first time by herself. She got her own passport. It was the beginning of women's liberation and she was going off to be the solid independent woman I always wanted her to be and I was scared out of my wits. Our congregation was just starting to give *aliyot* to women, and I called the Ritual Chairman and asked him to give my wife an *aliyah* because she was going to Israel. Unfortunately he did not tell our rabbi about the trip. Meryl got up and went to the Torah with her knees knocking. It was her first time and she was nervous. The rabbi went through the announcements, didn't say a word about Meryl and the trip, and Meryl sat there, poked me, and said, "You know, for ten years I sat with the congregation, I slept next to you at night, I listened to you do all that junk, wishing people well on their twenty-fifth anniversary, fiftieth anniversary, all kinds of occasions. I listened to you do all that stuff. I'm nervous about this trip and if he doesn't say anything and he doesn't bless me and he doesn't wish me well, I'm going to be as sore as hell." And she said to me, without another word, "You can't do it for me. You are not my rabbi."

Once a rabbi, always a rabbi. Once you've presented yourself in that symbolic role, once you've done a wedding, a bar mitzvah, you are always a rabbi.

In the course of my research one of the men who I interviewed had replaced another rabbi who had gone into the stock market. In his congregation the new rabbi was constantly being asked by the *balebatim*, "Do you think it is right for a rabbi to be a stock broker?" The rabbi asked them what they might have accepted as a legitimate change for a rabbi, and they said, "A social worker, you know, a non-mercenary kind of enterprise." The rabbi asked them why they felt that way, and they said, "Because you fellows are in the rabbinate. That's a lifetime calling, and there is no way out. There is something special about it and people depend on you."

What are some of the consequences for the rabbi and his wife? For those rabbis for whom the symbol and the self are really one, there is very little problem. They function very well in the pulpit for years and years and years, and they are some of the very great rabbis of America. But I found that over the years, there is a sense of being set apart that increases with time, a kind of loneliness in the midst of the crowd, a sense of living behind a glass wall, the rabbi looking out and other people looking in. The rabbi is often aware that he is loved for being what he appears to be and not for what he feels himself to be. The more he is rewarded for his appearance, the more his humanness becomes a source of embarrassment to him, and the more inadequate he feels in his ability to authentically fulfill expectations. You get a greater sense of discomfort and the glass walls become thicker.

I swore the first two years of my career that as I watched other rabbis living behind the glass walls that that would not happen to me. I would wear Bermuda shorts, which were fashionable at that time, play tennis, be a regular guy and be the rabbi. At the end of six years I found myself behind a glass wall. I didn't know how that had happened. Now I know.

There is another danger in addition to being set apart from others. When I had a pulpit, going to the kosher-style supermarket to get a carton of milk was hard work. I had to ask everyone about their families. If I didn't smile wide enough or if I ran through in a hurry to get milk, people would say I was cold. When I got back from Israel and was no longer in the pulpit, I discovered something very interesting. When I went to the same supermarket for a carton of milk, I said hello to some people because it was important for me to say hello to those people and I didn't say hello to others, and I couldn't have cared less.

A Reform rabbi explained that we rabbis are professional lovers. One thing about being a professional lover is that you're paid to love every sheep in the flock — and the measure of your loving is that your loving has to be authentic. You really have to love them all. What happens is you start to lose touch with your own feelings and that becomes very dangerous. There are rabbis who can't get out of the role.

Let me say something about rabbi's wives and families. There is no rabbi's wife who has not married a symbol. They all want to say that they married a husband who happens to be in the rabbinate. They also married a symbol and there is an overflow from the symbol onto their lives because if the symbolic expectation of the rabbi is that he be a special, caring loving kind of man, the expectation is also that he will have a model relationship with his wife and his family and that his family will be the exemplar of the Jewish family. His family as a matter of fact is the proof of the pudding that he really is the authentic kind of model that he has presented himself and laymen have perceived him to be. Thus the boundary between the rabbi's public life and his private life is a dangerously vulnerable boundary. The relationship with the congregation is a marriage, and the experience of splitting with it is a divorce. The rabbi has to pay first concern to his own family but that whole relationship puts extra stuff into the rabbi's pot.

Rabbis never belong in the communities in which they live. The rabbinic community is your community. The proof of that pudding is not only what happens in those communities. The proof of the pudding is that rabbis are an anomaly. When you ask rabbis to describe who their best friends are, they'll describe people they went to school with fifteen, twenty, twenty-five years ago.

Symbolic exemplarhood in the moral and religious realm provides the rabbi with a larger-than-life image. There is no way around it. Such an image is at the very core of being a rabbi. The rabbi is designated by others and volunteers himself to exemplify a caring, nurturing, involved moral person. He is in a profession in which it is crucial to appear to be something more than he is, while still maintaining ongoing contact with other people. He is the willing helper, the good father, the para-familial member of many families. To help him maintain this role, he is given significant protection, he is treated with respect and deference and shielded, overtly at least, from others' anger and vulgarity, and he is not subjected to many of the stresses that others are subjected to. Without such protection he could not continue to maintain close contact and still function as an exemplar of those attributes he is expected to symbolize. The price of this protection for the rabbi is a sense of otherness or loneliness in the midst of a crowd. Barriers erected by both layman and rabbi which create this insulated and isolated existence are made up of masks put on, words edited and emotions held in check.

I don't want you to go away with the idea of denigrating this symbolic exemplarhood. It is your symbolic exemplarhood which makes your words count. There are very few people who forget who officiated at their wedding. They may even remember the words the rabbi said. They will remember the experience of their bar mitzvah. It is your symbolic exemplarhood that makes it possible for you to do your work and the work of changing the future of the American Jewish community. It is the source of your power. One of the sad things I see from time to time is rabbis railing against it, wishing it wouldn't be, trying to destroy it, without the awareness that they would be destroying the very thing that gives them the ability to do what they do.

In my ten years as a congregational rabbi I did more important work, affected more lives, changed more people and made more Jews than I will in the rest of my career. I know that it was me and my symbolic exemplarhood role in the end that changed and moved these people. Every time you get up to speak, you do so as a symbol, not only as a man and as a human being. If you are really unhappy with it, then you may have to take a look elsewhere. To try to continue to be a rabbi and destroy the symbol will not be useful to you as a pulpit rabbi. Symbolic exemplarhood is inevitable, and it is a vitally useful way to live. It is that which gives you and every rabbbi the power and ability to affect and influence others. I don't think you will ever be free of being a symbolic exemplar, but knowing the burden, perhaps we can deal with it.

THE SEMINARY AND THE MODERN RABBI

ARTHUR COHEN

THE MODERN rabbi is the victim of a misalliance: the union of Western secular enlightenment and historical Judaism. The union could not be avoided. The misalliance was inevitable. The dilemma of the rabbinate is that now — nearly a hundred years after its office and its authority had been undermined — the American religious revival is insisting that it be restored to strength and influence.

This dilemma is compounded by the fact that the rabbi which the times demand is not the rabbi familiar to Jewish tradition. He is an aberration. The rabbi called forth by this moment in history is one consecrated to serve, not the interests of an unfulfilled religious faith, but rather one rendered sanguine by the triumphs and self-deceptions of the American scene. The rabbi is victim because he is the captive of what he can least successfully and prudently attack — the security and comfort which has, in part, returned him to life and power. He is perforce vulgarized because he is restored in order to rationalize the triumph of "Americanism." The rabbi is trivialized because the effort he must make to buttress all the ambiguous, vague and insupportable deceptions of American Jewry, cannot help but render him the slave of triviality.

The deeper tragedy of the rabbinate is that the destiny of Israel is incomplete; history is not yet redeemed; and Judaism is the unknown faith. They who know this most profoundly are least able, by circumstance and the harrowing of history, to serve their vocation.

If there is value in considering the desperate situation of the American rabbinate, it is to indicate the source of its present anguish and to supply some measure of unsolicited, but I hope, not unwanted, understanding and counsel.

I

Judaism, it has been observed, is a religion without defense in depth. This is not to suggest that Judaism lacks articulate doctrines. It is rather that Judaism has historically chosen to express itself by and large within the circumscribed ambit of the act, rather than in the open and endless universe

---

Arthur Cohen, the publisher of Meridian Books, is a frequent contributor to *Conservrtive Judaism*, and author of two forthcoming works, *The Anatomy of Faith — Theological Essays of Milton Steinberg* (Harcourt, Brace & Co.), and *The Making of the Jewish Mind* (Pantheon).

of thought and speculation. The biblical and rabbinic traditions are less preoccupied with what a man thinks than with what he does. It was considered sufficient to populate the thought world of the Jew with suggestive images and insinuations of the divine. The Jew knew the world of the *aggadah* — a world of hints and allusions, daring thrusts of imagination, trenchant exegesis and profound intuitions. But for all its richness it was not a world of thought in the conventional sense. It possessed a logic, but it was an infra-logic. Rabbinic thought is to be read between the lines. What is articulate is life; and הלכה is the vividness of life. The rabbinic world, the world of Yeshivot and legal dialectic, was a profound and penetrating world. It was nevertheless a world, strange and unknown, a *terra incognita* from which many returned, but from whom one received only confused and inconsistent reports. To some, it seems, it was a world of darkness and misery, of confusion and inconsistency. To others it was a world of sentiment and nostalgia. To still others it was a world of antiquation and dust — best left to historians and *shtetl*-experts to summarize.

The world in which the הלכה was central broke itself against thought and freedom — those twin monsters of the enlightenment. Lest it be misunderstood, thought is not alien to Judaism. Jewish thought however circumnavigates a Ptolemaic universe — indeed every theology does. Such a universe has its edges and foolish and intrepid explorers take the risk of falling over into the abyss. The rabbis cautioned against such folly and advised against querying who God is or how He functions. Enough, they argue that He has done this: given the Torah and the principles of its explanation.

The peculiar dilemma of the modern world is that the truths vouchsafed by Torah — simply conceived and understood — no longer afford us a self-sufficient means of conducting life. The world is no longer Ptolemaic. No traveller — whatever his folly or intrepidity — need fear again. Since the days of Spinoza, when the edges of the universe were made less cutting, and English and Continental rationalism, when man learned to keep his nose close to the facts and infer when the abyss was proximate, the rabbinic way has been rendered questionable. The Jew, unfortunately, has always lived in a telescoped universe, with a compressed space and an unleisurely sense of time. Time and space have tended to break forth upon the Jew — suddenly and without warning. One day all was closet and secret chamber and the next day the blinding sun was searching out the corners of his universe and laughing at his darkness. Western man had passed through Spinoza and the English rationalists, Christianity had already splintered and nationalism had triumphed before the Jew was formally emancipated.

One day there was genius at Vilna and throughout the Lithuanian academies and the next day there was Mendelssohn and Maimon, *Wissenschaft des Judentums*, scientific study of Jewish law and history, secular Yiddish and Hebrew literature, political radicalism, Zionism, civil equality and the strivings of freedom. The coil of Western history unwound slowly for the nations of the world. At the end — when the whole array of philosophies

THE SEMINARY AND THE MODERN RABBI

and polities had been displayed and the Jew was no longer devil or usurer, the Jew was allowed to enter the universe of the West.

It is no wonder that the Jew sought to master in a century what had been denied him for millennia. The human mind asks the question of truth last. First it quests experience and wonders — only when the experience is digested and there is a satiety of wonders is truth questioned. It may well be that in the end there is only truth in Torah, but it is only the fanatic spirit that refuses to breathe free air. The historic course of modern Jewish man was to become in the West what the West had denied him. Be it knowledge or wealth, power or possessions — the Jew succumbed. He became more learned or wealthy or powerful, because such lustrous prizes had been denied him in the past and were now available. Sociology aside and history for a moment ignored, there is a metaphysical coefficient to the Jew — without such a coefficient it is neither interesting nor meaningful to discuss the Jew as Jew. To the extent that he is Jew he must be seen within the context of that which gives him his grandeurs and despairs. As human being alone each man deserves our attention, but as Jew he may be — and God and history make him (whichever you will is unimportant) the bearer of greater meaning and significance. It is only in the sense that he was once thought, and compelled, to live outside history and to receive, with malignant purpose, its scoring and buffets, that he is now within history to suffer its contempts, its pettiness — the triumphs and failures of all men and all histories.

What makes the Jew and the rabbi important today is that the enlightenment is over, the honeymoon of freedom and emancipation is long since past, and the world is once again at its Ptolemaic edges. Now the Jew turns back and seeks to recall what it is he has forgotten, who he is and what he shall be. He cannot return the clock to its ancient hour, but he must at least know how time once was told when the heavens were scanned for portents.

The Jew turns back at this hour because history has played a cruel joke upon him. With all his emancipation and freedom, he has again been cut down and mutilated. With all his emancipation and freedom, he won himself a homeland shot through with dogmatism and dreams, with fanatics hungering for theocracy, realists working through bureaucracies, and ideologists endlessly thinking out the stratagems of culture (as though culture were made with culture departments.) It is no wonder then that the intellectual and spiritual crisis of Judaism should occur at this moment. The standards of the past seem broken on the rock of modernity; culture, Western or Jewish, appears attenuated and petty; Jewish scholarship becomes alternately arcane and incommunicable or pietistic and prayerful.

The puzzling and yet hopeful paradox of it all, however, is that at this very moment, literally thousands of third generation American Jews are looking back to the synagogue.

II

There are more rabbis in America than ever before and more Jews going to synagogues than ever before. As of 1955 there were some 3,000 Orthodox, Conservative and Reform rabbis serving American Jews in 1782 congregations. The rabbis seem puzzled by their current popularity. Where twenty years ago it was reasonably hard to gather a *minyan*, in many congregations now it is hard to manage the "overflow." The critical questions which face the rabbi are what to do with all these Jews, now that he has them.

Very often the modern rabbi, if he is nothing else, tends to be an ideologue — high ideology in many cases, but in others special pleading — offering an excuse for being in the rabbinate. Where once the rabbi might nurse the wounds of the *declassé*, serving a profession nobody respected, like the proverbial student who wasn't competent to do anything else except teach, he is now suddenly in demand. The rabbi has an audience. There is however an unaccountable inclination of many rabbis — only too often scored by rabbis themselves — to use the rabbinate to prove that they're not really *declassé* but Westernized, cultured, indeed as psychoanalyzed and secularized as their congregations. The rabbi is painfully aware that he is without focus. This is not the rabbis's fault. The insistence that the synagogue be all things to all Jews and that the rabbi serve every need, results more from confusion of the institutions and movements from which the rabbi emerges, than from his own inclinations and preferences.

We must take it at face value that the rabbi wishes to serve God, Torah and Israel. Though the quality of the service can be questioned, we take for granted the authenticity of commitment. It is the office which we will assess — not the man.

Until recently the rôle of the Yeshiva was clear. It was to train its students in the study of Jewish law, to render the rabbi equipped to fulfill two primary functions — to teach Torah and to judge events in the tradition of Torah. The student of the Law was to be Teacher and Judge. When the student passed the examinations of his masters, he was ordained and received the authority of his master to teach and to legislate. The rabbinate was an institution secured by God's gift of reason and knowledge of the Law. The epiphany which compels this view of the rabbinate is the rebuke of Rabbi Joshua to Rabbi Eliezer when the latter sought to decide a matter of Law by calling down the power of heaven to support his view. To this effort, Rabbi Joshua replied: "The Torah is no longer within the power of heaven." God gave it and it is no longer with Him — it is with man to determine its compass and it is with reason, in the tradition of revelation, to apply its principles. Thus the rabbi was to be a למדן and a פוסק. No pressure was needed in centuries passed to coax the Jew to pray. If indeed such coaxing was necessary, it was another Jew who did the urging — not the rabbi. There were always Jews to turn the gaze of heaven — a sympathetic nod, an icy stare — against the recalcitrant. Authority functioned well when it was believed that it was just and absolute and its origin divine. It faltered when the insinuations of the *haskalah* began. Orthodoxy struggled against enlightenment and reform. But authority did not win the day.

The Seminaries on the American scene — whether the Hebrew Union College, the Jewish Theological Seminary or the I. Elchanan Yeshiva — have in common their adjustment to the American scene (whether strident or *sotto voce*). Synagogues affiliated with the Union of Orthodox Jewish Congregations countenance departures from הלכה in matters of liturgical conduct and personal observance. The Reform movement on the other hand is not faced with precisely the same problems as Orthodoxy. It wishes the best of possible worlds — vigor of intellect, modernity of vision, a dispassionate (but not unambiguous) interest in הלכה, as well as the validity of its ordination.

This matter of ordination is important because it is the *terminus ad quem* of the breakdown of halakhic authority in contemporary Judaism. It is evident that the issue of ordination would have aroused more controversy if the legal authority transmitted by traditional orthodoxy had not collapsed. It is sometimes questionable — from the point of view of traditional Jewish law — whether divorce or conversion or other religious acts central to Judaism — are conducted properly within non-Orthodox groups in Judaism. The issue of ordination becomes crucial because if the rabbi is not properly trained in the praxis of Judaism, it is possible that he perpetuates error and brings confusion to the generations of Israel. The crisis of authority is, in large measure, that of ordination, since the history of Israel is now channelled through the office of the rabbi. It is he who dispenses justice, interprets law, determines practice. Yet if he functions without knowledge or training, not he alone, nor only his inquiring congregants, but the whole community of Israel may ultimately suffer.

The issue of halakhic authority, though the origin of the crisis, is at the present moment a penultimate issue. If one considers the reports of the various Law Committees of the rabbinical organizations — Reform, Conservative, and Orthodox — more than disagreement on halakhic practice, there is disagreement regarding the assumptions on which Law is founded — the nature of revelation, the eternal or mutable character of the content of revelation, the province of freedom and obligation in the religious life. Agreement is reasonably consistent in Orthodox and Conservative discussions regarding the *fact* of Law, but disagreement exists regarding the *nature* and *validity* of Law. Where Reform has long since discarded the disciplines of Jewish observance and must now recover knowledge of that fact by searching out the implications of prior theological theory, Orthodox and Conservative thinkers are moving from an acceptance of the facts of Jewish observance to an assessment of their presuppositions. In either case the three movements seem to be moving toward a discussion of theory. Where once the issue was acts and acts alone, this is no longer sufficient, for the *whatness* of the Law is immaterial in an age where Jews no longer observe the Law. If one is to recall therefore the meaning of the act, one must enter the relatively uncharted wilderness of

theory. It is theory — both as discussion of טעמי המצוות and pure theology —
that moves in the underbush of present day halakhic discussion.

* * *

The source of Jewish authority in American life is no longer the Law, but the movement. Torah is no longer from Sinai alone, but also from New York and Cincinnati. To be sure, the new Torah bristles with traditional sources, but essentially it is new, for the reason that the rabbi is no longer only trained to learn, teach, and judge, but to maintain and support the Movement.

It is perhaps inevitable, but nonetheless regrettable that the rabbinate's understanding of American life is not as sophisticated as is its comprehension of Jewish tradition. The common assumption of the three Movements seems to be either that Judaism is to be preserved as a dam against the breakers or sneaked in through the back door. In either case the triumph of Americanism is taken for granted. The only hope for Judaism is as a kind of cultural play-therapy (the literature on the Sabbath, for example as fun, joyous, relaxing, a counter-agent to the pressures of life is extensive). The tendency is to make Judaism available as a surrogate of Americanism, a compatible extension of values implicit in American life, a coefficient of American well-being, comfort, and self-assurance. This distortion of Judaism is the work of the Movement, and not of the rabbis. The rabbi is trained by the Movement, introduced to its values, and sent forth to serve.

But though trained at the Seminary, (from this point on I refer specifically to the Jewish Theological Seminary) which is the heart of the Movement, the rabbi encounters in his congregations a world which he finds difficult to understand, much less able to manage creatively. The Seminary curriculum focuses its emphasis primarily on Talmud and Rabbinics. It is moreover lamentable to learn that the Seminary's emphasis upon Talmud has recently received added impetus from the decision to grant deserving students Talmud Fellowships, whereby they agree to an utter parochialization of their religious education (in addition to regular Talmud classes, these Fellows are released from all other courses, except Bible, if they take six more hours of weekly Talmud instruction). The balance of the normal program is spread thin among a variety of subjects: homiletics, pastoral psychology, Jewish philosophy, history, medieval Jewish literature, modern Hebrew, Midrash, etc. The average student carries from twenty-five to thirty class hours a week. However, the prize of intellectual accomplishment is talmudic proficiency.

In theory the assumptions of the Seminary are valid, but they are valid for an age that no longer exists. Five years of talmudic studies, at six to ten hours a week, do not convince a rabbi morally, much less intellectually, that he is competent to be a halakhist. It is inevitable that the rabbi, in abashment, should succumb either to the temptation of rendering legal decisions which are sometimes incompetent or simply to ignore the problem of Jewish law altogether and concentrate on other things. Concentration on talmudic studies *per se* perpetuates a fundamental unrealism — the unrealism of assuming that its authority still obtains *de facto*. However, as each generation proceeds it becomes harder and harder to find Jews who construct their lives within the talmudic ambit. In contrast, however, it is clear to almost everyone — rabbis and laymen alike — that the relevance of apologetics, doctrine, and theology to the modern Jewish enterprise has not been emphasized nearly enough.

It is a fact that almost all rabbinical students have received their secular education in the discourse of the Christian West. Speaking from my own experience — which is not atypical — the Western secular discourse brings many to Judaism with a fundamental embarrassment and shyness, an implicit sense of the grandeur and strangeness of the Jewish way. Very few young rabbinical students at the Seminary arrive without fundamental gaps of training and reservations of intellect and practice. It goes without saying that were they not already non-Orthodox they would have gone to more Orthodox institutions. Characteristic of the Seminary is that its requirements of observance are minimal, rather than mandatory, so that it becomes more a question of not transgressing Jewish law in public, than of making positive efforts to develop, within institutional confines, the attitudes of piety and belief which seem to me indispensable to a public ministry. The resistance to such efforts to achieve a religious community are more noticeable on the part of the administration than on the part of the students. The present generation of rabbinical students appear, on the whole, more congenial and susceptible of spiritual influences — had such ever been made available — than their predecessors. They are aware, to the extent that they define their religious vocation in terms of the contemporary Western scene, rather than in the terms of classic Orthodoxy, that to meet the demands of their congregations and the world — without surrendering to the pervasive inroads of religious vulgarity — they would need inner habits of prayer and worship, study and piety.

Little formal assistance is afforded rabbinical students in search of such spiritual direction and counsel. Although there is a morning and late evening *minyan*, for example, at the Jewish Theological Seminary, there is little more. These *minyanim* are indifferently attended. It is hoped, but never known that the students don *tfilin* in the morning. Behind the assumption of such an attitude of *nolle tangere* is the palpable American attitude that religion is really a private matter of conscience. This may be the American view. It is certainly not the Jewish view. It is surely the conviction of the literature that habits of conduct, attitudes of prayer, inner spiritual vocation can be nourished, stimulated, and taught. If this were not true the vast literature from חובות הלבבות, and ספר המדע, ספר חסידים, מסילת ישרים, and the *Musar* and *Hasidic* literature would have never existed. As in other areas the rabbinical student is left to his own devices and the nourishment of great and abiding cynicisms. How can rabbis be expected to respond — deeply and meaningfully — to the plea for a more authentic Sabbath observance or a more attentive attitude to Jewish prayer and liturgy if habits of mind and spirit were left by their training institutions to chance. I should venture to say that the spirit is as crucial to the enrichment of modern Judaism as knowledge of Talmud.

What is equally difficult to understand in the curriculum of the Seminary is the fact that the major portion of the ideology or theory which *is* taught there today and has been taught there for many years now has been and is a species of religious naturalism which undermines the whole structure of Judaism and has been repudiated and rejected by Protestants, for example, for almost half a century now.

The paradoxical fact is that the Seminary is attempting to play a dual and inescapably self-contradictory rôle. On the one hand it claims to be an academy for higher Jewish learning. It must, of needs, therefore encourage independence of inquiry and freedom of research. On the other hand it claims to be a rabbinical school. It must, of needs, therefore, be committed to a definite point of view. The Seminary has never resolved this paradox; nor is it apparent that it has ever made sustained efforts to understand the nature of the paradox. The polarization which exists between the scientific production of its faculty and the definition of its curriculum indicates that rather than resolve the paradox it is content to maintain its schizophrenia. It can do so only so long as the objectives of inquiry do not interfere with the training of rabbis. Quite obviously such interference exists, is unavoidable, if not necessary. Now is the time, presumably, to make resolute decision. To do so requires that the issue of ideology and commitment be raised forthrightly and with courage.

It is clearly impossible to assess in the brief compass of this essay the manifold perplexities that the rabbinate confronts. We can catalog these perplexities, but little more. Surely his efforts to create an authentic community of responsive and serious Jews is handicapped when the rabbi is burdened with enormous congregations, an insufficiency of available, trained and well-paid staff, a tremendous physical plant to manage, frequently uncooperative boards and trustees, demands for contradictory conceptions of worship and liturgy. Compound these difficulties by the assumption that the rabbi is to be lecturer, book reviewer, ambassador of good will to the community, pastor on call, an educator.... Lastly where and when is it possible against the background of such excruciating conditions, for the rabbi to be what he has chosen to be: a student and teacher of Torah.

III

The task of the rabbi is to hear, interpret and communicate the word of God. Without pressing the difficulties of this statement (and I am only too well aware of these difficulties), it would, I think, be granted that the word of God — whatever its literal or non-literal character — is contained in Holy Scriptures and its commentaries. It is assumed that, however one interprets the text, the task of the rabbi is to make clear to himself and then to others what it is he hears in this tradition and what relevance this tradition has to the immediacies of contemporary life. If it has no relevance to him, he has no right to be a rabbi. Moreover, if its relevance can only be ascertained by reference to the prior validity of socio-cultural, psychoanalytic, or secular political concepts, then his commitment is not to the word of God, but to the word of man. Then, too, his right to be a rabbi becomes problematical. It is my assumption that to be a rabbi requires, first and foremost, a commitment to find and articulate one kind of truth — the truth maintained and transmitted by Judaism. Any other truth, except insofar as it serves an ancillary or corollary function, is secondary. It is, secondly, my assumption that Judaism is a religion founded upon God's calling to vocation. Any assumption, such as that of Reconstructionism, which qualifies or refines or sophisticates the selection of Israel and God's covenant with Israel, compromises Judaism and with it the Rabbinate. The two dogmatic presuppositions which I have stated are, I believe, indispensable to the rabbinate. They serve as correctives to the interminable vagueness and omnipotent principle of adjustment which is characteristic of American Judaism. What has bothered many rabbis about the much endorsed principle of adjustment and accommodation is that once the principle of change is enthroned, changes never cease, adjustment never finishes, the innovation is never over, and tradition is seldom reconstituted. Change itself becomes tradition, the innovation the fixity.

Using "dogmatics" as his point of departure, the rabbi must recover the sense of who he is. Only if there is theoretical clarity can there be prudential discrimination. The principle of discrimination and change has become in far too many congregations the weapon of the congregation over the rabbinate, the instrumentality whereby the rabbi is compelled to make Judaism over in the light of the moment. Change is indispensable, but in matters of religion every change is charged with significance and should be wrought cautiously and with due recognition of the fact that change is contagious, particularly when it is coupled with pervasive ignorance.

If the rabbi is bound by two commitments, the commitment to the teaching of the Word of God and the conception of Israel as a unique and holy people, he is inevitably compelled to become an apologist for God and Israel. Apologetics — long a distinguished branch of Jewish thought — is relatively moribund. Indeed, it has never been in greater need of revival. Not only are numbers of returning Jews retiring, after the first flush of religious enthusiasm, to indifference; but many, unsatisfied by what Judaism is currently offering, are looking elsewhere for religious commitment. Jewish college students, less perplexed by issues of הלכה than by issues of theology, are finding the rabbinate, by and large, singularly unprepared to handle the questions staged by the philosophic traditions of the secular and Christian West; moreover, intelligent adults find it more pertinent at the present time to ask questions of values and ethics, to query the foundations of the Jewish demurral from Christianity, to expect clear-cut interpretations of Jewish belief and eschatology.

Younger members of the rabbinate find in such a situation that their talmudic training is not sufficient. With the exception of some Orthodox congregations that maintain a traditional שיעור, the demands in adult education are for expositions of Jewish history, practice, and belief. Such demands can only be met by articulate, forthright, and theologically grounded apologetics.

It is clear that belief can never be separated from practice. The Jew is not justified by faith alone; but neither is he justified by acts alone. The Jew confronts the rabbinate with questions fashioned in the West. The rabbinate must answer with weapons fashioned in the Western forge. To do otherwise may be courageous, but disastrous. The modern Jew, whether second or third generation American, is, for all intents and purposes, a convert to Judaism. His is not the problem of the Law. To be sure, he may balk when confronted at the outset with כשרות or מקוה. To emphasize these laws, at first, reflects impatient pedagogy rather than sound apologetics. The initial task is to restore the uncompromised sense of pristine Israel, pristine Torah and pristine religious obligation and the response to the ritual demand will follow in due course. I say this only because it is my conviction that when a man comes to love God there is little or nothing he would not do. Since we do not begin with the love of God it must be grown anew. Invariably as not this seed must be planted in alien soil.

The painful paradox is that the rabbi very often must begin his work at precisely that point where his training leaves off. His training affords him the grammar and language of discourse. It does not supply him with a method of religious pedagogy. The sermon — the concern of so many rabbis — is neither sufficient nor reliable in this area. The real pedagogy and the true pedagogue are the same: the rabbi who is a self-liquidating Torah. He is the first contact with Judaism. It is his task to try and prevent himself from being the last.

How can the rabbi function, nevertheless, if he is in bondage to his congregation and on suffrance to his Board of Trustees. Their strangle hold can be broken only if congregations begin to see their religious obligations independently of their social status. To be sure this is a vicious circle. It can be broken only in the leadership of the Movement itself. If the Rabbinical Assembly would develop and implement a standard contract which, in addition to guaranteeing the obligations of the rabbi to the congregation, also articulated the province in which the rabbi and only the rabbi shall decide, then the foundation of a system of authority will have been provided. At present the most incredibly uninformed ritual committees function in numerous synagogues to determine the extent of Hebrew usage, the kind of prayers to be read, the extent and conduct of the Torah reading, etc. This should not be permitted.

Lastly, but not of least importance, is the fact that rabbi cannot be expected — given the variety and extent of his obligations — to know everything.

18

(On the other hand rabbis would do well to be chary of giving the impression that they do in fact know everything.) Few rabbis seem willing to restrict their field of competence to the one area in which their competence should be unquestioned and from which their authority should flow: Jewish religion. They fall too easily under the spell of their own vanity. The sermon, which should be marginal, triumphs over all, forcing them to develop *expertise*, facility and glibness in a variety of areas in which they are by and large not competent.

To bring the world under the dominion of Torah, the rabbi must first believe that it *is* under the dominion of Torah. This is the capstone of the problem, the source of the confusion, and the essential tragedy of modern Judaism. Too few Jewish leaders really believe that Judaism possesses transforming power. It is at this point that the renaissance of Jewish leadership must begin, and nowhere else. All the other problems of the rabbinate are secondary to this one. The problem of leadership, movement, education and the tyranny of the congregation can be met only if a sense of ultimate meaning is restored to the Jewish enterprise.

Not for a moment is it imagined that truth can be worn as a façade; that one can pretend to truth if truth is unknown. Truth is not a brave front worn in adversity. On the other hand if one does not make the effort to articulate what it is one believes and if belief is not marked with the signs of truth, the effort to be believed and to communicate belief fails utterly. In sum, there is reason to argue that the Seminary ought to lay more demanding emphasis upon the talent of speculation and thought, than upon the mechanics of Jewish authority. Since there is no authority if there is no belief in the sources of authority (both ultimate and immediate), there is no point to Talmudics, if Talmudics and Tradition are conceived in separation from the task of definition and validation. Rather than to call conferences to demonstrate the relevance of rabbinic texts to world ethics or world peace, it would be wiser to call less spectacular and more pressing conferences on the nature of Jewish truth, or the essentials of Jewish belief. Only if the rabbinate is reawakened to the speculative dimensions that bind one Jew to another in truth and service is there hope of reconstituting a Jewish community which is at the same time one and holy.

It would be less than honest to conclude without making clear some of the suppositions which make it possible for me to write as I have written. I make no secret of the fact that I am less observant than my teachers would have me. I make it equally no secret that I believe Judaism is far more true than some of my teachers dream its truth. Judaism has at present modest wishes — to be that secret, supporting, holy community that, like the ל"ו צדיקים, sustains the universe without the universe knowing it. If indeed Israel does make possible the endurance of this most grim universe, it should be made known. If, moreover, the secret of the world's transgression, the world's return, and the world's redemption is possessed by Israel, this should be made known. If, further, the religions of the world are swathed in idolatry, and are, by the canon

19

of Israel, imperfect — whatever their obeisance to a true God — this too should be made known.

Religion is a risky affair. It is risky to believe; it is very risky to believe (as it seems one must) that one has true belief. On the other hand it is absolutely immoral to have true belief and not to make it known. Judaism is being pressed by the modern world to rethink its foundations. Only against the background of such rethinking can the rabbinate be consecrated to its new vocation — no longer only the teaching of הלכה but that broader and more encompassing Torah that addresses all history.

IV

In his classic volume of sermons, *Understanding the Times*, the seventeenth century preacher and Rabbi, Azariah dei Rossi, turned to Chronicles to locate what he conceived to be the primary responsibility of the rabbi: "To understand the times and to know what Israel ought to do."

Presumably, Azariah was not unaware of the temptation to succumb to history, to prize the sense of historical events in disjunction from the duty of announcing the task of Israel. In certain ages the historical sense has tended to overwhelm the clarity with which the vision of Israel has been articulated. In other ages Israel has been willing to resist the incursion of history, to reject the demanding thrusts of the hour and retreat into the protective sureties of inherited tradition. Azariah was profoundly aware that the rabbi must maintain both the perspective of history and the inescapable recognition not only that Israel must act, but also how it must act. It is to such realism that Israel must return — a realism that faces what is over and past, a realism that awaits the future well-prepared.

THE FUNCTION OF THE RABBI

Nathan Glazer

It would be relatively easy to describe to you what the functions of the rabbi have been; what they are today; the extent to which they differ as between Reform, Conservatism, and Orthodoxy, and within each group. It would be easy for me to go on from there and to describe to you the discomfort of the rabbi: The conflict between old definitions of his role and new definitions; the conflict between his view of his functions, his teachers' view, his congregation's view; the confused question as to what the congregation owes the rabbi, and the rabbi the congregation. But I suspect concerning all these questions you know more than I do and I have decided not to repeat to you what is too well-known.

Instead, I want to place the question of the rabbi and his role within the largest possible perspective, and thus I have it in mind to speak of three different sets of developments. First, the social developments within the American Jewish community in the last ten years. Second, the developments within American religion in the last decade or so. Third, developments within American Judaism. Out of this analysis there flow a number of considerations on the role of the rabbi that I think may be of some interest. I do not have a solution to the complex problem of the role of the rabbi. Indeed, as is so often the case with complex social matters, there may be no solution. But I believe certain possible lines of action are suggested which may make the role of the rabbi more comfortable, less strained, and perhaps even less strenuous.

I have undertaken this examination of the American Jewish situation after a lapse of some twelve or thirteen years. In 1954, I explored the available literature on the social and economic situation of American Jews in a lengthy essay in the *American Jewish Year Book*. In 1954–55, I explored the religious situation of American Jews in my book, *American Judaism*. This discussion therefore represents for me something of a return to subjects which I once examined intensively. Fortunately, enough has changed so that I think it will not be necessary to repeat myself, even if I repeat others.

In 1954 the big new fact about the American Jewish community was its new prosperity. It was only ten years before, or less, that major Jewish defense organizations had been concerned with such matters as getting Jews white-collar jobs. There were still poor Jews in 1954 — there still are today — but there were amazingly few of them. American Jews had undergone one of the most rapid transformations in history, from a largely working-class community to a largely middle-class community. This transformation had had striking effects on the community and spiritual life of American Jewry. Thus, the representatives of the Jewish unions, who had played such an important role in American Jewish and American labor history, now discovered they were leaders without a mass following — in any case, a Jewish mass following. Inevitably, this reduced their role and their voice in the Jewish community.

Various institutions that had once been based on the Jewish working class were also declining rapidly in 1954. Thus, the long sustained hope for a Jewish community defined in purely secular terms was rapidly disappearing — in America, at any rate. The Yiddish schools, of various political persuasions, and in every case non-religious or anti-religious, were disappearing. The various kinds of Jewish labor movements, Zionist and anti-Zionist, religious and anti-religious, with their differing characters and rich internal differentiation, were also in decline. They appealed only to a rapidly disappearing nostalgia. Whether all these movements would have maintained their strength if a large Jewish working class had continued to exist is an open question. In any case, in the absence of a working class, they suffered rapid decline. Benefitting from their decline were the Jewish congregations, which took over the old educational and social functions.

Another kind of institution was also in decline — and I think we can trace this to Jewish prosperity too. This was the Jewish community center. Originally, it had been the settlement house, addressed to an immigrant clientele. The community center had managed to make a transition to a middle-class clientele. It provided recreation and meeting places for the entire Jewish community, rather than only its poorer part. Despite this, it was in trouble, not because it was insufficiently middle-class, but because Jewish prosperity permitted the synagogue and temple to challenge it, with similar facilities and a similar range of services. Sadly, one saw one of the major potential institutions for a single Jewish community on the local level weaken — not because it was insufficiently middle-class, insufficiently adapted to current Jewish interests, but because wealth permitted other institutions to expand and challenge it. Or was this only part of the story? Many community centers, we know, did fight the introduction of specifically *Jewish* interests. Perhaps Jews after all preferred rabbis to social workers as leaders. There may have been another factor. We know the synagogue and the temple reflect a certain social and cultural level. Did parents gradually shift their patronage from community center to synagogue and temple because they wanted children to be with their own kind, even among Jews? Was the weakening of the community center only another sign of new patterns of segregation in American life?

In addition to Jewish prosperity, and the decline of the Jewish working class, the observer of 1954 had to point to another striking fact — that the Jewish community, despite prosperity, maintained itself and policed its boundaries, particularly through the widely maintained disapproval of intermarriage. The intermarriage rates of 1954 remained remarkably low, even though Jewish communities in Europe that had reached equally high levels of prosperity had shown phenomenal increases in intermarriage. I do not have to remind you that this observation has now been challenged by new studies. The real question is what is the meaning of the unexpectedly high rates of intermarriage that have been discovered, particularly among the college-educated and third and later generations. I think it would be an error to interpret this — and the associated finding of a low Jewish birth rate — as indicating that the Jewish community is on the verge of disappearance, through low birth rate and high intermarriage. I think that what is happening is that many Jews are now finding new intellectual and cultural milieux in which religious identification changes its meaning and significance. They now find it possible to become another kind of Jew — a kind that unquestionably has much less to do with the temple and synagogue, and takes intermarriage for granted, but that still remains, for many social and political purposes, Jewish.

What is happening, I would suggest, is that new bases for being a Jew are being created, so that alongside traditional Jews, and non-traditional Jews who oppose intermarriage, we find other kinds of Jews who have no objection to the intermarriage of their children. But let us be clear about this: they do not raise objection not because they desire the disappearance of Jews or because they want to raise the burden of being Jewish from their children — after all, they scarcely feel it a burden — but because they are not willing to interfere with their children's freedom and with what comes naturally from allowing this freedom to flourish. I think we must distinguish between different kinds of intermarriage. To my mind, the kind that is now so prominent can be described as the natural concomitant of life in certain cultural milieux, for example, the university community. Thus it is an outgrowth of something that is itself positive, rather than of negative feelings of self-hatred, fear, and social climbing — even though of course all these feelings are also to some extent involved in intermarriage.

To pull these various observations together, I would like to suggest to you what may be the most important development among American Jews since 1954, and that is their diversification. This may seem a strange way of characterizing recent developments. As the Jewish working class has disappeared, as the great Jewish ghetto neighborhoods have shrunk and in all but the largest cities disappeared, have not all Jews been homogenized — are they not all middle class together? All suburbanites together? So it once seemed — and for this reason many observers assumed that a single American Judaism would emerge, overcoming the divisions of the nineteenth and twentieth centuries. But it turned out this analysis was too shallow. The middle class and the new suburbia have their own bases for diversification, and new forms of diversification maintain the old divisions and create new ones — and thus we have a divided Jewish community, certainly as divided in important respects as ever before in American Jewish history.

Thus, as Jews have penetrated new spheres of the economy, new kinds of Jews have been created. As Jews are no longer limited to retailing, the clothing trades, and a few other specialties, as they penetrate all spheres of the economy, new diversity is created. As they develop new economic interests, a new political diversity also becomes apparent. And as they become accustomed to affluence, accustomed to a relative absence of anti-Semitism, new ideological bases for diversity emerge — and these are perhaps the most important. There are now conservative Jews as well as liberal Jews, reactionary as well as radical Jews, racist as well as tolerant Jews, and all types in between.

We once thought, as all or almost all Jews go to college, they become more alike. Perhaps they do on some dimensions, and in comparison with the general community which contains large proportions of non-college goers. But among the college-going, new forms of division also develop. The Ivy League school is different from the state college, which is different from the junior college — all these develop their characteristic cultural tastes and styles of life. Thus I would suggest that while some bases of diversity have been overcome, new and by no means less lasting bases of diversity have been created. Indeed, I would suggest that we interpret the intermarriage figures in this respect. It is not that a massive sea-change is taking place in the American Jewish population and that it is shifting from abhorrence of intermarriage to tolerance of it. This would be the movement from one type of homogeneity to another. I would suggest rather that while large proportions retain an abhorrence and dislike of intermarriage, another very little segment of the American Jewish population is to be found that accepts it. The common error is to extrapolate, and to say that all of the first will become the second. Rather I would say that, whatever the sizes of the two groups, there will be two groups, strong and to some degree mutually intolerant, for a long time to come.

Let me now come to the religious situation. I think now we all suffered from a certain illusion in 1954 — the illusion of the religious revival. Of course most of us understood its limitations even then. But certainly there was a good deal that seemed exciting and new then. There was the creation of the vast physical structure of present-day American Judaism — the building of the synagogues and temples, the classrooms and the meeting halls, the parking lots and the sanctuaries. In part, this reflected, as I and others pointed out at the time, a number of non-religious features. One was simply the need to relocate in suburbia where the Jews were moving. The physical plant of the twenties, now given over to the Negroes, was being replaced by a new physical plant for the fifties and sixties. In greater part, this represented the impact of American suburbia, with its communal structuring of social life — and the communities involved which did the structuring were religious communities.

And yet among Jewish young people, among Jewish intellectuals who had no formal contact with religion, among many rabbis, and in all three major branches, there was a degree of liveliness in concern with the Jewish past, Jewish tradition, Jewish religion that has not I believe been maintained. I recall the enthusiasm that used to greet Will Herberg when he came to speak on campuses. By 1965, they were coming to hear Paul Goodman — also a Jew, and an old *Commentary* contributor, but certainly not a testimonial to the religious revival. By now they come to hear Stokely Carmichael and Timothy Leary. The audiences in all three cases I would guess were often very much the same, and prominent in all three were inquiring Jewish undergraduates. Certainly the formally religious, however re-interpreted and re-invigorated, has lost in the last ten years much of its appeal to the intellectually most active part of the American Jewish population.

I think in retrospect we can discern what happened. A generation that had been completely divorced from traditional Judaism — in mind and heart, if not in practice — suddenly discovered after World War II, generally at the instigation of the Christian world, that there might be something of interest in religion after all. The generation I have in mind is the second generation of East European Jews. In the post-war world, it emerged from various forms of disappointing radicalism to find value in old verities — American society, free enterprise, constitutional safeguards, and even religion. There was an enormous influence from existentialism, for even when it rejected religion it at least considered it. There was an influence from thinkers such as Kierkegaard, Simone Weill, Reinhold Niebuhr. There was the awesome destruction of European Jewry, which had to be given some meaning larger than that given by the acts of a madman. The discovery of a talented generation of an important heritage of thought inevitably led to some kindling, some sparks. Sadly enough, one feels that not enough heat was given off for light or comfort. There are much fewer sparks now. Compare the earlier with the later *Commentary*. The fact that we now have in addition *Judaism* and *Tradition* and the journals of the Reform and Conservative rabbis is not sufficient recompense — all these represent the strength of institutions, rather than the attempt to grapple with religion of young minds.

Nor have we seen anything more impressive on the Christian side. The Christian side is important, for if there is life and ferment in Christian religious life, there will be some reflection in Jewish religious life, too. But the life and ferment of the past ten years have been in areas that ironically enough are incapable of striking strong response from Jews.

There have been three areas of liveliness. The first is the controversy over the death of God. I think it is pretty clear why this has found little response among Jews. Personal belief has never been that much of a big deal among Jews. The issue has been the *mitzvot*. "Would that they would forsake me but keep my commandments." It was only among Reform Jews that the death of God might potentially strike a response. But Reform too was moving towards the right, towards a more traditional Jewish view. Israel was more important in this perspective — in terms of the emotions it aroused, the commitments it created — than God. Perhaps if someone had proposed a death of Israel theology, we would then have seen some lively response from Jews. Those who maintained the pure classic Reform position did potentially place a greater weight upon belief, but they placed an even greater weight on ethics — and that could survive the death of God well enough, thank you.

The second area of liveliness was the updating of the Roman Catholic church, and the rise of ecumenicism. This was an event of enormous significance. One large, frozen area of American religious life has been quickened into the most active life. And in part as a result of the renewal of Catholicism, the Christian world is actively engaged in the reconsideration of old divisions. But neither of these developments finds much reflection on the Jewish side. The revolution in Catholicism does not affect Judaism. This is in large part an organizational revolution — democracy replacing hierarchical control, laymen replacing priests, free thought replacing authoritarianism. Judaism has already undergone this revolution. We might consider Orthodoxy the most likely candidate for the kind of influence that might flow from the picture of a Catholic Church again undergoing change after frozen centuries. But Orthodoxy is totally unaffected. Its immobility is self-selected, autonomously chosen, exercised through the authority of freely chosen leaders, and without a strict hierarchical character.

As for ecumenicism — the divisions within Judaism seem stronger than ever. The moment is not ripe in Judaism, and the Christian example falls on unprepared soil.

Finally, the third area of liveliness in American Christianity is the way it has responded to new social and cultural movements. There has been an enormous impact from the civil rights revolution, which has swept up hundreds of ministers, and has on occasion seemed to be on the verge of revitalizing American Protestantism with a meaningful and special moral character. Indeed, it has done so to some extent. It is not without significance that Protestant religious leaders now play an important role in the peace movement, for example. This close identification of a significant stratum of young ministers with the civil rights and peace movements also has meant an identification with those who bore the brunt of these movements, the militant young. Thus their culture, their interests, their style of life, all have become relevant to progressive Protestant ministers, and Catholic priests. And thus pop religion with rock 'n roll in the sanctuary, and the new roving ministry to the hip areas of San Francisco and New York. Now we know that rabbis have played the same role in the civil rights and peace movements — these rabbis, including members of the CCAR, bear their scars from beatings and jailings. But is it unfair for me to say that despite this involvement, and the sympathy of their fellow rabbis, all this has had a much lesser impact on Judaism than it seems to have had on Protestantism?

Historically the synagogue and the temple, whatever the *positions* they have formally adopted, have never really engaged themselves, even to the extent of some Protestant denominations representing a less liberal clientele, in political and social issues. One can read CCAR resolutions, and good ones, on many important political and social issues. I think we can agree that little action has followed, on the rabbinical or on the congregational level. Similarly with Conservative rabbis. And Orthodox rabbis have very often not even bothered to pass the resolutions.

I can think of three reasons why this new involvement of religion with burning issues of morals, social justice, and political change did not have the same impact on American Judaism.

First, the Jewish religion has not for two thousand years sought to influence the world — that is, the non-Jewish world. It is ethnic, tribal if you will. Even Classical Reform suffered from a fatal ambiguity as to whether this fine, purified, moral religion should really be brought to the Gentiles. Jews are of course among the most active reformers and radicals. But they seem to have no desire to act as religious Jews in their lives as reformers and radicals. It is as if the vehicle of Jewish religion, because of long centuries of disuse, can no longer become a vehicle for social reform.

Second, the Jewish congregations are less directly involved in the major issue of this new wave of social concern, justice for Negroes. For the Protestant Congregations and Catholic Churches, there are direct moral challenges — integration in the congregation, integration in the parochial schools. The number of Negro Jews is too small, their Jewish character too ambiguous, for this direct challenge to be raised to Jewish congregations. Thus the liberal positions remain abstract ones — again, except for those rabbis who directly involve themselves and throw themselves into the struggle.

Third, because there are no strong missionary traditions among Jews, rabbis would feel odd following ministers and priests into the bohemian and hip quarters, to take up, there on the new scene, the new questions that directly concern the young — drugs, sexuality, work, and the like. And even though a good part of the new experimenting youthful generation is indeed Jewish, the rabbis do not follow them, do not confront them on the scene. That is not their style. But it is a significant style in Christianity. After all, look at Jesus. I can't think of an appropriate Jewish model.

Thus, new developments in American religion that have had an important impact on ministers, priests, congregations, and churches, have left Judaism quite unaffected.

And this brings me to developments within American Judaism itself. No great waves of religious change have swept through Judaism. What has not happened has been more important than what has happened. American Judaism has not changed organizationally — there has been no movement to bring various branches together. It has not changed theologically — there are new tendencies, new movements, but they have no impact on the congregations, and even little impact on the rabbis. There has been no change in style of public worship or of private practice. Israel has been created, and there a single hierarchical structure exists — but it has had no effect on American Judaism, except to exacerbate its divisions. There has been no transformation of Jewish education — though we have seen the development of Orthodox day schools.

What has happened is that every tendency has grown, has strengthened itself organizationally, has become somewhat more marked off from its neighbors. The social diversification I spoke of earlier has now been matched by a religious diversification. Indeed, perhaps the two most useful accounts of the religious situation in American Jewry, from a sociological perspective, confirm this view. I refer to Charles S. Liebman's lengthy essay on Orthodoxy in American Jewish Life, in the 1965 *American Jewish Year Book*, and Marshall Sklare's new book on *Jewish Identity on the Suburban Frontier*, which has just been published. The first deals with the situation among the Orthodox, the second with the situation among the Reform and Conservative. Both, interestingly enough, suggest very much the same conclusion. The social homogenization of American Jews, in terms of wealth, income, life-style, has not been followed by a religious homogenization. Indeed, religious diversity has grown, with an accompanying intolerance of really very small differences.

It is scarcely necessary to tell you of the variety of Orthodox groups, each developing separate rabbinical associations, congregational organizations, educational institutions. The intriguing discovery to me, from Marshall Sklare's book about a wealthy Midwest suburb, was the degree to which the same thing has happened on the Reform side. He describes four different Reform congregations in this small Jewish community — and they could not be more different. The largest represents the central tendency in Reform, the move from Classical Reform to Neo-Reform. Another represents the orientation of the most extreme Reform and in addition that of the American Council for Judaism. Another represents the new intellectual and theological interests that are strong among some Reform rabbis — and, in this case, they have found a response in a congregation. Another, the most right-wing, is smaller, less affluent, more communal, more *heimish* than the big temple. There are not many contacts between the congregations. Along with these differences, there are other differences: the kind of rabbi, the number and the type of auxiliary organizations, the social level of the congregational membership, the style of social life, the kind of public worship, and so on. The range of differences is astonishing.

One can find almost as large a diversity within Conservatism.

Thus, every congregation is a world of its own. Why this increasing diversification when religion means less, is less significant as a motive in people's lives? On the face of it this development is mysterious. I would suggest as an explanation that as the central tendencies and tenets of religion mean less, small things become more important. If faith, beliefs, the exact fulfillment of the *mitzvot*, become less important, but if some religious identification is necessary, then at least one might as well be comfortable. Thus one selects or creates a synagogue or temple with exactly the right proportions of ritual or Hebrew or formality or music so that one is not disturbed. This is one reason why indifference can be linked with diversity.

There is another reason. Since most of the members of congregations for the most part do not attend services, since their major interest is in the Jewish schooling of the children and in the personality of the rabbi for the occasional contacts they have with him, this means that the religiously involved in a congregation are free to multiply the grounds of their diversity. Thus, the rabbi and leading members of the congregation can create a congregation which reflects their specific interests and desires. Similarly, the rabbinical and congregational groups are free to emphasize their differences from other groups. Meanwhile the mass membership does not influence what the rabbinical associations and the institutions and the religiously involved do. But they do support them — they pay their taxes but don't really vote, except with their feet. So it becomes possible to spin out elaboration and distinction, at a theoretical level if not at the level of the practice of the members of the congregation, and to create barriers to a potential unity, and maintain defenses for greater diversity.

Charles Liebman, describing the pattern whereby we now have congregations of the Orthodox that are wealthy, suggests another reason. He points out we have been too deterministic in accepting the formula: poor is Orthodox, middle-class is Conservative, wealthy is Reform. Affluence need not mean the abandonment of tradition; it may mean the strengthening of tradition because the individual is now free to vote for and pay for his real tastes. I think Mr. Liebman has a point here. Just as the institutions have enough money and support to maintain themselves in their most distinctive forms, so too do individuals.

And of course, there is no tradition of hierarchy or authoritarianism in Jewish religious life, which might counter these tendencies.

In effect, we find an increasing pluralism in American Jewish life. And this brings me to the problem of the rabbi.

One kind of problem I alluded to at the beginning. As we all know, the traditional function of the rabbi has changed, and new functions have been added, without old ones declining. Inevitably this leads to a severe strain on the rabbi. Thus, he is still a religious authority — his old, central function. He is still a religious leader. A long time ago he added preaching to these functions. Then he added religious education, for despite the rise of professional Jewish educators, it is still the rabbi who has to decide key questions as to the nature of the school. He has added the function of visiting the sick and comforting the bereaved — traditionally, a Jewish community function, but following the model of Protestantism, now a Jewish rabbinic function. He has had of course to become an administrator, and in many congregations he is a representative of the Jews to the non-Jewish community, working together on civic and political and social matters with other religious leaders.

And above all, and perhaps it is this that makes the rabbi most uncomfortable, he has had to become a politician. He must become a politician beause the congregations are all-powerful and they are torn with faction — after all, the diversity we have described above is not limited to the creation of different kinds of congregations, it also exists within congregations. The grander political role may be within the general community. But this grand role will not exist if the lesser political role, maintaining his job within the congregation, is not carried out. Just as any politician must spend endless time keeping his fences in order, getting re-elected, so too must the rabbi. And he can always justify the time so spent; what good would it do to be the best rabbi and have the best program if he can't stay as leader of the congregation?

Added to all these traditional problems of the multiplication of roles, there is also the long-discussed problem of the education of the rabbi. His teachers still try to make him a religious scholar. And despite the new courses on pastoral psychology and the like he feels very poorly equipped when he is faced with the challenge of an actual pulpit which needs many talents, and needs religious scholarship perhaps least of all.

Now the analysis I have presented of the social and religious situation within American Jewry suggests to me a somewhat different way of looking at these old problems. I would suggest that one major problem in the rabbi's role is the very diversity within American Jewry, the pluralism we have described. Whatever congregation he goes to, it will turn out he was not prepared to handle that kind of problem, be that kind of rabbi to that kind of congregation. So the congregation is dissatisfied, or the rabbi is dissatisfied, and he has to find another congregation. But the diversity is such that he will find out his previous congregational experience did not fit him for that new kind of congregation either. And so the discontent and the discomfort are endemic.

There is always the dream of a fundamental improvement, and for religious men the dream must take shape of a true religion, a common faith, a common understanding, in which rabbi and congregation are happy and at ease. Conceivably this kind of religious transformation of the situation will occur, but I do not see how. I see rabbis and people adjusting and adapting to a post-religious situation, in which the institution of synagogue and temple is of some value, and in which the institutions are maintained for rather marginal gains for most of those involved, and with marginal investment. I have suggested that it is in part because of this marginal investment and marginal gain that diversity flourishes and has complicated the life of the rabbi. (I might also point out it eases the problems of many rabbis, too. Whatever distinctive orientation they may develop, they may find a congregation willing to accept it — and they won't have the problem of being cast into exile by bishop or synod.)

I would suggest that Reform may learn something from Orthodoxy, which has accepted this diversity, and in which almost every diverse branch has developed some strength. In other words, is it possible to make this increasing pluralism a source of strength and satisfaction to a greater extent than it is, rather than a source of troubles and hardships? In the past, after all, there was no such thing as the rabbi who did everything. Eastern Europe had a variety of specialized religious functionaries — the *Rov*, the *Rebbe*, the *Maggid*, the *Posek*. One governed the religious community, another gave religious inspiration, another delivered sermons, and another handed down legal judgments. I think the principle still has much to commend it.

Perhaps one of the problems of the Reform rabbinate is that a single institution still sends out rabbis to a multitude of diverse congregations. I realize there is diversity within the Hebrew Union College. And yet I think perhaps one path to consider is increasing diversity, even through institutional means. Suppose there were institutions of Classical Reform, of ethical culture, of people-centered Reform, of theologically-orientated Reform, of social justice-centered Reform. These might not be responsible for the total education of the rabbi. But they might serve as centers to give support and legitimation to certain distinctive styles of rabbi, and certain distinctive types of congregation.

I have the impression that despite the fact that Judaism has indeed been historically diverse, modern efforts to deal with our problems often dream of a unity and authority that to my mind is inconceivable and that I think would weaken a good deal of the strength and appeal that Judaism still has for the American Jew. Thus, I suspect that many rabbis, viewing their difficulties with congregations, with conditions of work, with respect for their authority, think in terms of a more powerful rabbinical association that would lay down and gain respect for uniform conditions of work and, even more than that, would promulgate a uniform and authoritative position as to the role of the rabbi in the community. I would not deny the value of the rabbinical association serving as a trade association — just as the American Association of University Professors does — and defending principles of tenure and minimum standards as to recompense and conditions of service. But I would not be happy to see a rabbinical association develop a position that was too specific as to the proper role of the rabbi. In the present religious situation I can see many proper roles for the rabbi, and some remarkably different. I can see rabbis specializing in roles they find congenial — and I believe that they will be successful in finding or creating some congregation that will accept *their* idea of what a rabbi may be. In other words, I find it difficult in the present situations, and in view of the amazing variety of functions that religion itself plays for an amazingly diverse people, to argue that any role which gives satisfaction to a congregation and a rabbi is illegitimate — and I include the roles of salesman, showman, administrator, politician, and all the other somewhat less respected roles, as well of course as the great historic roles of religious teacher, leader, law interpreter, preacher.

Is this position only a weak acceptance of the status quo? I believe not — for what I propose is a more positive attitude toward Jewish religious pluralism, which would give more opportunity for new religious forms, styles, experiences to emerge, and these developments may well transform the status quo. It is interesting to me that that branch of American Jewry which some years ago was weakest in developing central institutions now shows the greatest possible variety in religion — I speak of Orthodoxy — and in addition shows a good deal of growth and vigor. Is there not perhaps something to be learned here?

My model then is not of varieties of Reform battling with each other, but of varieties of Reform being encouraged to find their distinctive features, their most satisfying form. I admit it is not easy to make the distinction between the two situations, but we do have examples in which the different secular nationalisms respect each other and live in peace, as well as those more unfortunate examples where they fight with each other. I would hope the same thing would be possible with the varieties of Judaism.

I do not know what organizational form the encouragement of pluralism might take. I do see three areas however in which it would be necessary to encourage pluralism — if, that is, my hypothesis is right, and one important reason for the unhappiness of the rabbi is that the rabbinical role does not sufficiently recognize the legitimacy of this religious pluralism.

The first area which might be improved by a recognition of pluralism is the education of rabbis. I have already suggested the possibility of a variety of different types of training — and this might take the form of specialization within a single institution, or the development of limited institutions responsible for a part of rabbinical education, or the development of completely different institutions.

The second area in which pluralism could be included would be that of congregational life itself. Here the Reform movement might well experiment with creating and supporting a variety of different kinds of congregations. It is true these already exist, but I do not think the central institutions support or encourage the relatively unguided efforts of Jews to find styles of congregation and worship and Jewish expression that might satisfy them. I think here of the Unitarian experiment with fellowship groups, which has been very successful. Fellowship groups are not and do not plan to become churches. They consist of ten people or more who meet in a home, or in rented quarters, or even in a church; they may or may not have a minister, they may or may not have a religious school, and they are free to explore in their meetings all the religious questions that concern them. Nor are they simply secular institutions — for generally the members of fellowships are socially active people who have other places to which they can go to explore political and social questions, and to find social satisfactions. However, fellowship members do want to meet in a framework that is specifically religious — even though all that is left of religion is the desire to question it, and talk about it.

I think of the substantial Jewish groups in campus communities. I think of the substantial number of Jewish Bohemians. I think of the large number of Jews who feel unhappy because of the collapse of the secular, Yiddishist institutions. And I have the feeling a good deal of creativity is possible in experimenting with new congregational forms that might meet the needs of these and other groups.

And the third area, finally, in which pluralism might be encouraged is that of the rabbinical role itself — though pluralism here would naturally follow from pluralistic developments in the sphere of rabbinic education and congregational differentiation. Different kinds of rabbis would exist — not only those more or less successful in fulfilling the multifarious roles of the modern rabbi, but those who have chosen a last and have found satisfaction and fulfillment in it. Of course this pluralism already exists. There are rabbis who work with students only, rabbis who work in education only, rabbis who devote themselves only to organizational work in central institutions. But I would suggest that there are far more specialized roles in relating to a congregation than we formally recognize, even though we are informally aware of them. I would hesitate to formalize these different kinds of roles — theologian, preacher, legalist, comforter, and so on — with new titles, as was done with the varied religious functionaries of Eastern Europe. But I think one could do more to define these roles, and to insist on their legitimacy. Thus perhaps one might make vivid the possibility of different kinds of rabbinical careers, through describing the lives of men who have led that kind of career. Perhaps in the matching of congregation to rabbi one could be more explicit in profiling the kind of congregation, and the kind of rabbi — to the greater satisfaction of each. Perhaps, in developing this approach, one might even discover, as I hope one would, a place for a rather abrasive relationship between rabbi and congregation. One should not give up the time-honored role of the rabbi as flayer of the congregation for its sins. But I would hope we would discover what kind of abrasiveness was in some sense rewarding, for comfort is not the only objective of the rabbi, or the congregation.

To sum up: In looking at the state of American Jewry and American Judaism, today, one will find diversity and pluralism. One cannot pronounce this good or bad — only, in the present state of things, necessary. The functions of the rabbi, I am convinced, must be defined in the light of that diversity and pluralism.

The Role of the Rabbi Today

BY ROBERT GORDIS

This paper is based upon the address delivered by Dr. Gordis at the Commencement exercises held at the Jewish Theological Seminary, on September 15, 1946.

I.

IN a classic and unforgettable utterance, the medieval poet voices his love for God by declaring that he can flee only *mimmekha 'elekha* "From Thee unto Thee."

The full poignancy of the phrase was borne in upon me this past summer when a survey mission on behalf of the United States Government took me some ten thousand miles away from home, to Hawaii, Guam, Japan, China and the Philippines. Travel does more than reveal the unknown. It grants us a new perspective with regard to the familiar and commonplace at home. Leonard Feeney has said that we can never learn anything except what we already know. If this be true, travel in distant parts is not so much an act of discovery, as it is a process of self-rediscovery, leading to a revaluation of one's convictions and ideals.

Out of these experiences, apparently so remote from the American scene and from Jewish life as we know it at home, came an overpowering conviction that the Jewish people has not merely a duty to survive, but a vital function to perform in the world. To serve that end, the rabbi, who is the respository of Israel's tradition and should be the living voice of Israel's ideals, is charged with a sacred task of universal significance.

Superficially viewed, the civilization in which the modern rabbi is called upon to serve bears no resemblance to the world of the Prophets and Sages of old. Yet, as the French proverb puts it, "plus ça change, plus c'est la même chose". Then the world was united by the brute force of predatory empires; today it is the impersonal power of scientific and technological progress that binds men together, whether they will it or not. Then there was spiritual disunity among men, as evidenced in the multifarious forms of an arrogant and immoral paganism. Today mankind knows no real unity and little kinship of spirit, in spite of the theoretical adherence of hundreds of millions to one or another powerfully entrenched monotheistic faith.

In the days of the Babylonian Exile, a Prophet arose who declared that Israel was by a divine fiat a Witness to the Living God, and the truth of human brotherhood. Israel would do more than testify to the truth—he would suffer for it. He would bear the scars of persecution and misunderstanding in his own person, because of the spiritual immaturity of the human race. Today the broken body of the Jewish people is eloquent testimony to the fact that mankind has scarcely risen above the lowest rung on the ladder of spiritual progress.

It is the eternal glory of Israel to have enunciated the doctrine of human brotherhood as the basic law of the universe. This doctrine is a direct corollary of the basic Jewish teaching of the Unity of God. For cleaving to this idea, without compromise or modification, our ancestors suffered exile, discrimination and death. Side by side with this conception of the unity of mankind, Israel has recognized that human differences are not only natural, but legitimate, and that their existence adds to the variety and spice of life, when they are not permitted to serve as an excuse for mutual hatred and destruction. Judaism, always a national religion, has been steadfastly opposed both to national chauvinism, which seeks to rule other peoples, and to religious imperialism, which seeks to force its outlook and tradition upon other faiths.

The duty of the Jewish people today is clear—to enunciate this truth, underscore it, apply it and help translate it into reality. By the same token, the basic function of the Jewish spiritual leader is evident—to teach Israel its duty and thus make it worthy of the challenge of the hour.

II.

We hear much today of power politics in world affairs and the threat of Communism to this country's institutions. That threat cannot be effectively met by having our Government continue to act as the foreign office of the British Empire. There is neither justice nor wisdom in our seeking to preserve the spoils garnered in two centuries by the British Lion against the onslaughts of the Russian Bear. There is no enduring method of inoculation against ideas; no quarantine is enforceable against the effects of fear and hope on man's thoughts. We can buttress democracy in America, beyond the power of any force to destroy, by applying the universally avowed principle of the brotherhood of man to all men. Our experience of the past 25 years with democratic institutions in Europe demonstrates that partial democracy cannot survive. It is all or nothing. Here at least, half a loaf may prove worse than none.

That is not all. Judaism has always been a unique blend of realism and idealism, understanding the weaknesses of human nature without surrendering its faith in man's capacity for good. Hence it has known that freedom must be rooted in security, if it is to endure. America's Heaven-sent freedom and America's God-given economic resources are not distinct and unrelated facts. For the starving, freedom is a luxury that they cannot afford.

As soon as the traveller leaves the United States, he finds almost everywhere only two classes; the fabulously rich and the desperately poor. The sense of national unity is all but dissolved in the economic tension of classes, and with it too goes the moral stamina of the people. It was the Biblical sage who prayed:

ראש ועשר אל-תתן-לי הטריפני לחם חקי

כן אשבע וכחשתי מי ה" וכן אורש וגנבתי ותפשתי שם אלהי.

"Poverty and riches do not give me lest I grow full and decay, and say, 'Who is the Lord,' or lest I grow poor and steal and profane the name of my God." (Prov. 30-8).

No human being, least of all an American, will lightly surrender his liberty and self-government, his right to think, speak, write and worship God as he pleases, But man can easily be led astray by want and insecurity, as were our own ancestors in the wilderness, where they quickly and conveniently forgot the rigors of slavery, and remembered only the appetizing diet of Egypt. "We remember the dishes we had in Egypt for nothing." (Num. 11:5).

America remains the last, best hope of free men on earth. To strive to fulfill that hope is our sacred duty, before our entire civilization, and perhaps the human race itself, is wiped from this earth as a thing unclean, by the dark forces that man himself has unleashed.

This unity of mankind is not bounded by the Atlantic or the Pacific Ocean, nor limited to American citizens and native sons. This is truer today than ever before, because no man can tell where the soil of America begins or ends. In far-off islands with unpronounceable names, I have visited rows on rows of graves, where lads who died in the defense of our country now sleep under the Cross or the Shield of David. Their names bespeak their varied origin; their deaths, testify that they were Americans. During the first World War, the British poet Rupert Brooke, who later died in action, wrote: "If I should die, think only this of me, that there is a corner of a foreign field, that is forever England." If this be true, then every corner of the world today is forever America, fructified by American blood, sanctified by young American lives, and kept fresh by American tears.

In sum, when we teach Judaism and its world view, we are not expounding a parochial or insular view of life; we are making a direct contribution to the solution of the world's basic ills.

III.

This all-pervading sense of unity and inter-dependence applies with particular force to the Jewish people. A familiar Talmudic legend tells that God himself, in Heaven, like a pious Jew on earth, dons a pair of Tefillin each morning. While, however, Israel's phylacteries are dedicated to the glory of God, God's phylacteries proclaim the unity of Israel, containing the Biblical passage

מי כעמך ישראל גוי אחד בארץ

"Who is like unto thy people Israel, one people upon the earth."

It is true that my journey did not take me to the classic lands of Jewish misery today, to blood-soaked Europe, but rather to the more fortunate communities of the Pacific. Some, like that of Honolulu, are wealthy and well-established and have traveled a long way down the road of assimilation. Other Jews, as in Manila, are on a par in their privation and want with the rest of the population and no worse. Yet far-reaching as are the differences between them and the scattered remnants of Israel in Japan, or the tragic refugee community of Shanghai, the unity binding them all together is far more striking. They are united by a sense of kinship from the past, they share a common tradition in the present, and they know that a common destiny awaits them in the future.

If they do not know it from within, they are rapidly learning it from without. Shanghai has been the home of several hundreds of students of European Yeshivot, during the war years. By dint of extraordinary fortitude, these young men and some of their teachers escaped from Poland, and succeeded in creating an outpost of Torah in that strange environment. These students are now in process of transit to the United States. But the remainder of the refugee community, over 16,000 strong, may lay fair claim to being the "forgotten men and women of Israel." To describe adequately the squalor and poverty in which they live, is beyond my power. Take the worst American slum you know, and build a whole series of dilapidated tenements on both sides of a narrow alley, crowd a full family into each room, remove virtually all the sanitary facilities, add a liberal dose of all the odors of the not-so-fragrant Orient, sprinkle with a strong dash of malaria and cholera, and you have the physical environment in which Shanghai Jewry lives and strives to raise its children to maturity.

Their past under Hitler was agonizing, their present is dismal and their future even darker. For the situation is rapidly deteriorating. There is strong sentiment in Shanghai against all foreigners. Foreign residents of the French and International Settlements now live in great uncertainty and dread, having lost the protection of their own laws with the surrender of the concessions by France and Britain. Even the United States has been the butt of hostile public demonstrations, this at a time when millions of dollars of American supplies through the medium of UNRRA are helping to feed the Chinese people.

As for our unfortunate brethren, none are so poor as to do them reverence. There already have been riots and agitation against the Jews. The Chinese government has served notice that refugees in Hankow must vacate their miserable quarters to make room for the Chinese refugees who are streaming into Shanghai from the battle areas of the Chinese civil war. At the time of my arrival in Shanghai a few hundred Jewish refugees had completed all their formalities for emigration to Australia and were leaving by boat. Three days later we received word that the British Government had requisitioned their ship for a troop carrier, and that the hapless refugees were stranded indefinitely in Hongkong. Several thousands more are eligible for admission to the United States, even under our present illiberal immigration laws. The American Consul-General in Shanghai, Mr. Monnet Davis, a man of true sympathy and magnamimity of spirit, is anxious to do all in his power to expedite their emigration to our country, but his office is badly understaffed and the processing of visas proceeds at a snail's pace. Thus far, his pleas to Nanking and Washington for additional clerical help, have brought no results.

For many centuries, the tragic Jewish cry has been עד מתי ד' עד מתי "How long, O Lord, How long?" That agonizing question is still unanswered, but it has now been joined by another אנה ד' "אנה "Whither, O Lord, O whither?" On all God's globe with its vast open spaces, there seems no room left for the sons and daughters of Israel.

For us the war goes on. In truth, it has reached a far more critical stage than during the heyday of Nazism. Then we knew that our enemies were against us, but we had the hope that victory would bring us peace and honor. Now the victory has come and all but gone and we do not know who are our comrades. A few pious resolutions, no doubt sincerely meant, a gentle sigh or two of sympathy, and the world sits back calmly and serenely, waiting for time to solve the Jewish problem, preferably through the graveyard. Today we fight not against a concrete foe, but against the fog of numbness, the strange mist of apathy that envelopes our friends wherever Jews are concerned.

It is therefore my conviction, God grant I be wrong, that our generation face one of the most difficult periods in Jewish history. The next decade or two will try our generation in a crucible of pain unparalleled in the long experience of Israel. Perhaps that is what we should expect, for as Yehudah Halevi has said:

ישראל באומות כלב באברים

"Israel among the nations is as the heart among the other organs."

The body politic of mankind today is mortally ill: small wonder then that the heart is grieviously wounded.

IV.

To teach the truth that Israel is one people, and that every Jewish community, including American Jewry, shares a common destiny, is the call of the hour for every truly consecrated Jewish teacher. Variations in conditions abound, to be sure, but even the populous and well-integrated household of American Israel has manifold and pressing problems. Mordecai's great words to Queen Esther must be engraved on our hearts: "If thou remainest silent in this hour, relief and salvation will arise for the Jews from another place, but thou and thy father's house wilt be destroyed, and who knows whether it was not for a time like this that thou didst attain to royalty." *(Esther 4:14)*

Our problems here at home are neither remote nor imaginary. Our youth has learned to its dismay that discrimination, open and unabashed, has fastened upon our schools and universities, the guardians of liberty and truth, who now deny the ideals they were created to uphold. Employment opportunities for Jews, even in this period of labor stringency, grow less and less available and the end is not yet in sight.

In Palestine, the only other hopeful center of Jewish life in the world, where our brothers have written a noble epic in rebuilding their people's life upon the foundation of justice and freedom, the most sordid of selfish interests and the most cowardly of fears have united to rob us of our rights. The violence in Palestine, which every right-thinking human being must deplore, is at least as much the sin of Britain as it is of the desperate young extremists, who have lost faith in the sincerity of the promises and professions of nations and have come to believe that only force can command respect today. Throughout the dark night of Nazism, Palestine was the one ray of hope on the Jewish horizon. Now clouds have descended and the sun has been all but blotted out.

Where shall we look for guidance for our distraught generation? Our sages have taught us: הזהרו בבני עניים שמהם תצא תורה
"Be mindful of the sons of the poor, for instruction goeth forth from them." *(Nedarim 81a)*. It is not beneath the dignity of the prosperous and well-integrated Jewish community of America to turn to its brethren overseas for guidance and direction.

There is a message of courage and dignity in the life and action of the Yishuv in Palestine, which builds as it fights, and extends as it defends. Less spectacular, but equally moving, is the spirit that dwells in the dispersed communities of Israel the world over. The inmates of the displaced persons camps, the refugees

The Role of the Rabbi Today

waiting on the Mediterranean littoral for transportation to Palestine, the Jews of Shanghai, all testify to the unconquerable vitality of Israel. By and large, they have not yielded to despair. As one walks and talks with these Jews, one discovers in them an inner dignity and poise, which flight and persecution have been unable to destroy. A spiritual richness shines forth from their poverty. The American Jew may, in all sincerity, have come to encourage and help them; he leaves instead, inspired and helped by them.

As one learns to know our brethren the world over, one develops a new respect and love for our brothers, not only for the heroes and sages of long ago, but for the unsung heroes and unhonored sages of our own day. We are able to fulfill the the dictates of the Sages, who taught that love of Israel is greater even than the love of Judaism. Our brothers have redeemed themselves from death and from the degradation which is worse than death, because their lives are rooted in a great truth expounded in matchless form by the sages:

שלש מתנות טובות נתן הקב"ה לישראל וכולן לא נתנו אלא על ידי יסורין ואלו הן תורה, וארץ ישראל והעולם הבא.

"Three precious gifts the Holy One, Blessed be He, bestowed upon Israel and all were given only through suffering; the Torah, the Land of Israel and the world to come". *(Ber. 5a)*. Beyond our power to comprehend, our brothers have tasted the cup of sorrow. They have tasted the bitter wine of exile and imprisonment, of destitution and danger. But suffering has not been their sole Jewish experience; it has been the gateway through which they have entered upon their inheritance.

V.

First and foremost has been the gift of the Torah. It has been their study of the imperishable culture of Israel and their loyalty to its faith that has saved them and their children from moral collapse and despair. Travellers returning from Europe tell of their intense yearning for intellectual activity, their preoccupation with the life of the spirit. A copy of the *Jüdische Rundschau* being published in Germany by the pitiable remnants of our people came to my desk recently. From every point of view, the quality of the art work, the range of intellectual interests, and the depth of spirituality reflected in its pages it towers above anything published by the five-million-strong community of American Jewry. For the hundreds of boys I saw in the Talmud Torah in Shanghai studying the Bible and Rashi, the Talmud and the Tosafists, and for the girls of the Beth Jacob School being instructed in the tenets of the Jewish religion, Judaism is no vague idea or remote ancestral heritage. It is literally their life and the length of their days; it nourishes their mind and feeds their hearts, it gives them standards of conduct and a sense of brotherhood with their people.

But it is not they alone who need Torah. American Jewry needs it at least as desperately, especially because, to borrow a colloquialism, it does not know what it is missing. An old Hasidic story tells of a Jew who came to a Rabbi and said to him: "Rabbi, pray for me." "Why don't you pray for yourself, my son?" the Rabbi asked. "I don't know how to pray" was the answer. "Then, my son," said the Rabbi, "You have something else to ask before you pray for yourself. Ask God to teach you how to pray." Even more than the Torah, American Jewry needs

41

the love of the Torah, the hunger and the thirst for the word of the Lord, of which the prophet Amos spoke.

The superficiality and the partisanship that has American Jewish life in its grasp, and which is incidentally one of our chief perils, was revealed in the controversy created by Dr. Finkelstein's earnest warning several months ago against the inroads that assimilation was making among American Jews. Instead of being accepted as a sincere admonition, his words were attacked as partisan propaganda. Let those who will, continue to measure the vitality of American Jewry by the size of its fund-raising campaigns, the magnificence of its institutional buildings and the yardage of its publicity releases. The sober truth is much less comforting. The vast majority of American Jews are strangers to Torah, which is both the religion and the culture of the Jew, his law and lore and learning, his way of life and ideal of conduct. Having cast off the mantle of Torah, most modern Jews lack the spiritual strength to face the trials and dangers of an uncertain world. In the words of the book of *Job*, ערום ילינו מבלי לבוש ואין כסות בקרה "They are naked without a garment at night and have no covering in the cold." *(Job 24:7)* God grant that this unconscious description prove not an epitaph for American Jewry, which finds itself naked in the night of peril and lacking in shelter in the winter of trial.

But all is not yet lost in American Israel. Among our 5,000,000 souls, there is still a saving remnant, a loyal band of sons and daughters. Some of them I met overseas. In Yokohama, Jewish servicemen have created a religious school for the civilian Jewish children of the community. In Manila, Jewish GIs, under the guidance of the Chaplain, have organized the young people into a youth discussion group. In Tokyo, under the somewhat grandiloquent title of the Jewish Intellectual Society of Japan, a group of Jewish young men are seeking to grapple seriously with the problem of the Jews and Judaism in the modern world.

The central task of the Rabbi and teacher in Israel, his basic crown of distinction, lies in the study and propagation of the Torah. It is undeniable that young men in the rabbinate are often sent forth to communities which suffer in varied degrees from Jewish illiteracy. Therein lurks a great danger both to the shepherd and his flock. Raymond Clapper once said: "Never overestimate the knowledge of the people, nor underestimate its intelligence". The temptation to feel that Jewish culture is irrelevant to the modern world, because so many of our people lack any knowledge and appreciation of it, is ever present, but that way lies the road to decay and death for American Israel.

It is even more perilous for the rabbi as a leader and as a human being. To preach every doctrine except Judaism, to expound every book except the Bible, and to discuss all problems except those of the Household of Israel, means to court superficiality and intellectual sterility. One of the greatest poems written by a Jew in our century is the Yiddish epic "Der Geyyer"—"The Wayfarer" by Menachem Boraisha. The hero of the epic, Noah, who may be in part autobiographical, is a symbol of the Jew in our generation whose wanderings exemplify the spiritual conflicts and trends in modern Jewish life. At one point, Noah comes to the town of a Hasidic rabbi who lives in palatial style and keeps a regal court among his poverty-stricken disciples. Noah quickly sees that the Rabbi lacks learning and spiritual depth, and his first reaction is one of resentment. Then he understands that the Hasidic Rabbi performs a useful function in his way, but one charged with danger. Noah says:

"Most souls cannot raise themselves
By their own efforts even when they will it.
They suffer bitter pain to mount a single rung upon the ladder.
Hence they must not be given too much of holiness—A drop suffices.
For those upon the lowest level, even the bottom rung betokens ascent.
But therein lurks a peril all pervasive,
That they who grow accustomed to the lowest rung
May well remain upon that seat forever."

I cannot conceive of any more drastic decline than for the rabbi to cease being a teacher and to become an ecclesiastical functionary. That is the mortal blow to the innermost spirit of Judaism. Nor is it much better for the rabbi to be a mere spellbinder. Mere calls to loyalty may bring a temporary emotional glow, but they will not solve our problems.

Our task today is to find a way for the Jew to live in the modern world without isolation on the one hand, and without dissolution on the other. It is the Torah, rightly interpreted as a living influence, that can guide us. For traditional Judaism is the achievement neither of the Essenes, who cut themselves off from the world, or of the Hellenizers who were caught up in it and swept away from their ancient moorings. It is the work of the Pharisees, who stood with their feet firmly planted in their own spiritual country, but their gaze encompassed the world.

The consecration of the rabbi is no external act. It depends upon his inner dedication, manifested by his continual study of Torah in all its richness and depth, and if possible, by his creative enrichment of its treasures by his efforts. Therein lies his *Hattarat Hora'ah,* his right to teach. Only the student of Torah is truly a Rabbi. In Emerson's words: "I cannot hear what you say, for what you are speaks a thousand times louder."

VI

The second great gift which remains the hope and comfort of our afflicted people is Eretz Yisrael.

A short time ago the newspapers reported that Britain had celebrated the landing of the Romans on the site of the town of Deal, in 55 B.C.E., and that some of the speakers at the festivities had referred to Great Britain as the heir of the Roman Empire. With all one's heart, one prays that the analogy be not carried too far! One cannot help remembering the monumental work of an Englishman, called "The Decline and Fall of the Roman Empire." And one remembers too that the Romans conquered Palestine, exiled the Jewish people and then proudly erected the Arch of Titus to commemorate that triumph. Nineteen centuries later, many a Jew still lives and walks the earth, while the Arch of Titus is listed in the sightseers' handbook as a Roman antiquity.

There is room for legitimate difference of opinion as to the precise political structure to be established in Palestine, but whosoever has surrendered the love of Eretz Yisrael and stands aloof from the upbuilding and defense of the Homeland, has severed the vital link that binds him to his people, his faith and his culture.

Finally, life in the present is impossible without a vision of Olam Haba, the world to come. One of my most distressing experiences came recently when a sensitive and cultured American Jew, whose family has lived here for 150 years, showed me a picture of his son, who had been killed in action. As I looked at the photograph, the father said, in quite a matter-of-fact voice: "I wouldn't have my boy back if I could, I would hate to have him alive today in our dreadful world".

In many a dark hour, Judaism has kept alive the vision of a better world and stimulated Jewish energies towards its achievement. The young man who dedicates himself to the Rabbinate and undertakes, as his life's work, the interpretation of our tradition and its functioning in modern life, has not chosen an easy or petty task, nor has he withdrawn from the world's work. On the contrary, the true son of Israel is an authentic citizen of the world.

All that is most significant in Judaism, is, to be sure, rooted in the Jewish people, but often its origins are to be sought in the life and culture of its neighbors. What Israel has borrowed it has transformed by the alchemy of its genius and then has given it forth once more as a blessing to all the world. The Bible, the Talmud, medieval philosophy, all are rooted in the particular and flower into the universal. No wonder that the Torah, is compared to a tree, the roots of which are in the soil while its branches spread and encompass the heavens. We have but to reveal the light in Judaism and its refulgence will illumine the world. The day of travail may be upon us, but the tears can yet be transmitted into a shining crown of beauty.

As consecrated leaders, who go forth to preach and teach an ever-living faith to an eternal people, the Rabbis in Israel may find guidance and hope in the proud yet humbling realization that they stand in the noble line of teachers and sages going back to Moses, our Teacher. Is it too much to hope that the blessing he pronounced upon his faithful disciple, Joshua, will in some measure be fulfilled in the disciples of the wise of our day?

חזק ואמץ אל תערוץ ואל תחת
כי עמך ה" אלהיך בכל אשר תלך

"Behold I have commanded you: Be strong and of good courage. Be neither frightened nor dismayed, for the Lord your God is with you wheresoever you go."

THE RABBINATE—A RESTLESS BODY OF MEN

Ephraim Greenberg

I

"The Rabbinate is a restless body of men."

So writes Milton Himmelfarb in a recent review[1] of Mordecai Waxman's *Tradition and Change*. While many of us would dispute his critique of the book we have an obligation in all honesty to evaluate the implications of this indisputably valid observation. Although he points particularly to the Conservative rabbi, his remark is painfully true also of the other branches of the rabbinate as well.

Some of us will understandably take umbrage at Mr. Himmelfarb's words. His disturbing characterization hurts. It reminds us of too many things. Many rabbis will dismiss the whole matter by responding with well prepared defensive reflexes. We are accustomed to being misunderstood. And yet from many sources comes the disquieting evidence that Mr. Himmelfarb is not wrong. Marshall Sklare,[2] for example, quoting the proceedings of the Rabbinical Assembly points out that in one recent year as high as 40% of the Conservative rabbinate requested replacement in a new pulpit. Certainly anyone who knows the American rabbi could testify that the above fact has its parallel among the Orthodox and Reform as well. Why should this be so?

The Malbim, one of the great scholars of the nineteenth century was once asked why he held so many pulpits and was unable to settle happily for very long in any one community. He replied by saying, "מיטן אמת קען מען דורכגיין די גאנצע וועלט!" (Tell the truth and see the world!)

This is an answer which contemporary rabbis sometimes fall into in attempting to interpret their own participation, or that of their colleagues, in the annual game of "musical chairs" which large sections of the rabbinate play with the American Jewish pulpit. And yet it is an answer that few of us really believe exhausts the scope of the question.

Himmelfarb attempts an answer: "How are we to explain the Conservative rabbis' readiness to put up with the inconsistencies, contradictions, and ambiguities they have to live with? Those things hurt. One of the ways in which the rabbis try to soothe the hurt, unavailing but revealing, is to change congregations; the Conservative rabbinate is a restless body of men.... The average Conservative rabbi dislikes his job and dislikes the intellectual muddle." But this is by no means the whole of the answer.

It must, of course, be admitted that there are, indeed, circumstances which inhere in the unique amalgam we call American Jewish life which gnaw at

---

Rabbi Greenberg has recently been appointed Director of the New England Branch of the United Synagogue.

[1] *Commentary*, December 1958, pp. 540–542.
[2] *Conservative Judaism, An American Religious Movement*, 1955, p. 285, note 50.

the foundations upon which a rabbi stands. The "intellectual muddle" within which a rabbi functions is undoubtedly a major source of potential demoralization. There are also other matters. The ambivalence of the American Jew about his Judaism, if not his Jewishness, certainly spills over into his relationship with his rabbi and his work. The horror which many Jews, themselves active in the leadership of synagogues, might feel should any of their own sons choose the rabbinate as a career, clearly reveals the truth. Who has not heard the quip that "being a rabbi is no business for a Jewish boy?"

There is, moreover, serious tension between the kind of society America and its Jews are fashioning and the demands of Jewish religion.[3] The rabbi is in great measure caught between the rôle for which he has been trained, to be the teacher of a unique דרך, a religious *way of living*, and his rôle as administrator of an institution whose functioning is dictated largely by what Nathan Glazer has described as "the desire of laymen to acquire religious services more in keeping with their social status."[4] For a rabbi Judaism is *the* all-compelling דרך. But for most American Jews, even the synagogued,[5] being an adherent of Judaism is often more an indication of their social and civic status than a definition of their religious committment. As one rabbi put it so well, "here is the final tragedy . . . our theology dims to name calling; our law to high church postures; our preaching to reviews of books. Judaism demands the Jewish man, the Jewish people. And neither in Williamsburg nor in Riverton can he be found."[6] He describes himself, as many of us could, as "an uncertain rabbi in an other-directed congregation in a goyish suburb."

Another perceptive critic[7] has expressed also what most rabbis bitterly confess as the truth about the homiletic activity which occupies not only so large a place in their own professional economy and an even greater one in that of the congregant. "Exhortation, however moving, however beautiful, cannot really disturb the slumber of the soul. It may address itself to the husks of the psyche, but it cannot really enter . . . it can only address the heart and head that has learned previously to hear. It can draw forth from the soul only if the soul has previously been prepared to yield." Here too is the kind of religious quicksand upon which the rabbinate is forced to tread.

That these take a serious toll of rabbinical energy and morale and give rise to "restlessness" needs no documentation.

---

[3] See *Religious Revival and Jewish Family Life* by Sidney Aronson, Synagogue Council of America (1957), wherein he discusses the ease with which Jews have accommodated themselves to American life.

[4] *The American Jew*, University of Chicago (1957), p. 47.

[5] A study prepared in 1958 by Professor Leonard Reissman of Tulane University of the New Orleans Jewish community documents what many of us have long suspected that in this city, typical of many others, the Jewish attitudes of the synagogued and the non-synagogued Jews differed little.

[6] Rabbi Arnold Jacob Wolf in *Conservative Judaism*, Vol. XII, No. 4, p. 23.

[7] Arthur Cohen, *ibid.*, p. 42.

II

There are, to be sure, more personal hazards in the rabbinical situation. In one of the journals[8] published by a national rabbinic body, for example, an article recently appeared on the question "Can a Rabbi Have Personal Friends in His Own Congregation"?

There is something deeply shocking in this question. True, it is the kind of question which could theoretically have appeared in the journals of other professions, but it is difficult to imagine many other callings where such a question would have as much priority. To a layman unacquainted with the rabbinical life, such a query must be puzzling if not shocking. He is accustomed to thinking of a rabbi as the *very one* whose personal relationships especially with his own congregants should indeed be *more personal* and on deeper levels of friendship and understanding than the relationship of any other professional person with the individuals whom he serves, both within and outside of the formal structure of professional duties and services!

Several rabbis from different areas of the profession answer the question put to them. Most of them, to one degree or another, cautioned the younger colleague who had posed it to be circumspect in his personal involvements with congregants. They counseled him against seeking his personal friendships in the congregation and urged upon him an understanding acceptance of the large degree of social isolation in the very rôle of rabbi which his calling imposes upon him and his family.

Paradoxically, too, rabbis are involved in the same struggle for success as their laymen. But for the rabbi the conflicts are different and possibly even self-destructive. For example, he must rise or fall by how neatly his activities correspond to the popular image of the "successful" rabbi.[9] Himmelfarb, describing the Conservative movement as "centrist, diverse, eclectic and thriving," writes, "All of this has been very successful. But rabbis are intellectuals, or some of them are, and intellectuals are rather less certain than businessmen that you can't argue with success." A rabbi finds he must be vigilant. He must keep a sense of balance in evaluating his "success" at budget building and crowd gathering. The desire of some congregants for a "successful" rabbi causes the unwary to deceive themselves that an aggregation is a congregation; an audience, worshippers and affiliation, true belonging. Fortunately most of us know the difference and yet know also that a career that started as a "service of the heart" may often succumb under the pressure of American success values and degenerate into self-emolation at the altar of institutionalism and careerism.

[8] *CCAR Journal*, January 1958, p. 35.
[9] Speaking of some rabbis who have been "frozen in the post they now hold," Rabbi Bernard Bamberger observes "that his personal disappointment will be compounded by the judgment of his own people, however fond they may be of him, that he must be a second rater, for small congregations pride themselves on being stepping stones and the rabbi who stays too long has in a sense failed them." Columbia University Seminar "The Ministry as a Profession," 1951.

In all fairness to the rabbi must it be said, however, that the exigencies of the hour do demand that most abandon the classic rôle of scholar-saint for that of functionary. What caused this transformation? Undoubtedly the immigration of millions of East European Jews to America in the last seventy-five years resulted in many personal and social disruptions which inevitably were to be reflected in the new concepts of rabbinic status and rôle. Is it not, perhaps, remarkable that we have done as well as we have? And yet in spite of this change we continue to insist that our efforts and their scope are "*as much* a service"[10] as that of our rabbinic antecedents. Do not many suspect uncomfortably that this is not so, that we are actually a lesser breed than the rabbis of past centuries? Our most pointed evidence is the generally sheepish and indecisive attitude not only of the liberal element among American trained Orthodox rabbis but also of Conservative rabbis when it comes to taking independent action which might force them to assert a degree of authority parallel to that assumed by the rabbis of yesterday. We assume the rabbinical rôle but do not really act rabbinically. A rabbi is obligated to act independently and boldly in meeting the religious needs of his day. Why and when do rabbis shrink from this obligation?

Historically too the rabbi was primarily a scholar. But for the contemporary rabbi scholarship has become a luxury and for his congregants' viewpoint perhaps even a wasteful one. There are painfully few rabbis for whom the urgent pressure of inner need has restored learning to a place of primacy in their lives.[11]

III

To speak, however, of the situation of the American rabbinate as though it were merely a reflection of the dislocations and ambiguities of the American Jewish laity, or the generally inhospitable environment, is to state only a partial truth.

Our faults are not in our stars, but in ourselves.

A rabbi's professional experience mirrors his personal history. Certainly there are problems specific to the American Jewish scene, but no rabbi can be creatively effective who does not honestly recognize his own inner problems and can distinguish between his subjective responses and objective occupational hazards.

This is a difficult, but imperative, truth. Unresolved personal problems accompany the rabbi into the pulpit and the study.

During the past several years many rabbis have begun to recognize the

---

[10] Rabbi Abraham J. Karp, *Conservative Judaism*, Vol. X, No. 1.

[11] It is noteworthy to observe that the relatively small British Jewish community and its rabbis produced the Soncino translations of the Talmud, Midrash and Zohar, not the American rabbinate.

centrality of this matter in the rabbinical situation and have sought to come to grips with it. What I describe below are some personal impressions of efforts made in two eastern cities by groups of rabbis, one under the aegis of the local Psychiatric Institute and the other at the local Psychopathic Hospital. The purpose was to meet weekly for a period of several months in order to discuss rabbinical problems with colleagues in the presence of trained psychiatric authorities in the hope of gaining a better understanding of the unique situation of the rabbi.

Most of us enrolled in these sessions in order to receive certification to serve as chaplains in institutions. But once the group got under way the secondary desire with which many of us came, a need for help from colleagues in working out rabbinical problems which we were finding too difficult or too puzzling to handle well, became a more dominant motivation. We learned many revealing things about ourselves.

Our first insight was into the fact that for many of us unconscious factors were intruding upon our ability to function effectively as rabbis. The initial session of one of the groups illustrates the point well.

We commenced the first day with a sense of high expectation. Yet the very moment we began, we found ourselves entangled in serious contention. Those rabbis who were interested in learning pastoral skills and techniques were impatient with the pressing needs of those rabbis who came to discuss problems they had encountered either in their own functioning or in counseling situations. The first rabbi who brought up an experience which was troubling him deeply, a violent argument with a congregant the day before, was treated very unsympathetically by several members of the group. Everyone clearly knew that the purpose of the group was to enable us to share with each other this very kind of personal problem. Yet one heard such comments as, "if somebody needs psychiatric help let him go to a psychiatrist" or "rabbis should rise above these things and not let them get us down." Several members of the group expressed great disappointment in having to sit through an hour and a half listening to the problems of rabbis "who were not handling things well." There was a great deal of feeling that what was needed was a series of lectures by experts. Some suggested that we might bring into the group patients from the hospital to illustrate various kinds of cases. Others observed that each session ought to have a theme, and that each of us would bring in cases only on that theme. As one rabbi put it "then we could do some mental editing." There was also what appeared to be polite arguing over points of religious doctrine among rabbis of various schools of thought. After the first few sessions several rabbis dropped out.

At subsequent meetings we tried to understand what had happened. Why was there so much resistance towards doing what indeed we had *come* to do? It began to dawn upon the group that most of us found being asked to discuss our personal anxieties or inadequacies in the presence of other rabbis and especially in the presence of a psychiatrist was too threatening. It was too threatening to us to show how we really felt about ourselves and our work because it was a confession that we were a little less than the strong, happy, secure, all-knowing rabbis that we worked so hard trying to convince ourselves and especially our competing colleagues. How much safer to have impersonal lectures or to expose the personal life of someone else by sitting in judgment over patients in a mental hospital.

A doctrinal argument among several rabbis at the initial session on the question of "rabbinical integrity" proved to be, as everything else mentioned above, a dispute as to whether it was "really safe" to talk. In the same way as one retreats to the familiar in a setting which is new and disturbing, not knowing here whether it was really safe to talk or whether we could trust our colleagues, we had turned to the familiar approach to learning to which we had become accustomed, lectures where we could indeed feel safe.

We thus began to see that all of us were in many ways governed by unconscious feelings and motives of which we were frequently unaware. The question was: Were they intruding into our professional life? An understanding of our own "inner life history" as men was clearly necessary before we could possibly begin to approach and by teaching and example affect the "inner life" of our congregants.

There were many examples brought before the group which illustrated how, indeed, our own unconscious feelings often block our ability to function effectively. One man told of an experience, humorous only in retrospect, of being invited to conduct a Passover Seder at a Federal prison. He succeeded so well in impressing the inmates with the meaning of the Festival of Freedom, *and thereby relieving his own unconscious anxiety about their incarceration*, that the next day several of them were involved in a major prison break.

An example of a more serious nature, was the following: Two rabbis related similar but separate experiences concerning women in their congregations who had suffered severe depression, and their marriages great tension, following the arrival of a new child; in one case, a boy instead of a hoped for girl, and in the other a child who did not survive. What was significant here was the fact that the advice offered by the respective rabbis pointedly illustrated how often the rabbis' own life adjustments inappropriately influence the manner in which he gives counsel in situations which come before him. One of the aforementioned rabbis suggested to the couple who sought his help that they further enlarge their family by having yet another baby; he himself, it seems, *has* a big family. The other rabbi suggested that the husband act with great kindness and understanding, perhaps take her on a trip; those of us who knew him were aware that he was constantly doing such nice things for his *own* wife.

In considering the above we were concerned not merely with the fact that the advice was inappropriate to the situation, but primarily with the fact that it caused many of us to begin to realize that perhaps we too often were guilty of projecting into our professional experiences, patterns of feeling and action, likewise inappropriate. How many of us, we asked, were treating our congregation as though it were an extension of our family. Our attitudes towards congregational leaders and colleagues, were these simply a mirror of our attitudes towards our father or brothers? Some of us recognized these phenomona, for example, in their alternating feelings of anger and fear towards their synagogue presidents; others began to take a new look at their competitiveness even combativeness not only with colleagues but also with synagogue committees and boards. Were we more at ease with the women than the men in the congregation, or *vice versa* and why? In short, was the congregation but another stage upon which to "act out" the drama of our own family history and the feelings and attitudes with which it had left us, by inappropriately "assigning family parts" to people whom we encountered in our professional life! Some of us came to recognize that herein perhaps lay seeds for self-sabotage.

Further discussion revealed yet another fact of how our unconscious feelings frequently intrude into our rabbinic behavior. A congregant and close friend of one of the rabbis in the group had lost a son. The rabbi had at that time visited them, consoled them and told them "to accept their loss as God's will." He related how he had spent a great deal of time giving them the "Jewish philosophic interpretations of death" and yet he confessed that he was less than effective in helping them to lift themselves out of the darkness of their grief. Not long thereafter they lost their second son. When he came to their home the mother met him at the door and said to him "well rabbi, and what are you going to say this time!" The rabbi confessed that he was unable to handle the situation. He felt helpless and inadequate.

In discussing the case with the group he began to understand that there were two things that the mother was saying here. She was on the one hand punishing the rabbi for what she thought was the sophistry with which he consoled her the first time. On the other hand she was desperately looking for help. The key to the question of whether he could indeed help her, depended upon how he felt about himself. Did he mainly feel she was intent on punishing him or was she really desperately reaching out for help, but of a different kind than before.

If the rabbi in this case felt he was only being punished, he could be of no further use to this woman. If he was held in thrall by the urgency of unconscious needs of his own which demanded punishment or satisfaction, they would inevitably block his ability to help her. But if, instead of feeling thusly, he could *forget* himself for the moment and see her agonizing needs, he could perhaps begin to come to her aid. If he could bring himself to admit that he felt as genuinely heartsick, shocked and hurt as did the family, if he could show them how he *really* felt, he would soon discover that they in turn could respond to his own feelings because they would know them to be genuine and not spurious. *By how he reacted to her, the rabbi could "cue" the woman as to which of her twin needs she should permit him to approach.*

IV

The realization that we often unconsciously "cue" the congregant on how to respond to us and our work, led us to ask ourselves some basic questions.

What "needs" and what motivations and influences had caused us to pursue the rabbinate as our life's work; and what also of current needs and expectations? How indeed these cues often affect our work we soon came to recognize.

All of us have been asked by congregants "why did you become a rabbi"? And all of us have our stock answers. But are these the real answers? Did we drift into the rabbinate or did we choose it? Did we enter the rabbinate out of love for the children of Israel or out of anger with the children of Israel? Were we attracted by the opportunity to teach Torah or the power to command an audience? Did we become rabbis because father was a rabbi or mother dreamed her son would become a rabbi, or did we ourselves consciously select the rabbinate as the way of life in order to serve? Is a little of everything true? Did we have mixed motives?[12]

Many of the rabbis felt they were being "restricted" in being a rabbi. They felt that there were too many unreasonable restraints on a rabbi's freedom for "normal living." One man confessed angrily "I give up so much and do you think it means anything to them"? Another complained "I pound and I pound and it doesn't do any good!" Many traditionally oriented men were bitter about the non-observance of הלכה. Some of the latter admitted to profound feelings of anger and frustration and often even to disillusionment and despair.

In talking the matter through we began to understand the fundamental fact that *how we feel about ourselves we ultimately pass on to others*. If we are conflicted, ambivalent, angry or disappointed about being rabbis we shall pass these things on to our congregants. If the pulpit or the study, or for that matter the meeting room, become the dumping ground for the unhealthy projection of our own personal problems or the vehicle for the satisfaction of our unreasonable or improper needs and motivations, then we may be sure that our congregation will catch the feeling. As one member of the group put it well *"if we have contemptful, angry or poor opinions about our congregants we may be sure they will live up to them!"*

V

As our discussions proceeded they brought us also to a fresh look at the meaning of the wide gulf that is usual between the world of the rabbi and that of his congregant. That this was an inevitable experience in the life of the rabbi both because of the uniqueness of his training and the special rôle

---

[12] An interesting study of the situation in the Protestant Episcopal Church can be found in a pamphlet by Gotthard Booth, M.D. and issued by the Academy of Religion and Mental Health, New York.

he fulfills in the life of the Jew, was something we could largely accept. What we found disturbing, however, was the realization that the gulf was often wider than it needed to be.

To paraphrase what Paul E. Johnson has observed[13] of Protestant ministers but certainly not without parallel among rabbis: Many of us recognize that our approach to a congregation when first we arrived was something like this. A rabbi will ask himself where and with what shall I begin? He may say to himself as he surveys the situation that there are apparently a variety of pressing problems that demand attention. Then he proceeds to set up his agenda and to develop a system of priorities. He may recognize a need for greater synagogue attendance, a new building, a larger budget, improvement of the religious school, youth activities or adult education and so on. Or he may be concerned with the lay power struggle within the synagogue, etc. Having set up his agenda, he rolls up his sleeves and goes to work. Certainly the rabbi can keep himself very busy with these activities.

But such a rabbi is a *problem-centered* rabbi as contrasted with a *person-centered* rabbi, who sees that a synagogue is made up of people. *He sees before him not a series of problems, but a group of people.* Karl Menninger put it well when he said "the world is made up of people, but the people of the world forget this. It is hard to believe that, like ourselves, other people are born of women, reared by parents, teased by brothers . . . . consoled by wives, flattered by grandchildren, and buried by parsons and priests with the blessings of the church and the tears of those left behind . . . . It is easier to speak of fate, and destiny without realizing that people are trying to work out their own fate right now and in the immediate past and future."[14]

The problem-minded rabbi will frequently be superbly efficient but he is seldom effective. He will exhaust himself and his time with details but neglect the genuine needs of his congregants. He may brilliantly and successfully attack his agenda of synagogue problems, but he will never begin to really come to know and understand his people as people. He will meet people but always with his mind on his problems. He will see his people but only superficially either as enemies or allies in meeting *his* problems. He may be on a first name basis with them but all he will really be doing is sorting them out as to whether they are either for or against *his* policies and plans without ever really learning to know them or to take a genuine interest in *their* concerns. People may come to the synagogue with urgent spiritual needs in order more adequately to meet the tasks and burdens of life, but he will never pause long enough to attend to them. He will never speak to the people *where they are*, but will be consumed only with *where he is*.

To such a rabbi people are like chess pawns, something to push around, to use or to avoid in winning a strategic move! To approach our responsibilities as though they were a catalogue of problems is thus to become enmeshed in a web of exertions and mannipulations by which we miss the heart

---

[13] *Psychology of Pastoral Care*, Abington-Cokesbury, 1953.
[14] *Love Against Hate*, New York, Harcourt Brace & Co., 1942, p. 4.

of the matter. It should surprise the problem-centered rabbi little when he becomes painfully overburdened with his problems and is beset by feelings of anxiety, frustration and disappointment. Because he never reaches out to make linkages with people as people, but only with people as problems he will always inevitably be anxious about how his congregants feel about him and what they really think of him. Inevitably he must all but lose contact with them across a gulf needlessly and dangerously widened.

This is especially of concern to the contemporary rabbi because he is engaged in working against the tide of social and intellectual forces of our time in the Jewish community. It is a tragic fact that he can no longer build his work and make his place in the community at large as did the rabbis of generations past on the assumption of a basic and profound commitment to Judaism by the congregation and a widespread acceptance of הלכה and the observance of מצוות, because this is no longer true. Perhaps, therefore, with greater urgency than ever before he must build a person-centered ministry in his congregation; build a system of close and intimate interpersonal relationship with members of his congregation, entering with genuine concern and warmth into the personal lives of the families of his synagogue in order to build a personal bridge sufficiently strong to stand heavy strain of introducing ideas and values that challenge the social and religious patterns of his environment.

VI

There was yet another matter with which we grappled. During the advanced stages of these efforts there was much frank talk concerning the "worthwhileness" of the rabbinate. All of us confessed alarm at the decline in the religious life of our congregants, the disappearance of authentic Jewish living among our people and the dissipation of the once high level of Jewish learning. In this atmosphere many rabbis felt they "were struggling to breathe meaning into their existence as rabbis." Some men felt that they were carrying on "a massive holding action." Others lost themselves in the social pastoral and group work phases of their activity, while still others found areas of communal work outside the synagogue where their efforts gave them a measure of satisfaction and worth. We discovered that an unusually large number of us, disappointed with the level of religious life and activity in our congregations, had retreated to a peripheral area of rabbinic concern. But what was shockingly apparent by its absence was that *none* of us had turned for satisfaction to the area of study and research in the rich fields of Jewish learning. It seemed not to have occurred to many of us that if as rabbis we were less than effective in breaking into the current pattern of the American synagogue and its pseudo-religious world, then perhaps part of the trouble was that our own religious resources were not deep enough to provide for a sustained struggle whether from the pulpit or the study.

His books should perhaps have been the first place to which a rabbi ought instinctively to have retreated for strength. But for most of us it was the last place! We were strangely and shockingly content to wear the badge of busyness whereas we should have been donning the mantle of scholarship![15]

Can there indeed be a genuine revival of Judaism in America without leaders who study, men for whom the passion for learning is an overwhelming personal experience consuming primary energies and concerns? Clearly many of us had never asked such "basic questions" of ourselves. The essence of the matter, however, was whether we were indeed even troubled by such questions. That there were many paths to divine service was certainly true. That this one, however, of all paths, historically so much the heart of the life of the rabbi, should have fallen into neglect and disuse, we felt was a glaring revelation of the condition of the soul as well as the heart of many a contemporary rabbi. Perhaps even an indictment.

Very much in the same vein were several discussions on the subject of prayer. Some rabbis described how they frequently and spontaneously prayed either at a sick bed or with people who had come to their study with a personal problem. Other rabbis observed that they felt awkward about engaging in prayer with individuals at such times. To pray at a bed side or in the study with a congregant seemed to many, in the first instance, that it might be "too frightening to them," and in the second, "an awkward thing to do." What we came to realize, however, was this. *How a patient or congregant would accept our prayers and feel about them depended primarily how we ourselves felt about praying.* Many men felt no more strain and uneasiness or artificiality in praying in these situations than they did when in the pulpit. Nor was it a question only of theology. Whether we are advocates of a supernaturalist or naturalist understanding of God and prayer all of us *did* pray and at synagogue services even *lead* prayer. Why therefore should any rabbi feel ill at ease only when praying informally with individuals, but apparently not when doing so formally and with a group. Have not congregants the right to assume that for a rabbi prayer is *never* inappropriate, especially at a time when the urgency of personal crisis heightens both the need and the significance of prayer? Why is it that some rabbis can with such ease retreat from so superb an opportunity to teach the art of prayer at a moment a congregant was particularly "open"? This too was a question we asked of ourselves. Why indeed?

VII

These then were some of the matters with which we treated during these group therapy sessions. It is difficult to evaluate what results may have come from this "self-study." But for many it brought a better understanding

---

[15] Rabbi Arnold Jacob Wolf writes: "It is a question too seldom faced and never, to my knowledge, answered, why the rabbinate has not produced the seminal works of the last hundred years, at least the congregational rabbinate. Why was it German laymen like

of the "restlessness" so wide-spread in the rabbinate. Certainly this is not without genuine gain.

Most of us who participated in these efforts agreed that both because of the unprecedented burdens which the contemporary rabbi carries, and perhaps also, if one may dare to be hopefully optimistic about the future, because there are unparalleled opportunities on the American scene to create a sounder religious community, it behooves the rabbi to put his own house in order so as to be more adequate to the task. Self-study clearly is demanded of us.

Martin Buber tells the story[16] of the man, who when he got up in the morning, found it was so hard for him to find his clothes that, "at night he almost hesitated to go to bed for thinking of the trouble he would have on waking. One evening he finally made a great effort, took paper and pencil and as he undressed noted down exactly where he put everything he had on. The next morning, very well pleased with himself, he took the slip of paper in his hand and read: 'cap' — there it was, he set it on his head; 'pants' — there they lay, he got into them; and so it went until he was fully dressed. 'that's all very well, but now where am I myself'? he asked in great consternation. 'Where in the world am I'? He looked and looked, but it was a vain search; he could not find himself. 'And that is how it is with us,' said the rabbi."

And that, indeed, is how it is with us. Everything is in its place in the American Jewish community but many of us have yet to ask ourselves, "where in the world am I"?

"Our sages say: 'Seek peace in your own place.' You cannot find peace anywhere save in your own self ... When a man has made peace within himself, he will be able to make peace in the whole world."[17]

Eliminating or even reducing the "restlessness" which wastefully consumes so much rabbinical energy could make for a dramatic change in the effectiveness of the group of men who compose the American rabbinate. It could make a decisive difference in their efforts to fashion a Jewish community which is at peace with Judaism.

Hermann Cohen and Rosenzweig and Buber — why in America academicians like Heschel, by the side of those far less rabbinic like Will Herberg, Arthur Cohen and Maurice Friedman — who shape modern Jewish thought, while the pulpits are silent?" *Conservative Judaism*, Vol. XIII, No. 2, p. 23.

[16] *The Way of Man*, 1950, p. 33.
[17] *Ibid.*, p. 31.

THE RABBINATE AND THE JEWISH COMMUNITY STRUCTURE

Simon Greenberg

WHAT AND WHOM does the term "Rabbinate" designate? As the name of a profession, it is similar to such terms as Medicine, Education, Law or Engineering, The Rabbinate shares with all these the degree of tension that exists between each profession and the power structure of the community. No profession feels that the measure of power which it exercises in the community fully reflects the significance of the contribution it makes, or could make, to the community's welfare. No profession feels that it plays a role in the communal decision-making process commensurate with its own conception of the knowledge, skill and general competence of its practitioners. The basic difference between the Rabbinate and the other professions is that their roles in society are rather clearly defined, and their practitioners easily identified.

The practitioners of most professions want not only to determine for themselves the conditions under which they offer their services to those who *voluntarily* seek them, but also to influence the *entire* community to make more ample use of their services, honestly believing that in doing so they are not pursuing their personal advancement primarily, but are really concerned with the good of the community. The community, however, generally resists the well-intentioned advances of the profession. Hence the almost universal tensions between the professions—Education, Medicine, Social Work, etc.—and the community. The community feels that it is being pushed around and imposed upon; the professionals feel frustrated and mistreated.

The article beginning on this page is part of a paper read before the West Coast Region of the Rabbinical Assembly in the spring of 1968, by Rabbi Simon Greenberg, Vice Chancellor of the Jewish Theological Seminary. The paper was later circulated by Conservative Judaism to a number of colleagues in various parts of the country. A few of the reactions received will be found in the pages following the article.

The Rabbinate and the Jewish Community Structure / Simon Greenberg

The difference of opinion which exists between the Rabbinate and the Jewish community regarding the role of the Rabbinate in determining how the community should function is but another manifestation of the tension that inevitably inheres in the relationship between any profession and the community it serves. If we Rabbis are to appraise our own condition with even a minimum degree of objectivity, we must view ourselves as but another instance of this universal principle.

If the tension between the Rabbinate and the community appears *to us* to be more aggravated and to contain more paradoxes than the tension which prevails between other professions and the community, it is due, I believe, to two causes. In the first place, any degree of tension appears more unbearable to one who is directly the victim of it than to an outsider. But more important is the fact that the scope of the Rabbinate as a profession is not nearly as clearly defined, either in the minds of its practitioners or in the mind of the community, as are most other professions. The American Rabbinate, since it is young and serves a community which is living under political, social and economic conditions unprecedented in Jewish history, is still in search of its identity.

The trend in modern psychology is to place the search for identity at the very core of the inner problem faced by every human being: as Erich Fromm states it, "Man cannot live doubting his identity." Erik Erikson similarly points to a very interesting revolution which has occurred in our life-time: "While the patient in early psychoanalysis suffered most under inhibitions which prevented him from being what and who he thought he knew he was, the patient today suffers most under the problem of what he should believe in, and who he should be, or indeed might be or become." Does this not describe the difference between the frustrations suffered by an East European Rav living in America and our own frustrations? The Rav and his congregrants know what he is and what he should be. If he suffers, it is because he cannot fulfill himself as he knows himself. But we are in a different position: neither we nor our congregants are quite sure of what we are or should be.

How then shall we proceed in our search for a viable definition of the Rabbinate, and of ourselves as Rabbis?

who is a rabbi?

I suggest that we start by asking a deceptively simple question: Whom shall we identify as Rabbis? Shall we include all those who have been or-

53

dained and are now members of a recognized rabbinic association regardless of what they now are doing? Should we include members of accredited national rabbinic organizations who are now trading securities on Wall Street, or selling Israel bonds, or who are administering a philanthropic communal institution such as a hospital, a home for the aged, a Jewish center, or who are occupying academic positions in institutions of higher learning whether or not they are teaching a subject of specifically Jewish content? Or shall we limit ourselves to those who have been ordained in an accredited rabbinical school, are now members of an accredited national rabbinical association and have been called by a lay-maintained congregation to minister to it, or are serving as chaplains in the Armed Forces or in communal institutions, or are directing Hillel foundations at our colleges and universities? All of those in the latter groupings have at least one thing in common—whatever other duties they may be asked to perform or may voluntarily undertake, their indispensible responsibility is to conduct public synagogue services on the Sabbath and Holidays and to preach during those services. For the purpose of this theme, the latter description may help delineate the practitioners of the Rabbinate.

But if conducting public services and preaching are the indispensible identifying characteristics of the practitioner of the Rabbinate, they certainly do not constitute an adequate definition of the Rabbinate as a profession. Indispensible characteristics may distinguish one species from another but they give no adequate description of the species per se.

Let us then try to define the Rabbinate from the point of view of those whom it serves. A profession comes into being because it meets real, irrepressible, biological or psychological human needs. What human needs have called the American Rabbinate into being? I stress the fact that the human needs to which the Rabbinate is expected to respond are real and irrepressible and not artifically stimulated, because as far as I can see, there is no other way of explaining what it is that moves our people to build and maintain rabbinical schools and synagogues. I shall identify three such needs.

The most basic of the three is the usually unarticulated need felt by a very substantial portion of American Jews to relate themselves meaningfully, as individuals and as a community, to the universe and to human life—although many of our congregants would hesitate to admit to such a need and might even deny it.

The second element which brought the American Rabbinate into being is the conscious need of a very substantial portion of American

54

The Rabbinate and the Jewish Community Structure / Simon Greenberg

Jews to relate themselves meaningfully, as a community, to their non-Jewish fellow citizens and to the totality of American life.

The third is the instinctive group will-to-live as a religious people in the world, and as a distinctive community in the United States.

sense of dissatisfaction

Now THERE IS NO Jewish communal institution and no Jewish community function that offers any serious alternative to the Synagogue and the Rabbi in providing appropriate Jewish responses to the basic human need to relate oneself meaningfully to the awe and mystery of human life and the universe. The challenge to the Synagogue and Rabbi in this area comes primarily from extra-Jewish sources, from philosophy, science, technology, and from the other religions which today are so easily accessible to our people. And yet despite the ample dimensions of this realm which is universally conceded to the Rabbinate, the sense of impotence in communal affairs seems to plague the individual rabbi and the profession as a whole. Why?

I suspect that this dissatisfaction stems in large measure from two sources. The first of these is lack of faith in the supreme importance of the Synagogue and the Rabbi within the total community structure. Despite the fact that the Synagogue constitutes the most significant single segment of the total Jewish community structure, rabbis tend to judge the significance of their role by the number of people their work directly affects, by those who attend daily or Sabbath services. It is as if Isaac M. Wise or Solomon Schechter were to have evaluated their role in the history of American Jewry, or for that matter of world Jewry, by the number of students who attended their seminaries during their lifetime, rather than by the total long-range impact their few students had upon the whole of American Jewish life!

The second source of our restlessness is our profoundly felt sense of failure to meet adequately the need of our people for an intelligible and acceptable philosophy of life as Jews. I believe we have failed not merely because of the intrinsic difficulty of the task, or because of our lack of intellectual resources, but because our professional duties have been so numerous that we simply did not have the time and energy this task requires. When we started upon our rabbinical careers, most of us—and I include myself—did not have any real appreciation of the central role which study, meditation and prayer should play in our lives. Hence we did next to nothing to educate our laity to that central dimension of our profession. By our own choice of activities we taught

55

our people to think of us as fundraisers, organizers, Zionist propagandists, and apostles to the gentiles.

I think that from the historic point of view, we made the right choices at the time. American Jewry was seriously understaffed in professionals, and history had thrust upon us a multitude of simultaneous responsibilities, none of which could have been rejected or postponed. Had we not been fundraisers and organizers, millions upon millions of dollars to relieve suffering and to build Zion would not have been raised, and hundreds of synagogues would not have been built. Had we not been Zionist propagandists, the Zionist movement would never have taken on the character of a mass movement, and the State of Israel would not have had as many ardent friends in America. And had we not been apostles to the gentiles, the present favorable position of the Jew in America would not have been attained.

But these activities warped our own conception of our role, and certainly did much to distort the laymen's conception of our role. Our conception of ourselves was warped because in exercising the functions of organizers, fundraisers and propagandists, we were immediately rewarded with the sense of tangible accomplishments, the approbation of the masses, and the feeling that we were acting as leaders. Younger men who aspired to the Rabbinate in America judged their success by the extent to which they could emulate those rabbis who were acknowledged communal leaders.

need for reappraisal

BUT THE SITUATION has changed, particularly in the last two decades. We are fortunately no longer the only significant body of servants of the Jewish community, and we are not the only ones who seek to respond to the inner needs of the Jewish community. We should rejoice in the fact that we are no longer indispensible in certain realms of Jewish community life. The areas of fundraising and community relations have become highly specialized, and we can usually be of greatest service by helping other professionals.

Our first duty, therefore, to ourselves and to our community is to re-appraise our role in Jewish life honestly, and to re-educate the community to the nature of that role so that it can help us fulfill it satisfactorily. Our role is primarily to help the individual Jew and the Jewish community to relate "Jewishly" to the awe and mystery of life, and to live comfortably as Jews amidst our non-Jewish fellow citizens. That role requires that we be first and foremost students and thinkers

56

—students, not professional scholars; thinkers, not academic philosophers.

It has been emphasized repeatedly that within this generation more than half of American Jewish adults will be college graduates, and a very high proportion of them will hold higher degrees. The Synagogue and its recognized leader, the Rabbi, will stand or fall not by raising funds or spearheading inter-group relations or civil rights movements, but by serving this intellectual and spiritual elite of our people, by tapping its energies and promise. We should participate in inter-group and civil rights activities—but not because we think we may thus validate the role of the Synagogue or the Rabbi in our society. We should choose our positions only because we feel that we are not fulfilled as Rabbis if we abstain from them.

If the rabbi sincerely believes that by engaging in anti-war demonstrations, in civil rights marches and similar struggles (as I believe he should), and by urging others to engage in them (as I believe he should), he is fulfilling his primary task as a teacher and exemplar of Judaism's philosophy of life, then by all means let him engage in them. But there are two things he cannot do. He cannot deny others the right to disagree with him, and he cannot use his position as a Rabbi to commit his congregants without their consent.

I believe that by and large the Synagogue pulpit is about as free as any public platform can be. But the amount of freedom of speech and action enjoyed by the individual Rabbi today depends first upon the wisdom with which he uses his freedom—and no one can teach wisdom—and secondly upon the mood in the community as a whole, particularly the mood which he has succeeded in engendering in his congregation.

Some of our people will attack us for undertaking activist roles, and may even resign from the Synagogue. Others may be attracted to the Synagogue by such activities. These calculations of numerical gains or losses may, I suppose, legitimately be taken into consideration by each one of us individually as we decide to participate in any given action. But in the final analysis they should not be the factors determining our actions. Our primary concern must always be to equip ourselves to be readily accessible to our community. We must not be ivory tower recluses, but leaders with whom the people can identify, whose knowledge and spiritual and ethical integrity they respect, and in whose personal lives and spoken and written word they find helpful guidance for their own lives as human beings and as Jews.

If we are to serve the community effectively, however, we must re-order the program of our personal lives and re-educate the community

57

to our needs. It should become a self-evident truth that the Rabbi must have a goodly portion of every day available for undisturbed study and meditation, and at stated intervals, longer periods set aside for spiritual and intellectual renewal. Colleges and universities which do not make nearly the same demands upon the time and energy of their faculties provide vacations and sabbaticals. We must ask as much for the Rabbi. If we use our time properly, our congregants will soon discover that this is the best thing they can do for *themselves*, for they will have a far more effective rabbi. This does not mean that we should view ourselves as competitors of the full-time scholar. Our task is to study in order to communicate with our congregants, and to ensure that what we have to communicate is Jewishly authentic, currently relevant and personally persuasive.

the impress of the rabbinic identity

EVEN AS I WROTE these paragraphs, I seemed to hear voices of distinguished colleagues asking in dismay: Are you counselling us against participation in the large areas of Jewish life outside of the synagogue? Are you suggesting that we withdraw into the *daled amot* of the *beth hamidrash?* No, I am not counselling such withdrawal.

I do not consider any area of activity which has ethical consequences as being out of bounds for the Rabbi, but I firmly believe it to be a Rabbi's duty to see that his participation in the larger areas of Jewish or general concern bears the unmistakable stamp of his total identity *as a Rabbi.* He cannot achieve this unless he devotes regular daily intervals to study, to meditation and to prayer. He will then play a part in the total community structure not merely through his own direct participation, but also through the effect which he, as Rabbi, will have on his congregants, who are or may become leaders in the community.

The direct participation of the Rabbi in broad community affairs also calls for discussion. How shall we participate and how do we want the community to ask for and accept our participation? Do we want to participate as individuals or as an organized profession? Do we want Rabbis to sit on the governing boards of Federations or other organizations as representatives of the Rabbinic bodies, or do we want the Rabbinic representation on these boards to be chosen on the basis of individual merit? If a Rabbi is invited to serve a community institution as a representative of the Rabbinate, does he follow his own opinions, or does he try to implement the decisions or follow the directives of the Rabbinic body he represents?

The Rabbinate and the Jewish Community Structure / Simon Greenberg

I doubt whether any of us would advocate the latter procedure. We do not want, in fact or even in appearance, to function at all times as an organized clerical body seeking to impose its desires upon the community. We are the servants of a religion which is not clerically oriented, but is an essentially lay oriented, democratically rooted faith. Our authority as Rabbis is exercised only insofar as we have knowledge, and the power to persuade those who are willing to listen to us. The fact that we cannot persuade as often as we would like to, certainly does not add to our self-esteem. But let us remember that the *Guide* of Maimonides was publicly burned, and forbidden in practically all the yeshivot of Eastern Europe—and that the Gaon of Vilna could not dissuade the masses of Jews from following the Besht. That does not mean that the writing of the *Guide* and the denunciation of Chassidism were futile gestures, nor that the distinction of the Gaon and of Maimonides, or the dimension of the service they performed for their people, has been lessened because in their lifetime they experienced less than unanimous appreciation.

In a moment of unguarded speech Moses called our forebears "*mamrim*"—recalcitrant and "*k'shey oref*"—stubborn and unyielding. Let us not forget that we too are members of the same people. If we fail to be as stubborn and unyielding in advocating our ideas as the laymen appear to be in rejecting them when they disagree with us—then *they* are the ones who are running true to form, and not we. And it is precisely because our congregations are so free to reject our suggestions that we are absolutely free to suggest and try anything which we sincerely believe to be essential to the performance of our main task—that of presenting Judaism as a profoundly relevant philosophy of life for a modern American Jew.

Buber evaluated the life of Moses as having consisted of an unbroken series of failures which added up to success. I believe that this description can be applied to the American Rabbinate as well, if only we cease studying popularity polls, refrain from nursing resentment over our failures, and instead follow Abraham Lincoln's advice to act "with firmness in the right, as God gives us to see the right," and Solomon Schechter's admonition to "leave a little to God." When we feel secure in our own identity, we will find our professional relationship to the total Jewish community more readily definable, less subject to tension, and above all more enriching both to the Rabbinate and to the entire Jewish community.

59

ARTHUR HERTZBERG, Rabbi of Temple Emanu-el in Englewood, New Jersey and author of *The Zionist Idea*, is lecturer in history on the graduate faculty of Columbia University.

The Changing American Rabbinate

By ARTHUR HERTZBERG

A GENERATION ago, the overwhelming majority of the rabbis in America were either immigrants or the children of immigrants. Even the rabbis of English speaking congregations, many of whom were chosen in part because they appeared to be completely Westernized, were thoroughly at home in Yiddish, and with the exception of one segment of the Reform rabbinate, the rabbis of all persuasions were, overwhelmingly, fervent and devoted Zionists.

The great rabbinic careers of the last generation were not really made in congregations. To be sure, men like Solomon Goldman in Chicago, Abba Hillel Silver in Cleveland, and Israel Goldstein and Stephen Wise in New York were the rabbis of imposing congregations. Their careers did not, however, unfold on the stage of what they were doing within their synagogues. Several of these men did indeed, at some point, come to high office within their specific denominational groups, but that was incidental and often as a consequence of other battles. When Silver became the president of the Central Conference of American Rabbis (Reform), in the 1930's, that was understood within the Conference itself as symbolizing the turn of its majority toward Zionism. His elevation did not occur for internal, denominational reasons. In the minds of everyone the great rabbis of that period had individual synagogues as their base, but they served as such to exercise what was essentially political leadership, in the Jewish community and on its behalf in American politics and in international Jewish affairs. Silver is again perhaps the best example. He remained a factor in Republican politics, because he could and did produce the necessary Jewish votes in Ohio, especially for his friends in the Taft family. As a Zionist leader he translated this power into political leverage against Franklin Delano Roosevelt, when the latter faltered on Zionist issues. Stephen Wise led the Reform elements in New York against Mayor Walker. He was as much the leading Democrat among the rabbis of the country as Silver was the leading Republican, and the defeat of Wise by Silver for the leadership of the American Zionist movement in 1946 represented, more than anything else, the disillusionment of the Zionists with a policy of trusting the Democrats.

Perhaps the most illuminating analogy to explain the role of the leaders of the American rabbinate a generation ago is to be found in the career of

Martin Luther King. The generation of Negro ministers immediately preceding his own comprised men of the Negro ghetto, who were as incapable of speaking for the Negro to the rest of American society as were the *maggidim* of the East Side in the 1890's. King represents their children, with college training, largely at home in white society, but retaining deep roots within the misery of the Negro ghetto and profound identity with the aspirations of their community. It serves King well in the world that he remains a minister of a specific church, because thus the world must treat him with at least some of the respect that it professes for religion in general.

Nonetheless, King's role is that of a Negro political leader, and his career unfolds on the stage of his people's struggle for its rights. Should he ever become, as is quite conceivable, the president of all of American Protestantism for an elected term of several years as the head of the National Council of Churches, such an event would belong to the history of Race in America more than to the normal preoccupations of internal religious structure. Rabbis Wise, Silver, Goldman and the others represented a comparable phenomenon, at a comparable stage in the development of the American Jewish community.

THE AMERICAN RABBI of today is quite clearly a different phenomenon. There exist today many individual congregations as large as or larger than the congregations headed by Wise and Silver. Nonetheless, no comparably renowned rabbinic names have emerged. There are a few specialized reputations in Jewish scholarship, but it is a well known fact that the scholars among the rabbis have no real power in Jewish communal affairs. There is hardly one rabbinic figure today who commands the attention of the entire Jewish community. This is so at the very time when the majority of the Jews of America are formally affiliated with the synagogue, and when both locally and on a national scale American Jewish life has been prospering. The organized enterprise that the rabbis head, the synagogue and all its institutions, is more powerful than ever before, but the rabbis seem to be less so. Why?

Part of the answer lies in the very "success" of the synagogue. All enterprises in America today—economic, political and religious—have been undergoing the same shift from viable, small private enterprises to institutionalization. Careers which in the past were made through personal force and creativity, have now been transmuted into advancement for service to large organizations. The successful owner of a local grocery store of a generation ago is today the manager of a division for a chain of supermarkets, looking forward to the day when he will be a vice-president of the company as a whole. The very success of the religious institutions in America implies that the central bodies are now much stronger and that they have much more influence—to be blunt, they have many more favors to grant and they are much less beholden to powerful, individual rabbis. On the contrary, those individual rabbis who have the normal, human ambition to rise, must now take much greater account of the wishes and the needs of their central denominational bodies.

A generation ago, the central organs of religious Jewish life were largely dependent for moral and material support on the good will of potent individuals, both lay and rabbinic. Now these bodies are so large, that they are ever less beholden to any individual. They can, and indeed do, by-pass even the most powerful rabbi, and deal directly with his congregation and community. This means that status within the general community, and sometimes even within an individual congregation, is much more affected today by the relation of the rabbi to his denominational superiors than it was a generation ago. The result is that rabbinic careers today are evermore being made in semi-bureaucratic fashion. They tend to be safe rather than picturesque.

MANY RESULTS flow from the hugely increased size and power of the central denominational bodies. One obvious result (and the one that is heard most often in the mutterings of unhappy rabbis) is really the least important. To be sure, the road to a "leading pulpit" is smoothest for those in favor with the denominational higher ups, and it is more difficult for the nonconformists. Lesser favors, such as star speeches at denominational conventions and chairmanships of national committees, are also reputed to be likely gifts to those rabbis who do not rock the boat. These mutterings are not entirely justified. None of the structures is so monolithic, or so vindictive, that it really purges the oddball. The truth is that the rabbi of today has very few economic problems, because hundreds of congregations are now paying their rabbis more than decent middle class salaries. The rabbinate as a whole is shorthanded. Therefore, every rabbi with any ability is sufficiently in demand so that even his critics in the national bodies are glad to help him obtain a substantial pulpit. Nonetheless there is much unhappiness in the rabbinate, reflecting a frustrating sense of the decline of the importance of the individual rabbi—and this unhappiness does have something to do with the rising power of the denominations. What has happened has not been willed by the leaders at the top; it was an inevitability.

The growing denominational establishments continue to need increasing numbers of professionals to staff themselves. Many of the bureaucrats are lay people, but many of the jobs cannot be done except by rabbis. Even fund raising, that most secular of occupations, engages the efforts of some of the rabbis who are in the employ of the denominations. Our contemporary seminaries, and the institutions that are allied with them, are wisely following in the footsteps of a very ancient Jewish tradition, that the givers to schools of Torah feel closer to the ennobling purpose of the appeal if they give the money to a scholar. It is also self-evident that much of the educational and cultural work of the central denominations must be directed by rabbis. The various seminaries have required a number of their own graduates to staff their faculties, and that number increases as the schools grow. For that matter, there has been a remarkable growth in the last decade in the number of chairs in Jewish studies that have been created in various colleges and universities. Many, if not most, of these jobs have been occupied by ordained rabbis. One other economic consideration needs to be mentioned: the posts in the bureaucracies and the professorships, with preaching on the high holidays and lecturing thrown in, now pay as well as a middle range pulpit. Such jobs, therefore, appear more attractive to a large number of the ablest graduates than betaking oneself to an initial pulpit somewhere in the wilds.

Two things are happening within the congregations themselves that add to the discomforts of the individual rabbis. In the first place, the synagogues are becoming ever larger and more varied in their functions. In the course of one generation the synagogue school has come to supplement the independently maintained communal school as the dominant form of Jewish education. To almost an equal degree the synagogues have become community centers, and have thus acquired a range of activities that most of them did not have a few decades ago. The administrative responsibilities of the rabbi have, therefore, increased enormously. His predecessors of the past generation no doubt worked just as hard, but they had a free choice of their fields of activities. They had major energies left to devote to larger causes, because they were not running institutions which demanded that they attend an infinite number of regularly scheduled staff meetings, board meetings, committees, etc. The individual rabbi may want to study or to devote himself to some communal cause. He may even know that this is the only way to exert real influence on the broad American Jewish community. The obdurate fact remains that he is busy as institutional executive, and that his immediate constituents are justifiably demanding that he should not neglect his specific duties. But busy and tired men, who are running to keep up with what is immediately before them, do not make major revolutions.

THE PEOPLE who are occupying the pews of individual congregations also differ from their parents a generation ago. In the earlier relationships there was a distinct aura of respect for learning that suffused the encounter between the rabbi and his congregants. This involved not only Jewish learning; it also involved secular knowledge. The rabbi belonged to what was then a small minority of American Jews who had gone to college, and the shop-keepers who sat before him gloried in both his rhetoric and his English accent. On the level of secular learning, the congregants of today are as well educated as their rabbi. The congregations are studded with professional people who have spent as many years in graduate schools as did the rabbi, and some of them read much more widely than he does. In the mind of the congregation, the rabbi therefore no longer enjoys a unique estate. The congregants presume that the highest reaches of learning in the rabbi's profession, as in theirs, are not being cultivated by him, but by research students. On literary, social and political matters they delight in correcting his misquotations from Yeats, or from the lead article in the latest issue of a quality magazine. The rabbi is decreasingly a man apart. Like many of his congregants, he is in a service profession. (This point is even demonstrated by the rhetoric now in vogue for the announcement of new rabbinic appointments. In the past the rabbi was usually "called" to be the "spiritual leader"; nowadays he is generally "elected" by the board to "serve" as rabbi.)

This structure of denominational life, both within the national bodies and the individual synagogues, thus tends to depersonalize the rabbi. There is far less relationship today between the individual talents of the rabbis and the fortunes of their synagogues. A growing neighborhood, with a reasonably affluent Jewish community of child rearing age, produces, as a matter of course, a large and busy synagogue. Such synagogues succeed just as well as institutions with rabbis of little personal stature—men of drive and learning are not indispensable to their fortunes. A generation ago every major Jewish center in America had at least one rabbi whom people came to hear from all over the city, Sabbath after Sabbath. Joshua Liebman in Boston and Milton Steinberg in New York had the last such congregations, in which their particular pulpit was a sounding board which an entire community heeded. Men of equal capacity are preaching today. Within their congregations on a Sabbath one finds the same human material as in the pews of their more conventional colleagues: the small group of regulars, and the relatives of the Bar Mitzvah. But there is not a single pulpit in America today which leads opinion, precisely because the attendances are institutional rather than substantive.

THE DECLINE of the pulpit is part of a general trend in American life as a whole. The lecture platform and the mass meeting are no longer of great consequence in this generation. Mass audiences are addressed today primarily through television, and, to some degree, through the national press and publications. Individual rabbis do appear in dozens of communities on the religious programs of their local stations, but they have little access to national programs. The normal procedure for one of the networks is to turn to the New York office of the denominations, or to one of the secular Jewish agencies, when it needs "Jewish representation." The various national agencies are, indeed, quite competitive with each other, as they battle for the available invitations. Each national agency constantly bears in mind its own need to show to its givers that it, more than others, is doing an effective job in enhancing respect for Jews and Judaism in America. It is thus no casual concern to any of them, that an official clearly identified with his specific organization appear before the cameras to speak for Jewry.

Less parochial motives are also at play. Sensitive issues are constantly being debated, especially in "chat" shows. The national agencies quite properly feel they are excercising their responsibility to the entire Jewish community, when someone who is well briefed by them (which generally means someone in their employ or in their top elected leadership) does the talking. The mass media do occasionally select an individual rabbi, but these cases are atypical. Such rabbis are likely to come to the attention of busy program editors only if they have said something scandalous, e.g. that neither they nor their congregations believe in God. But in the normal course, the mass media, playing safe themselves, turn to the people they know, the staff representatives of the national Jewish organizations, for quasi-official Jewish opinion. The same situation obtains in relation to the wire services, the national newspapers, and the important magazines of mass circulation. They will cover the occasional rabbinic oddball with great relish, but they will tend to get their serious and continuing Jewish coverage from the officials of the national Jewish organizations.

No individual can make a reputation and excercise continuing leadership in a democratic society unless he can effectively and consistently broadcast his views. Effectively barred as he is from the general media, the individual rabbi has only one alternative, if he wishes to influence Jews outside his immediate bailiwick. It is the Jewish press. Here the picture is somewhat different, but not much brighter.

IN THE LAST generation the Yiddish press still had a national circulation of several hundred thousand, and its readers were in their forties and not, as today, in their seventies. It covered the Jewish news directly, and not by reprinting press releases and handouts. The reputations of individual leaders could be and were made within it. After 1910, Judah Magnes led the newer immigrants of the East Side against some of his immediate peers among the German Jews, by the power of the Yiddish press. A number of quite obscure young immigrants, such as Boruch Zuckerman of the Labor Zionists, rose in a few years to a leadership with which even Jacob Schiff had to reckon, because they could create a mass constituency. In the great battle in the early 1920's between Justice Brandeis and Chaim Weizmann for control of American Zionism, Brandeis lost the fight because both on the platform and in the press Weizmann swayed the immigrant Jewish masses. Even today there remains one segment of the American Jewish community in which some individual leaders, most of them rabbis, are effectively heard. What remains of Yiddish speaking Orthodoxy can still be reached, over the heads of any of the national bodies, including its own, through the Yiddish press, but this press is now irrelevant to the vast majority of American Jews. They may remember enough Yiddish to understand the jokes at Grossinger's, but what is published in the language does not shape either their opinions on issues or their estimates of individual Jewish leaders.

There are now a number of Jewish periodicals in English which circulate in hundreds of thousands, but not one is a newspaper. Almost every one of the national organizations has its own periodical. Some of them publish articles of substantial merit. However, they scarcely pretend to be anything but house organs. It is both their right and their duty to serve the needs of their immediate constituents. The news that is covered is therefore largely that of the sponsoring bodies, the purpose being to give a picture, in the most positive terms, of their activity. Controversy and criticism is not a staple diet of such journals. These are not the forums in which individuals can get a consistent hearing for any outlook that is at fundamental variance with the existing mood and structure of the contemporary Jewish establishment. The house organs, especially the religious ones, print many articles by rabbis. But even the most critical members of that breed are, of course, gentlemen; when they do write in these forums, they know that such occasions are not the proper time to embarrass one's hosts.

With a few exceptions the local Jewish weeklies that are published in all Jewish communities of any size, are not much more useful as a platform for an individual Jewish leader. Most exist to publish the announcements of the various local Jewish bodies, plus all of the Jewish "society" news. Their coverage of national Jewish affairs consists almost entirely of reprinting press releases. Most of their editors do not even read the few small, serious journals of Jewish comment, where critical opinions do get some hearing.

ANNUALLY the various denominations and other national bodies hold conventions, and there is debate. Dissenters do rise to speak their piece, but they are essentially muffled. I have before me a pamphlet containing the resolutions to be proposed for adoption at the biennial convention of one of the major religious denominations. This set of resolutions is typical of the sort of thing that serves as the basic convention agenda of the other denominations, synagogues and lay bodies. For that matter, substantially the same material appears annually at the meetings of the national secular organizations. The particular resolutions before me divide into two parts. There is, first, a series of statements representing Jewish-flavored, conventional liberalism. The convention in question will declare itself against the Arab boycott of Israel and for increased rights for Soviet

Jewry; it will support a liberal American immigration policy and express its concern about the separation of Church and State. The rest of the resolutions are self-congratulatory. The assembled delegates will vote their pride in all the many activities of the national body.

What is typically missing from all the convention programs is serious business. In the last two decades I have attended a few exceptional occasions, when someone arose to call some major activity or project into question. Such speeches were almost invariably greeted as disloyalty. The national conventions are not constructed to deliberate the working policy of the organizations. They are intended as demonstrations of strength. Budgets are indeed formally ratified, but are almost never seriously discussed. A small coterie of top lay leaders and upper echelon bureaucrats make the real decisions. The various little Jewish curias remain in continuous session, at the center of power. They may even endure a sharp annual barrage of brickbats, secure in the knowledge that the day after the convention they will continue to do pretty much as they please. The dissenter, even if he is a distinguished rabbi, will go home, where he has no regular access to the decision making process.

The only real check on the masters of national Jewish affairs is financial. Whatever the men at the top may decide to do, they must find the money for it, and this must come primarily from their constituents. In the past the dissenting rabbi was able to exercise some influence by refusing to cooperate with those appeals for funds which he did not approve. This last bit of veto power is now also vanishing. In the first place, the pervasive mood of the American Jewish community is not discriminating. The "givers" of today make their contributions without differentiating among Jewish sponsored causes, out of a feeling that all such endeavors are "good for Jews." When a dissenting rabbi suggests that a particular cause does not merit support, he is wielding a two edged sword. His own congregants expect that he lead them in being "warm," "good" Jews. It is an open secret, for example, that the American rabbinate as a whole is less than enthusiastic over the fact that a Jewish-sponsored, secular, non-sectarian university like Brandeis, raises more money each year than all of the national religious bodies and their seminaries combined. That this is so is in part due to the brilliance of Brandeis' leadership, but it is equally due to the fact that, unlike the Jewish scene of a generation ago, the climate of today is not hospitable to public criticism and to continuing debate about the values which Jews ought to be fostering with their money. Rabbis therefore are increasingly hesitant to attempt to exercise veto power by inhibiting fund raising in their baliwicks for causes they dislike.

WHAT I HAVE BEEN describing, so far, are aspects of social change in the American Jewish community as these have been affecting the role of the individual rabbi. Such is the new context of his labors; but it is not the heart of the matter. The essence of the problem that confronts the American rabbi today, much more sharply than it was ever faced by his predecessors, is the question of faith and purpose. To what end can the rabbi really lead?

The crisis of Jewish faith is a long standing one. It is at least two centuries old. In its starkest form, it boils down to the question: if one rejects orthodoxy, why be a Jew at all? This is the Jewish version of a question that has been confronting all of religion in the age of modernity: what is the role of faith among men whose primary concerns are of this world? The dominant answer among all the faiths has been that the contemporary function of religion is to play some significant role in the remaking of society. In the 19th century, and in the first part of the 20th, western Christianity addressed itself, in the name of the "social gospel," to the woes of the underprivileged. In America today the most advanced churchmen make it their prime business to be on the barricades in the battle for racial equality.

In Jewish circles the equivalent of this "social gospel" has been the continuing battle of the Jews to reorder their own situation in the world. During the last century the rabbinate has been in the forefront of the fight for Jewish equality. In America, this battle is now over.

The Jewish community itself has few tangible problems. It would be content to stop the social clock at this moment, so far as its own interests are concerned. The rabbinate, therefore, has no local Jewish social tasks left. The remaining issues concern the relationship of American Jews to other communities, especially to the Jews of Israel and to the Negroes in America. Both of these cares involve basic issues and Jewish commitments, and rabbis are inevitably in the middle of the several battles. Nonetheless, it scarcely needs demonstrating that the American rabbinate is very much less involved in Zionism today than it was two decades ago. It is equally clear, despite the presence of rabbis in places like Selma, that race relations are not today the major cause preoccupying the American rabbinate. There is nothing in the tenor of rabbinic involvement in the Civil Rights issue which resembles the urgency and singleness of purpose with which many of these same men picketed Great Britain twenty years ago, when they were still students at the seminaries. In their heart of hearts the majority of American rabbis are ambivalent, for very serious reasons, about all the immediate, tangible issues of this day.

Let us consider Zionism first. Ever since the creation of the state of Israel, the Zionist movement has been wrestling with itself in an attempt to find a new definition. On several levels post-state Zionism in America has inevitably collided with the immediate interests and concerns of the bulk of the rabbinate.

This is revealed most sharply in the area of Jewish politics. Whatever else the concept of the sovereignty of Israel may mean, it certainly has been made to mean this: that in the international Jewish community Israel will not share any real political power with Jewish leadership of the Diaspora. The crucial turning in this new direction happened very early and very melodramatically. Immediately after the creation of the state of Israel, there was a titanic falling out between two of its chief architects, David Ben-Gurion and Abba Hillel Silver. To be sure, it was also a case of conflict between two strong-willed men, but their battle turned on a fundamental issue. Ben-Gurion maneuvered Silver out of Zionist leadership, in order to put an end to any pretensions of the Zionist movement to real political power in Jewish affairs. In this, Ben-Gurion was eminently successful.

There is no Zionist politics in America in the sense of the 1920's to the 1940's. No one can today make a major career within American Jewry through Zionist political activity. Whatever barricades on behalf of Israel remain, are occasional ones, when a specific difficult moment arises, such as the Suez crisis of 1956. At such moments Israel has been finding support in the widest circles of the American Jewish community. It is true, as old-line Zionists have been claiming, that only they provide the kind of intense and passionate concern for Israel which used to prevail in the heyday of the movement, and that other American Jews are far more tepid, especially when the U.S. government happens to be opposed to some action or position of the Israelis. However, this argument is really irrelevant. Zionist politics will not again become an area in which rabbis make their communal careers, because today the only place where those who lead Zionist politics occupy the center of the stage, is Jerusalem and not New York.

Deprived of a political role, the existing Zionist structures in America have inevitably been moving in the direction of a primary concern with aspects of Jewish life in the Diaspora. This was symbolized very precisely by the slogan of the last World Zionist Congress, in December, 1964: "Facing the Diaspora." This emphasis has two possible meanings. The one preferred by the Zionist leaders of America is that Zionism should concern itself with a wide variety of Jewish educational and cultural endeavors of the "survivalist kind." Such a program inevitably sets Zionism on a collision course with the rabbinate.

SINCE the synagogue in America is, to a large degree, a "Parent-Teacher Association" of its religious school, the rabbis regard with alarm any serious drifting of Jewish educational facilities, especially those for the young, outside their orbit. There are no doubt sound reasons for this attitude. From ancient times, the synagogue has been conceived as a place of study. The rabbi is the one professional Jew best qualified by scholarship and training to concern himself with the perpetuation of Jewish learning and traditions.

However, counter-arguments from history and tradition are possible. In the past, Jewish education has been the concern not of individual synagogues as institutions which charge membership fees, but rather of the entire community of Jews resident in one locality. A good case could be made for the proposition that it would be "good for Jews" in our day, regardless of the economic consequences to synagogue institutions, that the total Jewish community organize a network of free schools for all Jewish children. Whenever such a notion is broached, it immediately becomes clear that there is one fundamental objection: the synagogues must oppose it. Regardless of the professionally treasonable thoughts of a few rabbis (these men are the rabbinic equivalent of the few American doctors who dare to say a good word for socialized medicine), the rabbinate as a whole will not stake its career in this generation on creating a new structure of Jewish educational and cultural institutions which will bypass their synagogues. That such a venture may be announced under Zionist auspices does not make it more likely to succeed.

For Israeli Zionists, and for a handful of American Zionists, cultural work means propaganda for *aliyah*, i.e., that even Jews in America live in spiritual exile, and that they ought to return to their natural home. The merits of this position need not detain us here. It is enough to state that, on ideological grounds, such Zionists have an excellent case, for Zionism does indeed mean that the idea of the Jews as a lasting minority outside their homeland is an anomaly. But the overwhelming majority of the Jews in America today regard this idea as subversive. For them, their rise to middle class affluence and to cultural acceptance in the last two decades has been the culmination of their dream of "at-homeness." The hundreds of synagogues that have been built were not constructed to be temporary. Here, the rabbi performs a new function. He is no longer the tribune of an embattled Jewry, as Martin Luther King is of the Negro, demanding justice on behalf of the "we" from the "they." The rabbi of today is expected to symbolize the new Jewish role as part of a new American "we." Such a rabbi may still have a good word to say for the *aliyah* to Israel of a handful of Jews from America, as a kind of continuing Jewish peace corps, but even that he will say with some circumspection. Being human, the rabbi knows that one of his bright young people might ask *him:* if *aliyah* is so important, why don't *you* go? Here, too, Zionism becomes a threat. The rabbi can maintain some peace with his Zionist past, or with some of his rabbinic frustrations in the present, by keeping a small candle burning for the notion of *aliyah*, but this, too, cannot be a Zionist career for the American rabbinate.

There is a more immediate sense, however, in which the bulk of the American rabbinate is currently made uncomfortable by Zionist and Israel realities. The overwhelming majority of the Jews in America belong to the Conservative and Reform groups and, with a few notable exceptions, a large majority of those rabbis who might be major communal leaders serve within these two denominations. Yet it is precisely these two groups that have no organizational connection with the institutionalized life of Israel as it exists today, or with the formal Zionist structure. Since it is not only fashionable but also expected today in the American Jewish community that Jewish leaders be "recognized" in Israel, this creates a vexing problem for the non-Orthodox rabbinate.

This problem assumes two major forms. One is related to the nature of the society of Israel, and the other is the result of the structure of the World Zionist Movement. Amid the complications of organized Jewish life that is so bewildering that only the specialists understand it, there has arisen a situation which provides comfort for the American Orthodox rabbinate, while leaving the others increasingly angry.

Jewish religion in Israel is, in the legal sense, an "Establishment," supported by the government, and entirely in Orthodox hands. It is a fact that the rabbinate and the whole of Israel's formal religious life are dominated by and represented by a political party, the Mizrachi. In the political structure of Israel, each of the political parties is a complete society, with everything from housing projects to banks, and, in the case of Mizrachi, also rabbis. But the official Orthodox rabbinate in Israel by law controls the entire gamut of personal status—marriage and divorce—for everyone in Israel. The World Zionist Organization, including its American branch, is organized largely by the counterparts of the political parties that exist in Israel. This means that the Orthodox rabbinate, through Mizrachi, is directly represented in the highest organs of both the state of Israel and of world Zionism, while the American Conservative and Reform Jews—and their rabbis—are on the outside looking in. This results in many annoying little rubs, and a few threatening big ones.

Let me mention a small matter, first. There is hardly a rabbi of any consequence today who has not visited Israel recently. There are several set-ups in Israel for the reception of American dignitaries. The Orthodox rabbis are received by the Israel rabbinate, and their hometown papers, somehow or other, tend to be very well informed of this. Their individual status is thus subtly enhanced by pictures of them visiting the Chief Rabbi, or lecturing at a Yeshiva, or of sitting on the bench as honored guests at one of the rabbinic courts. Their Conservative and Reform counterparts are received with great respect by the Jerusalem office of the UJA or of the Bond drive. If they have any academic connections, there may be a tea for them somewhere on the campus of the Hebrew University. Some even attain the ultimate honor that Israel can give—a visit with Ben-Gurion or Eshkol, or coffee with President Shazar in his office. But rabbis are rabbis. They will soon discover that they are not socially welcome to any rabbis in Israel, and, if such an encounter is indeed arranged, it becomes quite painful.

LARGER ISSUES are, of course, more important. There is an unresolved battle being waged between the Conservative movement in America and the rabbinate of Israel on the issue of religious divorces. Such documents, issued by the responsible tribunal of American Conservative Jews, in due and ancient form completely according with traditional Jewish law, have not been recognized by the official rabbinate of Israel as valid there. "Quiet diplomacy" has so far avoided a frequently threatened testing of the issue in the civil courts of Israel, but it continues to smolder. Whatever the official rhetoric on both sides, the real position of the Israel rabbinate is not that it doubts the correctness of the procedures of the Conservative tribunal. It is, rather, that the Orthodox refuse to recognize that any group of Conservative rabbis, no matter how learned and meticulously legalistic, have any authority in Jewish law and practice. *A fortiori*, this applies to the Reform rabbis. The reverberation of this in America is that it adds another stroke to a picture of a valid Judaism, dominant in Israel, and represented in America by a faithful minority of true believers—the "real rabbis"—i.e. the Orthodox. The rest of the rabbinate is pro-Israel and continues to labor for it, but inevitably, because it is human, with a little ambivalence.

More than mere personal pique accounts for the unhappiness of the bulk of the American rabbis with the religious scene in Israel. At the very root of the Zionist vision, even among many Zionists whose rhetoric was secularist, there was the hope that the faith of Judaism would be revitalized in Zion, and that this renewed vigor would help sustain the rest of the Jewish world. This may yet happen, but it certainly has not even begun to appear in the last eighteen years. The boldest American rabbi, Mordecai M. Kaplan, has confronted this issue by maintaining that the greatest single need of Israel today is a "religious mission" from American Jewry. What he means is that Israel needs a religious alternative to the two choices that are presently posed there, sharply and almost exclusively: Orthodoxy or doctrinaire secularism.

A few younger American rabbis have been working in various capacities to bring this about. Some have gone to serve as the rabbis of the handful of nascent non-Orthodox congregations; others have worked as teachers in schools and kibbutzim. This is far from a mass movement, and it is hardly likely that it will become one. No substantial number of American rabbis (let it be said in utter frankness) are prepared to leave posts of both considerable responsibility and material security in order to assume the personal risk, in obloquy and insecurity, in Israel, for the sake of a serious struggle for a middle-of-the-road Judaism there. Nonetheless, it is a pervasive mood among the American rabbinate that "something ought to be done." This is a far different stance from the one hoped for two decades ago, in which rabbis envisaged themselves as the channel through which Israeli creativity would flow to the Diaspora.

ON SEVERAL levels, therefore, the American rabbinate is ambivalent about important aspects of Zionism and the life of Israel. To be sure, the rabbis are of one mind about the fund raising activities in support of Israel, but that area of Jewish life must, in the very nature of things, be led by laymen who are men of large affairs. The inevitable result is, that the leadership careers of individual rabbis are, by and large, being sought elsewhere.

Today the most obvious place is in the arena of social action on the American scene—which means the problem of race. But here, too, the rabbis are in some tension. All of the leadership elements of the Jewish community have been drawn into this issue. A sense of moral compulsion is operating, allied with the feeling that no civic or religious leadership of any persuasion can avoid the question of the Negro without being reduced to irrelevance. The rabbinate has certainly been serving the Negro cause no less than any comparable group of liberal clergy in any of the denominations, and the organized Jewish community has been involved in the race struggle more, perhaps, than any other white group. Nonetheless, it is hardly likely that the American rabbis in their various pulpits will find an adequate outlet, both within the Jewish community and in the country as a whole, by espousing the cause of the Negro.

In the first place, no white spokesmen of any kind can be more than allies to the Negro in this battle. The day is gone when that community will allow anyone who is not a Negro to be a major spokesman for him. For example, the beating up of Rabbi Arthur Lelyveld in Mississippi a few months ago was a scandal, but so many other people have been beaten and murdered there that this incident has really not made an enormous amount of difference. Twenty years ago a prominent white clergymen, after such an event, would have been speaking for the Negro cause all over the country. It is common knowledge that Rabbi Lelyveld has been fighting a courageous battle in his own town of Cleveland for Negro rights. That qualifies him as a notable and useful ally. He would not claim, nor would he even want to maintain, that he is a leader of the civil rights movement. It is today inconceivable that any white man can head a major civil rights organization, as Spingarn did for an entire generation, as the founder of the NAACP.

In the second place, the rabbinate is far from having solved a certain "Jewish" aspect of the race struggle. Here the hidden, and not so hidden, prejudices of their own constituents are not the issue. Indeed, if that were the only question, the rabbis of America would be in excellent position. They could reassume the mantle of prophets and engage in battle with the prejudices of their congregants. This would no doubt bring some immediate discomfort in various individual synagogues, but anyone who knows the rabbinate at all may be sure that its best men would be delighted with such a battle. The essence of the problem is that the rabbis themselves share in at least some of the ambivalence about the Negro that abounds among the laity.

Like their congregants, the rabbis are worried about intermarriage. They, too, have the feeling that a totally open Jewish community, that is primarily involved in larger social issues, is one that might vanish as a separate entity. The most liberal Christian ministers are comforted by the knowledge that the Negro is a Christian. Such men are willing to accept, and some even to urge, inter-racial marriages because they regard such an attitude as the highest expression of a contemporary Christian faith. It is true indeed, that the Christian inter-racial couple of today does not need to be lost to the Church. The synagogue is just beginning to face the problem of the Jewish-Christian inter-racial couple. It has certainly not yet arrived at the point of welcoming the phenomenon.

THE RABBIS who hoisted the standard of Zionism a generation ago, during the Hitler years, did it for a variety of reasons. One motive that was certainly a factor was that what they were doing would serve to bring Jews, who were on the periphery of the Jewish community, back to allegiance to it. The situation of the rabbis confronting the Negro problem is more ambiguous. On one level they are convinced that it is their moral duty to help the Negro advance. The rabbis even know that their presence in the Civil Rights movement is making them encounter many Jews, especially of the younger generation, who are entirely committed to this struggle What makes the rabbis uneasy, and what, therefore, makes it impossible for them to find their fulfillment in civil rights, is the feeling that they are not thereby bringing peripheral Jews back to any of the parochial Jewish concerns. On the contrary, a rabbinic effort to identify contemporary Judaism primarily with the struggle for justice may well serve to confirm a notion that few rabbis could possibly want to strengthen: that all that is "in-group" within Jewry is irrelevant and dead.

Out on the picket lines carrying the banners against segregation, many rabbis have been asked by young Jews they never see in synagogue: why should we survive as Jews? This question has been asked, prominently, since around 1950. For a few years the most contemporary voices in the rabbinate looked for a sense of purpose in a revival of theological thinking. Martin Buber, who had been almost unknown in America, suddenly came to occupy the center of the stage, as many of the younger Jewish intellectuals flirted with religious existentialism. But it became clear almost immediately, at least to rabbis, that modernist Jewish theology simply could not sustain the burden they were trying to put on it. The most that one could derive from Jewish religious existentialism was a highly personal sense of encounter with God and with other men. Hassidic texts especially could be an intriguing source for such emotions, but they were not necessarily the only ones, for many of the young could, and did, wander around among Buber, Zen and even Catholic mysticism.

The religious situation of the American rabbi is the most difficult that it has been in modern times. Almost the whole organized enterprise of Jewish life in America is today running less on passion and conviction than on momentum and on emotions about togetherness. What the rabbis are doing at this moment amounts to a holding operation. They are using every technique they can muster to relate individual Jews to some function or service provided by the Jewish community. This is why the rabbis are so busy. In this age of anxiety and insecurity people need counseling, so the rabbis have all become pastoral psychiatrists. Since Jews will not come to synagogues in great numbers to pray, the rabbis have devised family services in which birthdays, anniversaries and the like are honored. Book reviews of best sellers, antique shows, amateur theatricals —the list could be extended at will—are omnipresent. All of these are now much of the business of Jewish life, not because the rabbis really care about any of them, and not, as some of their critics have been maintaining, because the American rabbis have become vulgar.

The rabbis know that the Jewish religion is, to them, a source of unique spiritual experience, that it represents that by which they are commanded— but they have not the language with which to define such a uniquely Jewish commandment and to convince others to live under its yoke. Therefore, they keep themselves busy, and they keep others busy, with the myriad tangible acts of Jewish life. The corporate enterprise thus continues, while everybody can lay aside, most of the time, the disheartening ultimate questions.

CAN THE RABBINATE survive in its present form and with its present functions?

I think not, because we are now at an historic turning. The rabbinate that Jews have known for two millennia ended in America within the last decade. This hardly noticed event is as historic a turning as the beginnings of the rabbinate in ancient Israel, when the priests of the Temple lost the leadership of Judaism to the nascent class of Pharisaic teachers.

The rabbinate arose then as a new leadership, which the Jews were willing to accept, because the rabbis were the arbiters of a system of religious values which commanded their assent. While the early Pharisees were rising to dominance during the last years of the Second Temple, the priesthood remained, and it continued to perform ritual functions, but these activities became ever more vestigial. The business of Jewish life then became the cultivation of the values commanded in the Talmud, as interpreted by the scholars within that tradition. At the dawn of Jewish modernity, in the nineteenth century, the rabbinate secularized this role for a century or so, as it led the Jewish community in the name of immediate "this world" values which an oppressed minority shared: its quest for freedom and equality.

The rabbinate today is, essentially, neither judge nor leader. It is the agent of a remaining powerful and pervasive emotion about Jewish togetherness. The purely religious function of the rabbi has been becoming ever more vestigial for many decades. Indeed, it is as far now from the center of Jewish mass consciousness as were the ritual functions of the priesthood of old. The rabbi's more contemporary role as leader of the Jews in a hostile world, or as moral guide to their political action, is constantly diminishing. He has become peripheral to the major social struggles of this age.

The rabbinate thrived for many centuries by offering Jews a vision of themselves as the servants of God. It then carried on, for a relatively short time, by holding up the dream of the Jews as servants of their own quest for freedom and, therefore, as trailblazers for all the oppressed. The Jewish community within which the rabbis are working today sees itself, for the most part, as the servant of its own survival. There are no great, individual rabbinic careers, because there are no shared Jewish purposes on the American scene grand enough to evoke them.

And I see no sign of such purposes on the horizon.

The Intellectual and the Rabbi

MILTON HIMMELFARB

Because I was conscientious, I had trouble preparing this address. I had hoped that I would be able to be original and come up with some *ḥiddushim,* but then I spoiled things by reading Rabbinical Assembly literature, and that disabused me. I shall be saying things that you should already know, if only because most of them are to be found in your literature. I especially want to pay tribute to that remarkable collection of papers that emanated from the Conference on the Moral Problems of the Rabbinate last year.

To justify my title, "The Intellectual and the Rabbi," and especially the disjunction implied in the word "and," I can only plead Jewish precedent. If Sholom Aleichem could distinguish between a *shnayder* and a *mentsh,* then it is my privilege to distinguish between an intellectual and a rabbi.

Jews—and, I suppose, rabbis especially—need to be reminded that "intellectual" is not necessarily honorific. After all, it was a very intelligent man who coined that wonderfully contemptuous term "egghead." Intellectual is not synonymous with intelligent, or with educated, or with thoughtful. Intellectual is not even synonymous with university teaching. There is an overlap. Some, not all, university teachers are intellectuals; some, not all, intellectuals are university teachers. Certainly there is no necessary identification of intellectuals with doctors, lawyers, engineers, teachers. And once again, no moral or even intellectual superiority is implied when we speak of the intellectuals.

The essential characteristic of intellectuals as a group, since they emerged into history about two hundred years ago, during the Enlightenment, has been their alienation from the societies in which they live and from their communities of origin. If there is one slogan that has always characterized the intellectuals, it is this: "The enemy is at home." Even the university campuses have not been the same since the intellectuals starting pouring in. A generation or two ago the university faculties consisted almost ex-

---

Mr. Himmelfarb is Editor of the *American Jewish Year Book.*

[118]

clusively of academics, not intellectuals, while today they include many intellectuals. Ever since these began to infiltrate the university faculties, we have been regaled with I don't know how many novels every year, all exposing university life. When the intellectual went into the army, he was busy writing that little novel in his mind to expose the army after he got out. Now that he is in the university, he is busy exposing the university. The Jewish intellectual, alienated from his society and his community of origin or identification, is busy exposing the Jewish community.

To show that this is not a particularly Jewish characteristic, I will cite only the instance of the English writer Christopher Isherwood. Recently Isherwood said that when he was a young man in England in the 1930's, he was so totally taken up with hating his teachers, and the Establishment they represented, that he had no mind or energy to spare for hating the Nazis. The enemy was at home.

Rabbis, and affirmative Jews generally, tend to criticize Jewish intellectuals on the wrong ground, and are wont to call them victims of self-hate. But a psychological interpretation of the other man's point of view, or a psychological dismissal of the other man's reasoning, is not particularly useful. Freud himself disliked that way of arguing. In one of his essays Freud says that if two people are having a debate, it is destructive of rational discourse for one of them to psychologize the other. If you call someone a victim of self-hate, he will retort that you are overcompensating. You cannot have a productive discussion that way.

What is more, the assumption is wrong. It is not true that Jewish intellectuals have a greater animosity to the Jewish community than other intellectuals have to their communities. Let me cite some names of people who have worldwide fame as intellectuals, none of them a Jew: William Faulkner, Edmund Wilson, Jean-Paul Sartre. Faulkner and Wilson do not say nice things about America. In fact they say rather nasty things about America. If America has *nakhes* from them, it is because they are great writers, because these great writers are Americans. The fact that they say nasty things about America gets ignored. Similarly France is proud of Jean-Paul Sartre, but if I were doing a kind of low-order propaganda job for France, I do not think I would refer to his works to prove French greatness. One explicit message of his is that France is not an ideal society. Much the same sort of thing is even true of the maverick Soviet intellectuals. That is

[119]

the way it is with intellectuals, and that is how it has been for a long time.

As for self-hate, the prime example of an intellectual with self-hate is not a Jew. Arnold Toynbee, non-Jewish and perhaps anti-Jewish, who is white, Western, and English, is anti-white, anti-West, and anti-English. (He is also Christian, at least by birth and tradition, but many consider him to be anti-Christian.) Jewish intellectuals are not preeminent for self-hate.

Actually, if we were to look at this problem coldly and objectively, and from the outside, it would have to be turned around. The problem would no longer be why the Jewish intellectual is so alienated from the Jewish community and Jewish tradition, but why he is not *more* alienated than he is. *A priori,* that is what one would expect.

First of all, Judaism is a religion and a tradition, and an intellectual would obviously be alienated from that. The intellectuals are the heirs of Voltaire, and you will remember that Voltaire's fondest dream was of the day when the last king had been strangled with the entrails of the last priest. The horror of monarchy (and all that monarchy symbolizes) and the horror of priesthood (and all that priesthood symbolizes) still characterize the intellectuals, two hundred years after Voltaire.

On top of that, the Jewish intellectual has a specific reason for distancing himself from the Jewish community and tradition. *Es iz shver tsu zayn a Yid.* If a theological or a philosophical argument cannot be made for the superiority of Christianity to Judaism, there is an esthetic argument that can be made, and one that may be expected to appeal to many intellectuals. After all, Christianity has Gothic architecture, Renaissance painting, the poetry of John Milton, the music of Bach. We Jews have not. Thus not only is Judaism a religion and tradition—which for the intellectual would be bad enough—but also, by the criterion of relatedness to the high culture of the West, it is distinctly second-best to the religion and tradition of most Westerners. Yet the alienation of Jewish intellectuals is only moderate.

One finds Jewish intellectuals respectful of the Jewish tradition—in a distant sort of way, of course, but respectful nevertheless. Surprisingly often, when they criticize Jews and the Jewish community it is by the standards of Jewish tradition: the Jews are seen as falling short of their own tradition. That is an implicit moral of the novels and the stories, say, of Philip Roth, who

[120]

criticizes his Jewish characters not because they are insufficiently American—"American" is no term of praise for him—but because they are insufficiently *mentshlikh;* and *mentshlikhkayt* is well defined in the Jewish tradition. That is true not only of Roth. There is a real respect for the Jewish tradition as that which teaches how to be a *mentsh,* which is concerned with being a *mentsh.* In their way Jewish intellectuals affirm that tradition.

Still, it should give us something to think about that the direct source of the knowledge or perception of this tradition among many Jewish intellectuals is not the Bible, or rabbinic literature, or a synagogue experience. A cursory examination leads me to believe that for many of them the direct source of this tradition is Yiddish literature (in translation, of course), and you know that Yiddish literature is ambiguously Jewish in any religious sense.

It is pointless to tell you about the tensions between the rabbi and the intellectual, because you know about them. Whether those tensions are implicit or explicit, potential or actual, they are there. From the intellectual's side, a major trouble with the rabbi is that he is (or is imagined to be) an Establishment man, and almost by definition the intellectual is against Establishments. The rabbi is thought to be an Establishment man in several different ways: in belief, in thought, in conduct, and in the kind of society he apparently upholds and seems to be happy in.

As we have seen, the intellectual is alienated. But of course, that is an ambiguous statement, because today there are so many alienated intellectuals that they can form a rather cozy society or subsociety of their own. (You may remember that immortal cartoon in the *New Yorker* where the artist's girl friend says to him, "Why must you be a non-conformist like everyone else?") It is possible to have a society of the alienated, and thus to have the best of both worlds. You have the stance of alienation and yet you are not terribly lonely because there are so many like you. Or again, as we have seen, the intellectual is untraditional. But that, too, is an ambiguous statement, because by now untraditionalism is itself a tradition more than two hundred years old.

Yet, for whatever comfort it is to a Rabbinical Assembly, it is my impression that among all clergymen the rabbis are the least—what is the word I want?—rejected by the intelligentsia. I think that for intellectuals the priest is the primary clerical enemy. First of all, to many he is an uncanny figure, on account of

[121]

celibacy. And there is always the image of the priest as persecutor and bigot.

As for the Protestant minister, he is dismissed with a kind of contempt as being a hick. Over and over again people have told me that when they were in college, everyone knew that the smartest students were in physics, the next smartest in engineering, and so on down the hierarchy of smartness, to the least smart students in the divinity school and the teachers' college. I do not know whether this represents reality, but at the very least it represents a well-established mythology.

The rabbi, for his part, is exempt from all this. Whatever stereotype there may be about the rabbi, it is not a stereotype of flabby intellect or lack of education. Basically, he is regarded as intelligent and learned—though, of course, in the wrong way. There is respect for the learning and the intelligence; let us understand that. But I do not think that the respect is increased when rabbis try to deemphasize what is specifically rabbinical. Lord Melbourne was an eighteenth-century survivor, quite lacking in Victorian piety. During the course of a debate in the Lords on some ecclesiastical matter, which was monopolized by the Bishops' Bench, he was not impressed by their knowledge of the subject they were discussing or by the manner in which they were discussing it; so he turned to a fellow peer and murmured: "The silly fellows don't know their own silly business."

Sometimes clergymen are tempted to sound like alienated free spirits, very emancipated and liberal. That does not work. I do not think, for example, that rabbis, generally—and I say this candidly—have done much good for themselves, and perhaps even the Jewish community, by the way they have expressed their feelings about church-state matters. A rabbi should not talk about church-state matters in the same way that secularists do. You may want the Regents' Prayer abolished—although I personally would not—but at least let your language be your own. Do not think the secularists have any greater respect for you when you talk their lingo. They either think you are hypocritical—a secularist pretending to be a rabbi—or a dupe.

Or again—and here I am glad to say that rabbis have not been conspicuous—there is a temptation to sound liberal in certain kinds of so-called censorship cases. Recently *Lady Chatterly's Lover* was on trial in England, and the Anglican clergy made fools of themselves. Some of them, including a prelate or two,

[122]

said: "Not only are we opposed to censorship, but also we consider this to be a deeply moral book." That is nonsense. It seems to me that if a rabbi were to express himself on the issue of *Lady Chatterly's Lover*—and I do not know that any has done so— he ought to say that it is an immoral book. He might add that that has nothing to do with whether it should be censored, that there is a difference between sin and crime, and that not all sins are crimes, to be punished as crimes. But he should also say that the book is sinful, in that it preaches adultery, and pagan, in that it teaches a priapic philosophy, which is the very essence of paganism. For a clergyman to say that the book is a deeply moral book does not win him respect, even from those who do not believe that adultery is a sin, or who laugh at the very idea of sin.

Let us end the digression. Much of the prejudice of the intellectuals against the rabbis is justified, according to your own literature. Some rabbis *are* too Establishment. Some rabbis *do* approach their congregations' tastes too closely. There has been plenty of rabbinic self-criticism on this score.

However, what is peculiar is that in their attitudes toward rabbis, intellectuals are often like the congregations they would not dream of joining. For instance, they both attribute to a rabbi, as rabbi, all kinds of primitive and nonsensical beliefs that in fact he does not have. What intellectuals do not realize is that more often than not they are in full agreement with the rabbis. They seem to think that the rabbis like their congregations, but you yourselves have repeatedly said that you would not join your congregations, either. (This leaves me in a peculiar position. I belong to a Conservative congregation.) If the intellectuals only knew it, they need not bestir themselves to document the awfulness of bourgeois Jewish life. The rabbis have already done it, and it is all there in the RA and the CCAR *Proceedings*.

It seems to me that part of the rabbi's resentment of the intellectual—and it exists—must come from envy. And really, the intellectual's position is enviable. He is free, free of responsibility. He can say what he pleases. How tired a rabbi must be of carrying the burden that has been put on his shoulders, and how often he must yearn for the freedom to say what is in his heart. Over and over again in your conventions the talk has been of the conflict between your priestly and your prophetic roles. You say that you really prefer your prophetic role, but, alas, your responsibility ties you down to your priestly role. What you probably

[123]

mean is that you would like to have the freedom and the lack of responsibility of the intellectuals. Who would not?

One final point about intellectuals, before we turn our attention to the students. From one point of view, the tension between rabbis and intellectuals is the outcome of a state of affairs that dates back not two hundred years ago but two thousand years ago. The hostility of the intellectuals to the rabbis is a kind of poetic justice, a punishment for an ancient and persistent rabbinical crime. That rabbinical crime is the contempt of the *talmidei ḥakhamim,* the *sheyne Yidn,* for the *ammei ha-aretz,* the *proste Yidn.*

In America the intellectuals are the children and grandchildren not of the *talmidei ḥakhamim* but of the *ammei ha-aretz,* for a simple reason which we American Jews, in our prosperity and glory, would like to forget. After all, who went to America? Overwhelmingly, it was not the elite of learning, piety, or money, but the *shnayders,* the *shusters,* and the *ferd-ganovim.*

Repeatedly, throughout Jewish history, there has been evidence of the vindictive resentment of the *am ha-aretz* against the *talmid ḥakham.* And the resentment was justified. You remember the notorious, unforgivable passage in *Pesaḥim* (49b):

לעולם ימכור אדם כל מה שיש לו וישא בת תלמיד חכם. לא מצא בת תלמיד חכם ישא בת גדולי הדור. לא מצא בת גדולי הדור ישא בת ראשי כנסיות. לא מצא בת ראשי כנסיות ישא בת גבאי צדקה. לא מצא בת גבאי צדקה ישא בת מלמדי תינוקות. ולא ישא בת עמי הארץ, מפני שהן שקץ, ונשותיהן שרץ, ועל בנותיהן הוא אומר (דברים כ״ז, כ״א): ארור שוכב עם כל בהמה.

It is an old class struggle, and we have paid dearly for it since the time when it was probably a major element in the rise of Christianity. In the past century it led to anti-religious movements among Jews and to a situation where workers who might themselves be pious nevertheless supported Jewish parties or unions that were anti-religious. The immigrant *ammei ha-aretz* in the United States valued education: after all, they were Jews; but what they gave their children was a good secular education. In their resentment of the *sheyne Yid,* they neglected or even contemned Jewish education for the same children.

The irony about the passage in *Pesaḥim* is that today it is impossible to distinguish between *ammei ha-aretz,* on the one hand, and *gedolei ha-dor, rashei kenesiyot,* or *gabba'ei tzedakah* on the other hand. Only the *melammdei tinokot* retain their old

[124]

position at the bottom of the ladder—in the eyes of the rabbis as well as of the laity. Altogether, of the *talmidei ḥakhamim* it may be said: כי רוח יזרעו וסופתה יקצרו.

Hebrew teachers and Jewish education are a good transition to a discussion of our younger educated generation (college students and the like), as distinct from the intellectuals. Immediately we are confronted with a problem. You remember the old joke about the propaganda man who comes from Moscow to a *kolkhoz* and tells the peasants, at great length, how good everything is. Afterwards he asks, "Are there any questions?" Of course no one wants to say anything, but finally an old man raises his hand and says, "Yes, I have a question, Comrade. If everything is so good, why is everything so bad?"

In a sense, that is our problem with our college youth. They are a postwar generation, and it is in their time, as you well know, that Jewish children in America were reached by Jewish education more than at any other time in American history—about four out of five.

When we add to this that not only Jews but Catholics, too, have discovered that college apostasy is always preceded by high-school disenchantment, then it is clear that the problem of the college youth is not a problem of the college. It is, rather, a problem of the synagogues, the congregations, the Hebrew schools—and the homes—which presumably have some influence on the young people before they enter college.

What the Catholics call apostasy we would call alienation. (Let us hope that it is only a temporary alienation.) It has some obvious causes. First of all, there is adolescent rebellion. One reason for going to college is to get away from the family. The Jewish family today is not what it used to be, but it may still be perhaps slightly closer-knit than the American norm, and at some point the close-knit family can be perceived by its members as a stifling family. So you escape to college and there you try out your grown-up stance. And since Judaism is very closely identified with *mishpokhe,* to get away from *mishpokhe* the most sensible and obvious thing to do is to get away from Judaism.

Next, there is a style-of-life conflict between the younger generation and the middle-aged Jewish Establishment. Let me use this as an illustration. We are here in this resort, but we could just as well be at the Concord or Grossinger's. Those are the kinds of place to which middle-aged Jews like to go. I do not think that college students like to go there. They would go to a ski resort. Note the difference. Grossinger's or the Concord is lush, soft, luxurious: one eats a lot, there is much emphasis on eating. The ski resort may be just as expensive, but it is more strenuous: you go out in the cold, you fall into the snow, your face is red and chapped. It is a very different sort of thing. Or again, the older generation, if it has the money, likes a Cadillac. I do not think the college generation does. It likes a sports car, which is not nearly so cushioned, though it can be just as expensive. The styles of life are quite different.

Many of our synagogues are, in this sense, middle-aged and Grossingerish, and the best symbol of that is the primacy of eating in the synagogue. The *Kiddush* after *Musaf* on the Sabbath, the bagels and lox of the brotherhood on Sunday morning, the reign of the caterer—these all attest to the style of the middle-aged consumer (in a literal sense). An institution where that style prevails is likely to antagonize the young. Conservative Judaism was founded by people for whom the style of life of the old-fashioned Orthodox *shul* and its people were unacceptable. Can it be that our younger generation now finds our institutions, which we created rebelliously, to be as inappropriate as we once found the Orthodox *shul*?

My friend and colleague Marshall Sklare is doing an extraordinarily interesting piece of research in a well-to-do midwestern suburb, where the way in which some Jews are living in the 1960's may point to the way in which the rest of us will be living in the 1980's. He asked a local rabbi how he would briefly characterize the difference between his present congregation and other congregations he knew. The rabbi thought for a moment and came up with a totally unexpected answer. He said: "You know, I believe that the women in my congregation are the thinnest, slenderest synagogue women in America. In my previous congregations the women were very conscious of diets: they talked about diets all the time, and some of them even followed diets. For the women in my present congregation food is not even a temptation."

I pause on this triviality because I think that it is symbolic of much more. I believe that there is a style-of-life conflict between us and the younger people which is rather hard for us to perceive, because we too speak English without an accent and because the difference between them and us is not nearly so marked as the difference between us and the immigrant genera-

[126]

tion. But for our college children the difference is not small, and that is one reason why they find themselves uncomfortable in our adult institutions.

There are still other reasons. I will not mention the horror that all rabbis feel, and all intellectuals feel, about the vulgarity of the middle class. Sometimes I think we exaggerate that horror, because there are sins worse than vulgarity. But that does not make vulgarity a virtue, and it does not mean that vulgarity should get incorporated into synagogue life and be explicitly or implicitly approved—as, for instance, in the form of New Year's Eve parties in the synagogue, with an advertising campaign that stresses free setups.

We joke about Bar Mitzvahs, and of course they are a joke. The one person we tend to forget when we talk about the awfulness of the Bar Mitzvah is the Bar Mitzvah boy himself. He is thirteen years old, he is in junior high school, he is not a fool, and he is thinking. In the *Commentary* symposium that Rabbi Kahn mentioned, one participant had not yet recovered from the total revulsion that was created in him by his Bar Mitzvah years earlier. It was easy to poke fun at what he said, but even while I was poking fun I realized that something was there which could not be laughed away. Let us never forget the effect all this has upon a Bar Mitzvah boy. He may not think of it now, but five or ten years from now he will think of it. He will remember that right after the Bar Mitzvah ceremony, with the prayer and the Torah reading and the sermon, everyone started dancing the twist.

College students and, more particularly, intelligent high-school students are said to be as devoted as ever to Salinger's *Catcher in the Rye*. *Catcher in the Rye* has a simple moral or theme—sincerity, honesty, hatred of phoniness; and it is that moral or theme that means so much to our young people. They hate phoniness. But there is abundant phoniness in the Judaism that they know. And the phoniness can be not only obvious, as in the case of the Bar Mitzvahs, but also insidiously present, in the very best that we do. Indeed, the better the job we do, the more reason there is to fear the effects of whatever phoniness may creep in. *Corruptio optimi pessima*.

For example, you preach as if you really believe what Hertz says in those *Ḥumashim* that your congregations use. But some of your young people are going to find out that you do not really agree with Hertz, and what will happen then?

[127]

Another instance. I have mentioned my friend Marshall Sklare. His children are the only fourth-generation Conservative Jews I know. (Dr. Sklare's grandfather was one of the founders of a Conservative synagogue in Chicago.) A son is now attending a Conservative day school, and what could be better than that? But the boy is only ten or eleven now. Soon he will be sixteen, and what is now troubling him only vaguely or inarticulately will have become clear and articulate by then. He studies Genesis and the teacher expounds the creation story exactly as it is written. But the boy is a middle-class American child. Like others of his kind, he has read—he owns—a large amount of the children's literature that is practically inescapable in America today: for example, the Book of Ancient Man, the Book of the Dinosaurs, the Book of Geology, the Book of Astronomy. (The books may actually be in the school library.) By the time such a child is ten years old, he probably knows those things better than you and I. This boy comes home and asks his father: "Daddy, if Adam and Eve were the first human beings, where do the cave men come in?" He had asked the question in school, and he got an evasive answer. When he is older and thinks back, it will be hard for him not to assume one of two things: either his teachers were dishonest, teaching what they knew to be not so, or else they were fools and actually believed what they taught.

So the child goes to the best of schools, and yet may come to think of his Jewish education as phony. Evasiveness *is* phony.

A final instance. My daughter has a fine teacher in her fine Hebrew school. This woman is Orthodox, a graduate of the Stern College for Women, and I thought I had learned to make my peace with that. But recently the principal, pleased with a composition that my daughter had written, showed it to me. When I read it I hit the ceiling. Martha had written: "Abraham was the greatest Jew because he was the first man to learn about the true G-d." I cannot stand that spelling.

What this does is to drive my daughter into a more Orthodox direction not only than her family—that in itself might not be bad—but also than her synagogue, whose school she attends. So that right then and there she is experiencing a certain kind of phoniness. It may not prove to be irremediably damaging in the long run, but on the other hand it may. Precisely because the school is good, it is all the more vulnerable to phoniness.

[128]

Something has happened not only to our children but to us also. I like the Rabbinical Assembly *Siddur:* I like the fact that it has altered the prayer for the restoration of the sacrificial cult, and I like the Conservative prayer for the government. To refresh my memory about the Orthodox prayer for the government, I went to look it up in the latest Orthodox *Siddur*. I discovered that the Rabbinical Council of America *Siddur's* prayer for the welfare of the government is very much like that of the Rabbinical Assembly *Siddur*. Something has happened. Even the modern Orthodox avoid the traditional *ha-notein teshu-a:*

... מלך מלכי המלכים ברחמיו יתן בלבם ובלב כל יועציהם ושריהם
לעשות טובה עמנו ועם כל ישראל ...

We are all emancipated Jews. We can no longer tolerate the kind of headline that reads: "Plane Crashes, Two Jews Killed." And if we do not accept that for ourselves any more, then certainly our children do not accept it for themselves.

In a well-known study that compared the attitudes of Jewish adolescents and parents, a remarkable difference was found between them on one score. The parents were prepared to agree that *shiker iz a goy* might be a true statement, but not the children. In principle, the parents may have been more nearly right than the children, but the children could not say it or believe it. Call the reason what you will—the American creed, which they have internalized and made their own, or democracy, or modernity. Whatever the reason, that is the way things are.

So we talk to these young people and we warn them against intermarriage. What we say to them, basically, is this: "Marriage is hard, you don't know how hard it can be. If you marry a gentile boy, or a gentile girl, the first time you have a fight—and you will have fights—why, scratch a gentile and find an anti-Semite." Or if we do not use those blunt words, we say, " . . . you will find anti-Semitic sentiments being expressed."

I think that, instead of being persuaded by such talk, our young people are repelled. It implies that there is something inherently defective in gentiles, that every gentile is doomed almost biologically to be an anti-Semite. Factually, our young people may be excessive in their rejection of the idea of a gentile propensity to anti-Semitism. Nevertheless, it antagonizes them. Speaking to them in language that sounds like that will not persuade them.

As for us of the middle-aged generation, while in our refusal

[129]

to say the traditional *ha-notein teshu-a* we are modern, in the matter of proselytism we are not modern at all. The *Neturei Karta* oppose Israel because Israel should have been established by the Messiah. We, for our part, are opposed to proselytizing because we say that the Messiah should come and proselytize for us. Yesterday your president discussed a certain kind of cultural lag among rabbis on how Christians now regard Judaism. There is another kind of cultural lag, and that is a reluctance, a distaste for engaging in the enterprise of winning over Christians to Judaism. I believe that our young people would respond better to a call for proselytizing than to our present exhortations against intermarriage. In any event, they are obviously paying less and less attention to those exhortations.

We are told that proselytizing is untraditional, and it is hinted that those who favor Jewish proselytism have been unwholesomely influenced by Christian modes of thought. But as I read the recent scholarship, the Jewish distaste for proselytism is not so ancient or traditional as all that. Bernhard Blumenkranz says that Jewish proselytizing did not end in Christian Europe with Constantine but with the crusades, i. e., in the twelfth and thirteenth centuries, not the fourth. Either way, the prohibition against proselytism was imposed upon the Jews as a disability and had to be enforced with the death penalty. Ironically, now that we are free to proselytize we have come to regard abstaining from proselytism as being alone authentically Jewish. The analogy that comes to mind, *le-havdil,* is the behavior of certain Chinese after Sun Yat-sen's revolution, when they refused to give up the pigtail. They had forgotten that the pigtail had been imposed upon the Chinese as a token of conquest and subjection by the Manchus in the seventeenth century. By 1912 the pigtail had become a sign of Chinese-*kayt,* and they did not want to relinquish it. And so, I think, it is with us. Our attitude to *gerei tzedek* partakes of the same thing.

We do not realize how unique America is in this regard. Dr. Eichhorn did that study ten years ago about conversions to Judaism, and you will remember that he said that in the latest year, Reform and Conservative rabbis had solemnized 1,500 to 2,000 conversions. The conversions were more or less spontaneous, nearly always in preparation for marriage, and Dr. Eichhorn thought the trend was up.

What is more, our profit from such conversions is qualita-

[130]

tive as well as quantitative. I have been told, by one who should know, that our imports are better than our exports.

In the entire history of the Jewish people since the crusades, conversions to Judaism have been anecdotes, with a story here and a story there. We, who have the *zekhut* to live in a time and place in which conversion to Judaism has become statistical rather than anecdotal, should be glad. Instead, we are suspicious. We still talk about intermarriage and conversion as if we were in Germany in 1850 and not in America in 1963.

Or again, if we are really serious about survival, why do we not think about another set of statistics? One never hears sermons advising American Jews to have more children. Instead, we are told—as if Jews needed the hint—that our tradition permits or actually encourages birth control. But demographically, we are a dying group in America. We are not reproducing ourselves. We are not only losing relatively, in our ratio to the population as a whole, we are also losing absolutely, in numbers. One would think that we should be concerned with little things like that.

Why mention these matters—proselytism, birth rate—here? They are important in themselves, but also, and more relevantly, what we have been doing and saying about them, or not doing and not saying, is apt to strike our young people as having an element of the phony about it. And that, as we have seen, can be fatal.

The time has come for *divrei neḥamah*. The end of the speech is in sight.

Despite all these worries of ours, our young people are a better generation of Jews than any we have known in America for a long time—probably more healthy emotionally, certainly better-educated generally, and perhaps also better-educated Jewishly. And they have the advantage—which we did not have in my day nearly to the same degree—of knowing, or being able to know, many rabbis who do not merely tell them what it means to be a cultivated, humane man and a good Jew, but who actually show them, by the kind of life they lead and the kind of people they are. And the force of this example, which is remarkably widespread—not least in the Hillel Foundations—is not to be underestimated. It is one important reason why the Bernard Berenson phenomenon is less likely now than it used to be.

I will end by quoting from an impressive young Israeli journalist, Shabbetai Tevet, who was in this country a year or two

[131]

ago on a UJA tour and probably saw more Hillel Foundations and college campuses than anyone who is not in the Washington office of Hillel. He wrote a book about his American travels called *Shefa Vḥaradah,* "Affluence and Anxiety." One unintended effect of that book is to show how complete has been the defeat of all modes of Jewishness other than the religious.

In 1957, at the Moscow youth festival, the young Israelis, invited to the pitifully few synagogues, did not know what they were supposed to do when they were honored with an *aliyah,* and they began to be ashamed of their Jewish illiteracy. When they returned to Israel the *toda-ah yehudit* program was instituted in the schools to teach Israelis about Judaism. When Tevet visits America, he finds that America, too, teaches the necessity for Israelis to have a *toda-ah yehudit.*

Tevet is talking about a Hillel service he attended, and he does not like some of the things he saw, like skipping back and forth in the *Siddur* and the poor attendance, but then he goes on to say this:

אף שקבלת־שבת כזו . . . היתה מעוררת בי גיחוך, חשתי נחיתות מסוימת בפני הסטודנטים המעטים שידעו את זמירות השבת. כי עד לבואי בפעם הזאת לארצות הברית, מימי לא הייתי בבית כנסת לקבל את השבת ולא ידעתי היטב גם אחת מהזמירות. אפילו חשתי בצער על שילידי ישראל, כמוני, במקרים כה רבים חונכו וגודלו ללא זיקה כלשהי למסורת היהודית של קבלת־שבת. אחרי הכל, "לכה דודי" ו"צאתכם ל'שלום" חשובים בהווי היהודי לא פחות מאשר השינון הנעשה בבתי הספר בישראל של אילו פרקי תנ״ך, וודאי שהם חוליית־קשר חיונית בין יהודי ישראל ליהודי התפוצה. הנה אף על פי שאנו הישראלים מחונכים על ערכי יהדות יסודיים כתנ״ך וכדברי־ימי היהודים, וחיים אנו במסגרת מדינית־ריבונית שההווי שלה מצוי מהיהדות, . . . מקופחים אנו, אפילו לעומת הבורים בסטודנטים היהודיים שבארצות־הברית, במה ששייך למסורת היהודית שנרקמה בבית הכנסת. אם נרצה בדו־שיח עם הסטודנטים היהודיים האמריקאים, לא נוכל לנהלו בלשון משותפת לנו ולהם ללא זיקה משלנו להווי של הפולחן היהודי. יתכן מאד, נדמה לי במסעי, כי הגשר האיתן היחיד בינינו לבין הסטודנטים היהודיים בארצות הברית . . . הוא ב"לכה דודי" ודומיו, כשנדע אותם.

There is still a great distance to go, of course, but we have come a long way.

[132]

6

The Synagogue in America

WOLFE KELMAN

I

The formal history of the organized American Jewish community is customarily traced to the establishment in 1654 of Congregation Shearith Israel in New Amsterdam, by twenty-three refugees from Brazil, who were compelled to flee their tropical home when the Dutch were expelled by the Portuguese. However, for several centuries thereafter, the Jewish community of North America remained small and insignificant. Indeed, it was not until the nineteenth century, which witnessed mass migrations to the United States from both Eastern and Western Europe, that the American Jewish community as we know it, with its particular institutions and varied religious life, began to assume shape. Typical of congregations which were established in the nineteenth century was the Central Synagogue in New York City, which recently celebrated its one hundredth anniversary. Central Synagogue, founded in 1870 by a group of middle-class merchants who had emigrated to New York from Bohemia some thirty years earlier, is unusual in that it is still situated in its original location. Few American synagogues of similar vintage can make that claim; most have moved from one location to another, following the migration of their members from the first areas of settlement to areas of greater affluence and, eventually, to the suburbs. In places like Newark, Baltimore, and Cleveland, synagogues have abandoned the inner city altogether.

155

The Synagogue in America

The featured speaker at the dedication ceremonies of the Central Synagogue, on December 14, 1870, was Rabbi Isaac Mayer Wise. This was the same Isaac Mayer Wise, also a Bohemian immigrant, who shortly thereafter was to found Reform Judaism in this country with the establishment of the Union of American Hebrew Congregations (UAHC) in 1873. The Conservative movement traces its formal beginnings to the establishment of the Jewish Theological Seminary in 1886, a development prompted in large part in reaction to the promulgation the year before of the so-called Pittsburgh platform enunciating the official positions of classical Reform. The United Synagogue of America, the congregational arm of the Conservative movement, was founded in 1913 by Solomon Schechter, the second President of the Jewish Theological Seminary. It was hoped that the United Synagogue would serve to oppose the innovations of Reform, but it soon found itself outflanked by the mass immigration of Eastern European Jews which led to the development of an organized Orthodox community.

In its founding statement, the United Synagogue declared its purposes as follows: "To further the observance of the Sabbath and the dietary laws; to preserve in the service the reference to Israel's past and the hopes of Israel's restoration, and to maintain the traditional centrality of Hebrew as the language of prayer and in the curriculum of the religious school." The concluding section of this statement reflects the tensions which still exist, although in diminishing degree, within the Conservative movement: "It shall be the aim of the United Synagogue of America, while not endorsing the innovations introduced by any of its constituent bodies, to embrace all elements essentially loyal to traditional Judaism and in sympathy with the purposes outlined above." This deliberate ambiguity reflects a not entirely successful attempt to establish a movement which would be hospitable to a wide variety of traditional congregations and yet not exclude those which had introduced some departures from historical Jewish practice. This compromise formula, of course, did not satisfy those synagogue leaders who were opposed to any innovation at all and who had joined in the establishment of the Conservative movement as a counterforce to Reform. Thus it happened that synagogues like Congregation Zichron Ephraim, Kehillat Jeshurun, and the Jewish Center of Manhattan, which were modeled on the Orthodox synagogues of Western Europe, with their large sanctuaries, choirs, and rabbis who preached in a variety of languages, and had originally been served by alumni of the Jewish Theological Seminary, are now identified with Orthodox Yeshiva University and led by Yeshiva alumni.

It is revealing to trace the growth in the number of congregations and their denominational affiliation during recent decades. Volume 31 of the *American Jewish Year Book* (1929) lists 3,118 congregations in existence as of 1927, without mentioning their denominational affiliation. Volume 39 (1937) lists 290 temples affiliated with the UAHC, claiming a membership of 50,000 families, and 250 synagogues affiliated with the United Synagogue of America, claiming 75,000 families. Volume 51 (1950) lists 392 temples affiliated with the UAHC, claiming 150,000 families; 365 synagogues affiliated with the United Synagogue, claiming 100,000 families; and 500 synagogues affiliated with the Union of Orthodox Jewish Congregations of America (UOJC), claiming 100,000 families. Volume 62 (1961) finds the United Synagogue with a larger number of affiliates than the UAHC, with 700 congregations as opposed to 605. Volume 64 (1963) contains a statement by the UOJC claiming a membership of 3,900 congregations in the United States and Canada. In addition to the *American Jewish Year Book* listings, both the UAHC and the United Synagogue publish lists of all their affiliates. (This practice is not followed by the UOJC, and it is therefore difficult to verify the accuracy of its stated number of affiliates.) In 1970 the UAHC listed 698 affiliated congregations; the United Synagogue, 832 affiliates.

As for the rabbis who serve these congregations, the Conservative group draws its rabbis, the majority of whom are graduates of the Jewish Theological Seminary, primarily from the ranks of the Rabbinical Assembly, which claims over 1,000 members. About 200 congregations affiliated with the United Synagogue, most of them in smaller communities, are served by rabbis, graduates of various *yeshivas*, who are not members of the Rabbinical Assembly. To further confound the observer, a substantial number of members of the Rabbinical Council of America, the largest of the English-speaking Orthodox rabbinical organizations, serve in congregations presently or formerly affiliated with the United Synagogue. Congregations affiliated with the UAHC are served primarily by members of the Central Conference of American Rabbis (CCAR) (predominantly graduates of Hebrew Union College-Jewish Institute of Religion). The Orthodox situation is less clear. It is impossible to determine exactly who are the rabbis serving the various Orthodox congregations, since there are numerous Orthodox rabbinical associations as well as many rabbis of

157

Orthodox synagogues who have chosen not to affiliate with any rabbinical organization.

II

Suburbanization, assimilation, and secularization were the most dramatic developments to mark the American Jewish community in the years following World War II, a period which witnessed the virtual departure of Jews from the inner cities to the suburbs of the major metropolitan areas. Accordingly, the past twenty-five years saw hundreds of synagogues established in new suburban communities. Most of these tended to identify themselves with the Conservative movement and, to a growing extent, with Reform. Orthodox Jews, who depend on a network of religious institutions for their religious needs, including a synagogue within easy walking distance, were less likely to move to suburbs lacking in such basic Jewish institutions as day schools, Sabbath-observing groceries, and *mikvahs* (ritual baths). Even in those urban communities which underwent fundamental demographic changes, the Orthodox synagogues were usually the last to leave. For example, the Hasidic residents of the Crown Heights and Williamsburg sections of Brooklyn (surrounded by black and Puerto Rican ghettos), under the leadership of the Lubavitcher and Satmarer *rebbes*, have insisted on remaining. The *rebbes* have used every moral and political pressure to persuade their followers not to abandon the institutions they had so painfully established.

The postwar period witnessed another development. In the larger cities, numerous synagogues which had not formerly been served by rabbis, or had been served by Orthodox rabbis, switched their affiliation from Orthodox to Conservative. Other synagogues postponed this change until they erected new buildings in more desirable residential areas. In the suburbs themselves there was a mushrooming of hundreds of synagogue-center buildings which soon became the focus of all communal, as well as religious, Jewish activity.

Jewish families who moved to the suburbs made the adjustment to their new surroundings—the ranch houses and lawns and car pools—with relative ease. It was more difficult to perpetuate an attachment to the living reality of historical Jewish tradition and memory. Almost immediately the new suburbanites joined a synagogue, not so much

158

for their own needs as for "the sake of the children," since synagogue membership provided handy Jewish educational facilities. Attendance at Hebrew school or Sunday school, in turn, qualified the children for *Bar Mitzvah, Bat Mitzvah,* and Confirmation (with all the attendant lavish trimmings). These adolescent occasions, however, frequently marked the end of both the children's attendance in religious school and their parents' expensive membership in the temple or synagogue.

This fact leads to a frequent misreading of the statistics regarding synagogue affiliation and membership. The percentages may fluctuate from area to area and year to year, but the statistics often reflect the rotating nature of suburban synagogue membership. Many families join a synagogue only for the period during which their children are required to attend religious school, until *Bar Mitzvah* or Confirmation, after which time they resign their membership and are replaced by other families with children who have reached the age of preparation for *Bar Mitzvah*.

Thus, "child-centeredness" became a feature of postwar American Jewish religious life. Jewish parents, members of a "lost" Jewish generation, became seized with the hope that their children would somehow find in the local synagogue, during the few hours a week allotted for the purpose, enough knowledge and commitment to grow up into members of a secure, rooted, "returning" generation. The hope, unfortunately, was rarely realized.

Aware of the shortcomings of the existing Jewish education, the Conservative movement, shortly after World War II, established a Commission on Jewish Education to devise standards for and to service the growing number of religious schools under congregational auspices. One of the first standards adopted by the Commission was the requirement that a child, beginning at age eight, attend religious school for a minimum of six hours per week (two hours three times a week), and that such attendance be a prerequisite for *Bar Mitzvah* and *Bat Mitzvah*. This standard was enthusiastically supported by Conservative rabbis and educators, for varied reasons. Some welcomed the suggested requirement in order to prevent their synagogues from becoming *Bar Mitzvah* factories for children who had been hastily prepared by professional *Bar Mitzvah* teachers to recite mechanically the requisite *Torah* blessings. Others welcomed this requirement as an incentive for more intensive Jewish education than could be offered in a one-day-a-week, Sunday-morning religious school.

However, the attempt to impose the Commission's standards was not always welcomed by either the lay leadership of the synagogues or by potential members, who regarded this as an unwelcome addition to the suburban child's already overburdened schedule. Some parents were also affronted when their children came home from religious school with information about rituals and demands for observance which were inconsistent with home patterns. Such families often joined the local Reform temple and, in some instances, Orthodox and Conservative synagogues which did not press the particular educational requirements or create unwelcome conflicts.

Although the suburban synagogue boom is a recent phenomenon, occurring only within the last twenty-five years, already it evokes a distant and hollow ring in recollection. As with so many strands of the American dream which inspired so much individual and institutional energy for a generation, the current mood does not seem to find satisfaction in contemplating the achievements, results, and consequences of maturity. As has often been noted, most problems are the result of solutions; pursuing a goal or ambition is often more satisfying than a realized dream. Thus, children raised in permissive affluence envy the struggles and denials of their disadvantaged neighbors. American Jewish children, offspring of parents who sought integration into a society which placed high values on the WASP virtues of dignity and conformity, in many instances now prefer to search for the roots of their Jewishness as well as for other forms of ethnic identity.

An earlier generation abandoned the "old-fashioned" synagogues where the men were segregated from the women and replaced them with modern ranch style, multifunctional buildings decorated with the latest art styles. But apparently this was insufficient to stimulate or retain the religious interest of their children who, along with so many of their peers, became full-fledged participants in the Age of Aquarius. The realization began to dawn that antiseptic buildings, responsive readings in the vernacular, and so on, were not the panaceas that might attract the disinterested back to the synagogue. In this context, one can understand the growing attraction of Hasidism and its romantic appeal to the yearning for the intimacy of a small fellowship and the excitement of the exotic. Similarly, disenchantment with the suburban synagogue helps to explain various recent attempts among Reform and Conservative synagogues at liturgical experimentation, from new High Holiday supplements to rock Sabbath services.

It is difficult, though, to speak with any real authority about the state of the present-day American synagogue. Until recently, there have been relatively few studies in this area, although some communities and synagogues have published histories and a few rabbis have written pertinent memoirs. There have also been scattered attempts at preparing studies of the religious constituency of the American Jewish community (most of them, curiously, under secular sponsorship, like The American Jewish Committee). There are, in addition, the Lakeville studies by Marshall Sklare,[1] which contain considerable information about the religious affiliations and attitudes of the residents of an affluent Chicago suburb. (It is questionable, however, whether "Lakeville," with its high income Jewish residents belonging to four Reform temples and one Conservative congregation, can be considered representative.)

The UAHC-commissioned study on its congregational constituency, by Leonard Fein of Brandeis University, was published in 1972. Not to be outdone by the lay arm, the Reform movement's rabbinic organization has also recently published a study by Theodore Lenn covering a wide "range of rabbinic procedures and thinking, congregational attitudes, personal conceptions of the rabbinate, the behavior of boards and congregants, changes in ideology."

The Conservative rabbinate has also conducted a self-study. At the Seventieth Annual Convention of the Rabbinical Assembly, in March 1970, the members debated the role and function of their calling. A resolution was adopted establishing a representative committee to include the various age ranges and regional distribution of the membership in order to study the status of the Conservative rabbinate. That study by Martin E. Segal was completed in 1971. The congregational arm of the Conservative movement, the United Synagogue, has so far refrained from indulging in such exercises, although individual congregations have commissioned studies for particular purposes.

III

Some light may be shed on the condition of the American synagogue by observing the changing role of the American rabbi, which obviously varies from one end of the religious spectrum to the other, yet

[1] Marshall Sklare and Joseph Greenblum, *Jewish Identity on the Suburban Frontier* (New York: The American Jewish Committee and Basic Books, Inc., Publishers, 1967).

retains certain constant factors reflecting contemporary reality.

The rabbi's traditional role, first as religious authority, then as teacher and communal leader, diminishes in descending order as one moves from the committed Orthodox Jew, who still looks to his rabbi for guidance in ritual questions, to the member of a Reform congregation, who rarely troubles his rabbi about such matters. In ascending order, the contemporary rabbi is expected to conduct religious services which will retain the loyalty of the regular worshipper and attract those who never acquired or have discarded the habit of regular prayer; deliver sermons; be expert in the arts of synagogue and school administration; represent the congregation in the broader community and, increasingly, in efforts on behalf of Israel; and, above all, fulfill a pastoral function.

The changing role of the American rabbi must also be seen in its proper historical perspective. One criterion for measuring the vitality and self-sufficiency of a Jewish community is whether it is dependent on other older or larger Jewish communities for its rabbis and teachers, or has matured sufficiently to establish its own academies of higher Jewish learning. History informs us that the various "Golden Ages" of Jewish life, in Babylon, Spain, and Northern and Eastern Europe, developed only after the scholars and leaders who had migrated to those areas from older Jewish settlements had been persuaded to stay on and establish centers of Jewish learning and train a succession of native cadres of rabbis and other Jewish scholars. Those communities that continued to import rabbis and teachers remained in a sort of satellite state, reflecting the traditions and conditions of the communities to which they looked to supply their needs. Viewed from this perspective, American Jewry is only now beginning to emerge as an independent center of creative Jewish religious life, able to train an increasingly adequate number of rabbis, cantors, and scholars of sufficient stature to assure a continuing supply of professional religious personnel.

Until fairly recently, most of the rabbis of American congregations were either immigrants trained abroad or the children of immigrants. A substantial majority were the sons of rabbis, cantors, and other religious functionaries, whose family circumstances were far from affluent. The American rabbinate recruited few native-born Americans of middle-class background. This led to the unwarranted generalization that anyone who chose the rabbinate had been unable to enter the preferred professions of law, medicine, or education.

Within the past two decades, however, a change has occurred in the manner in which aspirants for the rabbinate see themselves and are seen by others. During this period of unprecedented economic, academic, and social mobility for American Jews, anyone who chose to prepare for a Jewish rabbinical career was more likely to have done so after considering the many other professional opportunities which became open to Jews. The period in question also witnessed the filling of faculty appointments in seminaries and *yeshivas* by their own graduates. American-born and trained Jewish scholars, like Louis Finkelstein and Boaz Cohen (at the Jewish Theological Seminary), or Julian Morgenstern and Nelson Glueck (at Hebrew Union College), were no longer exceptions among faculties dominated by scholars born and trained in Europe. The latter could never fully reconcile themselves to the realities of the American Jewish community, or overcome their suspicion that Jewish life in America was inferior and lacking in real substance and a viable future. It will be interesting to observe the changes in relations between faculty and alumni of seminaries with a growing proportion of faculty trained in the very schools in which they are now instructors.

None of the major Orthodox *yeshivas* are as yet headed by Talmudic scholars born or trained in America. Almost without exception, the present heads are products of the major Lithuanian Talmudical academies, with their emphasis on study by and for an elite and very little concern for the training and calling of the congregational rabbinate. However, it will also be interesting to observe what changes in orientation may be wrought by the graduates of these *yeshivas* who are increasingly assuming positions of leadership in their own schools as well as in those which they are establishing throughout the country. Will these *yeshivas* continue to produce alumni who view their years of study as a necessary prelude to careers, other than the rabbinate, which will allow them to raise families and to establish communities with a maximum Torah atmosphere and the least possible association with any group which might dilute the intensity of their own religious commitments and environment? Or will some alumni of the *yeshivas* follow the model of charismatic leaders like Rabbi J. B. Soloveitchik and the Lubavitcher *rebbe* who encourage their gifted disciples to seek positions of religious and communal activism beyond the perimeters of those already committed to a life guided by Torah as taught and lived in their *yeshivas*?

Turning to another area of advanced Jewish learning, one must take

The Synagogue in America

note of the unprecedented rise in the number of chairs and departments of Jewish studies, all staffed by Jewish scholars, in American universities and colleges. Such chairs and departments have multiplied in the past fifteen years until today there are over 200 full-time Jewish scholars teaching a full complement of Jewish studies (Hebrew and Yiddish language and literature, history, Talmud, Jewish philosophy, sociology) in private and state universities, as well as in a growing number of colleges under Catholic and Protestant auspices. In addition, almost 1,000 rabbis now offer part-time instruction on an undergraduate level in their local colleges. This growth of Jewish studies on the campus level will undoubtedly have its effects on the future of American Jewish religious life. Synagogues are bound to feel the positive impact when graduates of Jewish studies programs show up on the membership rolls.

As for the American rabbinate in general, it is reasonable to predict that the proportion of rabbis born and trained in the United States will continue to rise to a point where the fraction born or educated abroad will disappear or become insignificant. History, much of it tragic, provides the reason. There simply are no Jewish communities left with facilities to train rabbis for export to America. Eastern Europe, excluding the Soviet Union, is in the process of becoming virtually empty of Jews; even should a mass Soviet-Jewish emigration come about, there would be no rabbis forthcoming. Western Europe depends for its rabbinical leadership on a diminishing corps of aging graduates of its seminaries and *yeshivas*, on the handful of rabbis who can be lured from America and Israel, and on those North African rabbis who migrated to France from Algeria and Morocco. Israel, for a variety of internal reasons, has ceased being a source of rabbinic supply for America. On the contrary, growing numbers of American-born and trained rabbis, scholars, and educators are settling in Israel and finding a ready market for their special skills. Approximately sixty members of the Rabbinical Assembly are already permanent residents of Israel, and a similar pattern is developing among both the CCAR and the Orthodox rabbinate.

One can therefore assume that the pattern of American rabbinical education and orientation will dominate not only the American Jewish community but, increasingly, the Jewish communities of Europe, Israel, Latin America, and wherever else Jews will be permitted to establish religious institutions of their own choice. Returning to North America, one can even now draw certain conclusions. The next few

164

years will witness some crucial transitions. The generation of rabbis and their leaders and teachers who grew to maturity in the period between 1950 and 1970 will gradually replace the present aging leadership. Venerable leaders of American Jewish religious institutions deserve credit for guiding their organizations and schools during an unprecedented period of expansion and growth. Their successors will assume the leadership of institutions which are in the process of consolidating a more mature and stabilized community. They are also likely to bring a different perspective to their tasks, the result of their having risen to leadership during a more self-confident era of Jewish history.

Whether Orthodox, Conservative, or Reform, the new leaders are more likely to have been trained and recruited from the institutions which they will be heading. (Indeed, this is the case with the Jewish Theological Seminary and Hebrew Union College-Jewish Institute of Religion, which have named their own alumni, Professors Gerson Cohen and Alfred Gottschalk, to head their respective alma maters.) Each group, from the Satmar Hasidim to ultra-Reform, has developed institutions which tend to retain the loyalties of their young, especially those seeking careers in the rabbinate and related pursuits. Thus, *yeshivas* and seminaries find themselves training an increasing proportion of the children of their own alumni, or of families affiliated with congregations ideologically related to these schools. The Reform Hebrew Union College and the Conservative Jewish Theological Seminary now rarely receive applications from *yeshiva* dropouts and no longer depend on Orthodox sources for either faculty or students, since both are adequately supplied from the ranks of their own alumni. All the movements of American Jewish religious life are now almost totally self-contained and self-perpetuating regarding their educational and organizational institutions.

On the other hand, there has been an intensification in the practice of militant separatism among Orthodox groups regarding their organizational and individual relationships with Reform and Conservative Jews. An earlier generation of members of the Union of Orthodox Rabbis would have refrained from public denunciation of Conservative and Reform rabbis, since the majority of the latter were often their own sons or the sons of their congregants and neighbors. However, in 1954, eleven *yeshiva* heads, led by their extremist spokesman and ideologue, the late Rabbi Aaron Kotler, issued an *issur* (prohibition) against Orthodox cooperation with non-Orthodox rabbis and synagogues, especially in such "interdenominational" efforts as the Synagogue Council of America. Subsequently, the situation has deteriorated even further, as exemplified by the picketing by *yeshiva* students of a Synagogue Council of America dinner honoring Rabbis Samuel Belkin, Louis Finkelstein, and Nelson Glueck, then heads respectively, of Yeshiva University, the Jewish Theological Seminary, and Hebrew Union College-Jewish Institute of Religion. However, one should not draw inevitable conclusions about the future of these relationships. As racial segregationists and other fundamentalists have learned, there is no slogan as evanescent as "Never!" Which rational observer of Christian relations would have had the temerity to predict the present ferment and crisis in the Catholic Church even months before the election of Pope John XXIII?

IV

The relative stabilization of American Jewish residential patterns and congregational affiliation has resulted in a marked decline in the building of new synagogue facilities. During the past five years, virtually no new Conservative congregations have been established anywhere in North America, a startling contrast to the activity of the previous decades. The increase in the number of United Synagogue affiliates in recent years reflects more the enrollment or merger of existing synagogues than the establishment of newly organized congregations. The UAHC reports the continuing organization of new affiliates, particularly in the older suburbs. However, it is difficult to determine whether this reflects a rise of interest in the Reform movement or a growing disenchantment with existing Conservative synagogues, whose membership dues are higher and whose religious schools are not only more costly but have more demanding standards. Then again, the rise may be due to the more vigorous activities of national and regional executives of the UAHC in promoting, assisting, and subsidizing groups interested in establishing new Reform congregations.

Although there is less exact data available for the Orthodox wing, it is possible to draw some general conclusions based on informal observation. The number of *shtiblach* (private houses of prayer) in the larger metropolitan Jewish centers has not declined, although such synagogues have moved to more concentrated areas of Jewish settle-

166

ment and now attract many American-born worshippers. They also tend to draw a more learned and observant type of member than used to be the case. There has also been an increase in the number of synagogues of the Young Israel type, appealing to Orthodox businessmen, professionals, and especially scientists, who have revived many a moribund Orthodox synagogue in academic communities like Boston, Washington, and Berkeley. But one rarely hears nowadays of new large Orthodox synagogues, of the kind that used to feature star cantors, being established in the major cities. The constituency for such synagogues has diminished appreciably. As for the smaller communities which once boasted small Orthodox synagogues reflecting the countries of origin of their founders (for example, the *Russishe* or *Galitzianer shul*), it is rare to find the children or grandchildren of the founders willing to continue to support these "ethnic" congregational efforts.

The declining Jewish population of the smaller communities, the rising cost of maintenance and other professional services, even when available, have led to a growing number of mergers between former fiercely independent and ideologically hostile congregations. First the small Orthodox *shul* might become a Conservative synagogue, with mixed seating, late Friday evening services, and a Seminary-trained rabbi. Recently, more and more of these Conservative synagogues have considered or consummated mergers with Reform temples, which were also suffering from a decline in membership, to say nothing of the dwindling of doctrinal difference between the two sets of congregants.

Assuming no drastic reversal in present American trends, no major upheavals in the Middle East, or catastrophic disruptions in other Jewish communities, one may expect no sharp changes in the number, size, and locations of American synagogues. The mass exodus of Jews from the inner cities and the influx of disadvantaged minorities (black, Puerto Rican, or Appalachian) into the large urban centers both appear to have run their course. The suburbs no longer offer guaranteed immunity from overcrowding, pollution, inferior schools, and other urban ills. One even detects a trickle back to the cities of young families as well as older couples who have no further need for their large suburban homes. Many young people of the generation for whom doting fathers endured the discomforts of commuting are not planning to repeat their parents' trials.

It is rare to find a second or third generation of the same family who are still members of suburban congregations to which their fathers and grandfathers belonged. This is due in part to the unprecedented mobility that has come to mark American society. Another factor is the rising proportion of salaried professionals among the Jewish community, who have neither the need nor the opportunity to strike roots in one place for any extended period of time. They move easily among locations as their tastes, circumstances, and employers dictate.

This change in Jewish occupational distribution is likely to have serious consequences in a variety of areas affecting the immediate future of American Jewish institutional life, particularly the synagogue. In earlier decades, synagogues were most often dependent on members of the free professions—doctors, lawyers, and so on as well as on owners and managers of business enterprises. This successful class provided the synagogue with its basic financial support and stability. The enterprising energies of these men, harnessed to a tradition of generosity and communal noblesse oblige, created synagogues which afforded hospitality to those in less fortunate circumstances. The rabbis and lay leaders of these congregations often went to great lengths to attract the less affluent and to imbue them with a sense of communal obligation as the latter's circumstances improved. Now the picture is changing, and one hesitates to predict what effect the rapid turnover in population and the growing ranks of relatively rootless salaried professionals will have on the future stability of the synagogue and on the ability of a particular community to build and maintain its congregations.

National synagogue groups have for some time encouraged their affiliates to adopt uniform patterns of worship and school curricula in order to provide a familiar context for the family moving from one area to another. They are also beginning to urge their affiliates to credit newcomers to the community for membership fees, High Holiday seating, and building assessments which had been paid in former congregations. It is hoped that this trend will lead to greater regional and national responsibility and to coordination of synagogue planning, building, and budgets, and a diminution of local autonomy and responsibility. Already there are signs that this is happening. The New York Metropolitan Region of the United Synagogue has offered help in sponsoring and subsidizing a synagogue for the middle-income residents of the mammoth Co-Op City project in the northeast Bronx. The residents of Co-Op City, mostly "refugees" from other parts of the

Bronx where they had abandoned synagogues and temples built by an earlier generation of escapees from the Lower East Side, were not in a position to establish their new synagogue without outside, regional help. Similarly, Yeshiva University sponsored the synagogue that was recently built in New York's Lincoln Center area. Most of the members of this congregation had already given years of labor and donated substantial resources toward the building of synagogues in their former communities and were not prepared to repeat the process. The Reform movement has had a longer and more varied history of encouraging and subsidizing new temples from a rotating fund, which has enabled the establishment and maintenance of scores of congregations.

As already noted, there has been an increase in mergers between congregations of similar orientation. But mergers have also taken place between congregations of different denominational affiliation. The trend began in the smaller communities and is now apparent in larger centers of Jewish population as well. For instance, the Orthodox, Conservative, and Reform congregations in Duluth, Minnesota, with separate buildings but some overlapping membership, have merged into one congregation with a new rabbi of Conservative background. In San Francisco, an aging Conservative congregation in an older part of the city merged with a struggling new Reform suburban congregation whose rabbi now heads the new congregation. (There has been an intrasynagogue merger development as well. For example, in Philadelphia eight Conservative congregations have merged to form four. The partners in these mergers consisted in most instances of an urban congregation and a younger suburban one, with the former selling its property to join the latter.)

However, as a counter to the trend toward merger, we also find occasional instances of institutional dissent among the synagogue movements. It is perhaps most pronounced among Orthodoxy which, apart from its innate resistance to associating with groups that do not share its outlook, has avoided organizational centralization on the local, national, or international level. (Reform and Conservatism tend to be more accommodating to diversity within their ranks.) Orthodoxy, moreover, remains suspicious of anything that might smack of a *Sanhedrin*, a supreme religious court which might interpret the *halakha* (religious law) on the basis of a vote by a committee and lead to the toleration of ritual innovations. It was for this reason that the attempt of the UOJC to establish a world organization of Ashkenazic and Sephardic congregations (as a counterpart to the Reform-sponsored World Union of Progressive Judaism and the Conservative World Council of Synagogues) did not succeed. The opposition feared that a world organization might encourage the minority of Orthodox modernists in Israel and abroad, who favor a *Sanhedrin*-type of rabbinic authority, to deliver lenient rulings on the unresolved *halakhic* problems which have accumulated in a technological society and a sovereign Jewish state. This may also be the reason why so few (only a small minority) of Orthodox congregations have affiliated with the UOJC. The vast majority of Orthodox congregations remain unaffiliated and restrict their institutional loyalties to their own synagogues, to certain *yeshivas*, and to certain charities.

The Reform and Conservative groups, products of a different history, have a different outlook. Both began their careers with a central seminary for the training of their rabbis, and quickly developed effective centralized rabbinic and congregational organizations. There have always been tensions among the seminaries, their alumni, and the congregational leaders over the distribution of power, prestige, and the allocation of budgets, but these tensions rarely led to splits or the establishment of rival schools or groups. Usually, the hospitable temperaments of both groups have permitted a latitude broad enough to accommodate a wide range of views and practices. Dissent and critical inquiry have not been discouraged, and academic freedom is safeguarded both in the classroom and from the pulpit.

The Reconstructionist movement is a case in point. For many years it considered itself a philosophical fellowship exerting an influence on Conservatism and Reform from within those two movements. Its recent establishment of a rabbinical seminary in Philadelphia and its talk about becoming a fourth denomination in American Jewish life is a departure from the traditional Reconstructionist posture. Professor Mordecai M. Kaplan, the founder of Reconstructionism and a member of the Jewish Theological Seminary faculty for almost fifty years, has enjoyed freedom as a "house" critic within the Conservative structure.

V

It would appear that the current ferment in Christian circles and the emergence, for want of a better term, of the "underground church," with its radical, anti-Establishment clergymen, has encouraged a comparable, although not parallel, Jewish development. Its guiding spirits are drawn primarily from the ranks of Jewish Theological Seminary alumni and dropouts. It is a matter of conjecture as to whether these dissenters develop their ambivalence about Jewish tradition and the organized Jewish community after they enter the Seminary or whether the Seminary, by its very nature, tends to attract a greater proportion of students with unresolved conflicts between their reverence for traditional forms and rebellion against them. In any event, there is a growing vogue for Seminary alumni to establish rabbinical schools, academies, and fellowships known as *havurot*. For some reason, we rarely find Yeshiva University and Hebrew Union College alumni among the leadership of these groups, perhaps because they are afflicted with fewer unresolved conflicts.

The most widely publicized of the radical groups is the *Havurat Shalom*, founded by a group of young Conservative rabbis and a Reform Hillel director in the Boston area and presently located in Somerville, Massachusetts. It has attracted a group of students and teachers, with a high dropout rate, from an odd mixture of pacifists, educational innovators, and dissenters from the institutional synagogue. One should note, however, that the *havurah* members have not lacked for a platform from which to air their views. The organized Jewish community—synagogues, centers, and national organizations, the Jewish "establishment," in short—has vied to provide occasions at which members of the *havurah* might vent their spleen at their elders. I, myself, am inclined to believe that the significance of the *havurot* has been highly exaggerated and it is merely a passing fad, not unconnected with the more egregious manifestations of the so-called "youth culture" that emerged in the late 1960s.

A more serious demonstration of American Judaism's concern with the social issues of the day was evinced by the widespread participation of rabbis and synagogues in the civil rights movement of the early 1960s. Prior to that time, social activism, among Christians as well as Jews, had been restricted to individual clergymen, men like John Haynes Holmes, Reinhold Niebuhr, and Stephen S. Wise, who, in their sermons and writings, inveighed against social evils and thus helped to sensitize the social conscience of their generations. The organized church and synagogue, especially denominations with a tradition of social concern, usually confined themselves to adopting occasional resolutions at conventions to express their views on the problems of war and peace, race relations, and similar issues. Insofar

171

The Synagogue in America

as they allocated material resources and assigned personnel to help the needy and disadvantaged, it was through conventional forms of charity and services.

In the early 1960s, however, organized religion, the clergy in particular, became actively involved in the whole range of social concerns. One may trace this development in part to the general encouragement of religious activism and ecumenism inspired by Pope John XXIII and to the charismatic model of Martin Luther King. This new development was dramatically launched by the Conference on Religion and Race in Chicago in January 1963. Cardinals of the Church and assorted religious establishment figures mingled and shared platforms with emerging religious, social, and political activists like Abraham Joshua Heschel, Martin Luther King, and William Stringfellow. Later that year, scores of rabbis, together with many priests and ministers, joined Dr. King in demonstrations at Birmingham, Albany, Georgia, and Selma, Alabama. Many were arrested. The brutal repressions in the South aroused unprecedented religious engagement. By the winter of 1965, hundreds of rabbis joined thousands of other King sympathizers in Selma to prepare for the historic march to Montgomery.

In the following years these same social activists participated in the peace movement. However, many rabbis, as well as congregants, halted their public involvements in the peace movement when they found it awkward to explain their support of a "hawkish" American role in the Middle East and a "dovish" role in Southeast Asia. They were also forced by internal and external Jewish pressures to mute their selective opposition to militarism. Gradual disengagement by the Jewish religious establishment and by individual rabbis from a program of active social concern was hastened by the racial riots in Watts, Detroit, and Newark, where Jewish shopkeepers were often the first victims. Other events, such as the New York teachers' strike in 1968, added to the disillusion of many Jews with participation in radical causes.

It is difficult to generalize about shifts in Jewish political and social orientation on the basis of religious affiliation. "Conventional" opinion on this matter is often contradicted by personal encounters with Orthodox Jewish radicals and Reform reactionaries. There is in existence an unpublished study by Louis Harris on "Black-Jewish Relations in New York City," sponsored by the Ford Foundation shortly after the explosive New York teachers' strike. The study was based on

172

a total sample of 634 respondents, distributed among 16 percent Orthodox, 32 percent Conservative, 21 percent Reform, and 31 percent non-affiliated Jews, broken down by boroughs. Harris attempted to draw distinctions in attitude based on income, age, and religious affiliation, but I doubt whether such a limited sample, restricted to New York City, excluding the suburbs, and taken immediately after a highly publicized confrontation, can be considered a reliable indication of national trends.

One can also be misled by the greater publicity accorded the radical, militant young Jews of SDS, the Weathermen, and so on. One hears less about the million or so Jewish youths who are not involved in these movements and who probably tend more to emulate the patterns and models of their parents than did an earlier generation. In a recent synagogue bulletin, published by the largest Conservative congregation in Houston, Texas, for distribution to its college students, there are excerpts from four talks prepared by college students for delivery to the congregation at Sabbath services. One of the students, a senior at the University of Texas, commented as follows:

Sociologists today speak of the lack of communication between generations, and it appears to me that with respect to our present lifetime, these words are somewhat exaggerated. If you want to know what a generation gap really was, go back two generations to our parents and grandparents. Most of our grandparents came to these shores not knowing the language or customs. Their children learned a language different from their mothers' and fathers'. They learned customs, traditions, and mores of an American community entirely foreign to their parents. Now, believe me, that was a confrontation of two worlds. Nevertheless, in spite of this social gap between the two generations, their differences were merged in an atmosphere of respect, reverence, and understanding. We see the result of a truly first-generation American Jewry, a foundation laid by the generation we criticize.

I accept this view as far more representative of what Jewish young people think than all the frenzied talk about the existence of a "generation gap."

VI

In conclusion, what can we expect of organized Jewish religious life in the future? It is safe to predict that there will probably be a continuation of the growing cooperation between Reform and Conservative congregational and rabbinical groups, already hinted at by several recent joint study sessions of the Rabbinical Assembly and the CCAR. In addition, education commissions of the Reform and Conservative movements are sponsoring a cooperative pilot textbook publication project.

The differences in Jewish observance and in attitude to Zionism that used to divide Reform and Conservative congregants have narrowed. The number of Hebrew Union College students who observe traditional religious practices is increasing. Jewish Theological Seminary students, reared in decorous Conservative congregations, who, at the moment, cover their heads with prayer shawls at services, Orthodox fashion, may only be indulging a passing yearning to rediscover the life style of their grandparents. Yet both examples point to a more positive probing attitude toward their heritage than was prevalent among their older colleagues when the latter were rabbinical students a generation ago.

Yeshivas for all age levels are likely to multiply and to expand the scope of their activities, although it is possible that they have already attained their potential in reaching their loyal constituency. Reform and Conservative day schools will increase in response to the growing demand for more intensive Jewish education. The assumption that such schools are being filled primarily by "refugees" from racially mixed public schools in the North and South is unsubstantiated. Parents who seek to protect their children from the rigors of an urban public school education either move to the suburbs or send their children to private schools which do not burden their students with a double curriculum of both general and Jewish studies.

It is fashionable to speak about Jewish education in America as a disaster. I disagree. It is my feeling that there has never been a generation of young Jews in the United States who have received a more intensive Jewish education, taught by more qualified teachers employing better educational materials. I believe that greater parental and communal concern, combined with greater financial assistance, will serve to increase the number of young people receiving various forms of Jewish education, from the nursery to the postgraduate level, as well as enhance the quality of the instruction.

Nostalgia has exaggerated both the quality and depth of Jewish knowledge and loyalty of earlier American Jewish generations. Was there really a higher proportion of learned, rooted, or pious Jews in

America thirty years ago than are to be found now? Was knowledge of Hebrew and observance of the Sabbath more widespread then? There are other myths and fallacies which bear little relationship to reality. One is that rabbis are deserting the congregational rabbinate in droves either after a brief period of active pulpit experience or as soon as they are ordained. Actually, most students who enter Hebrew Union College and the Jewish Theological Seminary with the aim of becoming congregational rabbis fulfill their intention after ordination.

It is reported that the Hasidic Master, Rabbi Meir of Premishlan, once discussed the ambiguous merits and definitions of modernity with his disciples. He reminded them of one of the oldest extant *midrashim* which Jews recite in the Passover Haggadah: "In the beginning our fathers were idolators, but now the Omnipresent has drawn us to His service." This is not an unfamiliar mood to a generation eager for service and suspicious of idols which seduced an older, more optimistic generation less certain about both their Jewish and American identity.

The established churches are in crisis and Christian theology is in ferment. Jews are too easily tempted to view their situation in a Christian mirror. Perhaps we should learn to measure Jewish reality in a more authentic Jewish context of qualified optimism and the mature posture of a people who have experienced 4,000 years of recorded history and civilization.

I once concluded an article on the Jewish religious scene in the *American Jewish Year Book* (1961) with the following affirmation: "Each generation somehow manages to surprise its predecessor and foil predictions of doom. Perhaps with a bit of luck, and an enormous amount of anonymous dedication, Jewish religious life will witness the dawn of a genuine renaissance in the years ahead." I see no reason to revise this opinion now.

CHAPTER 21: THE END IS WHERE WE START FROM. . .

Judaism may be perennial, but its work changes according to the cultural conditions in which the rabbis and their congregants live and think. And the cultural conditions, spurred by the rapid growth of the secular city, the piercing strides of modern technology, and suburbanization, have wrought their havoc on all our social institutions, including religion.

> Ever since the Age of Enlightenment there has been a tension between the traditional religions of the West - Judaism and Christianity - and the secular world then beginning to merge: its science, technology, economics, politics, and, in general, its attitude toward life. And since the modern-secular world would not go away and could not be wished away, its effect on orthodox belief was one of crisis - whether orthodox belief declared itself under total siege, ventured the odd sortie, or even undertook a wholesale assault on the alien territory and in so doing became itself transformed. By now, this crisis has existed for so long that it has become a permanent condition of religious belief in the modern world; and most of the recent talk about a brand-new religious crisis in our own age merely reflects the permeation of the old crisis into nearly all parts of modern society.*

The findings of the present study concur with Fachenheim that if there is a crisis in religion (particularly the religion of Reform Judaism), it is a crisis more by definition than by fact. By _fact_, it is simply a component of continuum.

---

*Emil L. Fachenheim, "On the Self-Exposure of Faith to the Modern-Secular World: Philosophical Reflections in the Light of Jewish Experience," Daedalus (Journal of the American Academy of Arts and Sciences), Winter, 1967, p. 193.

Religion, like philosophy, is first and foremost a mental discipline. The cultural lag theory tells us that what usually ails a modern culture is that the material accomplishments of man move ahead too fast for the non-material accomplishments to keep pace. An example would be to look at our atomic and nuclear accomplishments. We have created powerful forces, but as of now we have employed them mostly in ways that threaten our very existence as a human race. Our mental capacities have not yet worked out ways for living in a manner that would include the harnessing of these forces for human betterment.

So much for the cultural lag theory as it pertains to the overall situation. Let us extract religion from our mass society, just to examine it in terms of a further problem. As a mental discipline, with no empirical underpinnings to support it in the eyes of the pragmatist, it suffers even more than other "non-material" bodies of knowledge, such as art or literature. From the latter we expect no required rules of human conduct, only ideas. But with religion, we deal with ideas _and_ rules for living. The ideas aren't so much what is giving us trouble. We either accept, partially or completely, or we don't. The _rules_ are the troublemakers. The problem is akin to what philosophy started to confront many decades ago.

> It is not merely that the cultural aggrandizement of the investigative or phenomenological sciences has gradually threatened the very existence of philosophy and has progressively worked to dispossess it of its ancient home; worse, and in consequence, the prevalence of positivism today requires the philosopher to face an audience radically skeptical of anything he may say, doubtful even that he can say anything worth listening to it all.*

---

*Mortimer J. Adler, A Dialectic of Morals, University of Notre Dame Press, 1941, p. 3

But now we confront the white-hot core of the problem. Not only does religion "face an audience radically skeptical of anything (it) may say," but a good deal of this same skepticism abounds within the very ranks of organized religion itself.

Let us examine some specifics. At a CCAR Regional meeting, a prominent HUC-JIR rabbi-professor was invited to address the assembled members of the rabbinate. The speaker began his presentation by asking his audience of rabbis what they would want him to speak on and what they would want to discuss with him. The first question that the group put forth was "What is our position on God?"

Only 10% of the total rabbinate are able to agree categorically with the statement, "I believe in God in the more or less traditional Judaic sense." It is to be noted immediately that another 62% can agree with the statement once we add to it "as modified in terms of my own views of what God is, what he stands for, etc." This means that 28% of our rabbinate can be described as skeptical to say the least. If a rabbi is a teacher and preacher of an overall pattern of human behavior whose watchword is "Hear O Israel, the Lord Our God the Lord is One," how can it be done if he does not accept the very existence of the one God?

At another rabbinical meeting, a former CCAR president made this statement: "We (the Reform rabbinate) still have a long way to go in establishing a theology that would be acceptable to the Reform Movement." Throughout the study, this same concern was expressed over and over again. A Reform Shulchan Aruch does not exist.

If a Reform Shulchan Aruch does not exist, then what is the code of law that prescribes the pattern of behavior that the Reform rabbi teaches and preaches? And what would a Reform Shulchan Aruch mean to the 28% who express skepticism about God? If a rabbi cannot or will not accept God and the role He plays in Jewish heritage, will he accept a <u>Shulchan Aruch?</u> And if not, what steps is the CCAR prepared to take to invoke sanctions? At the present time, there is at least one Reform rabbi who a few years ago, <u>publicly</u> renounced God. He continues to remain a member in good standing in the CCAR.

To be sure, it is an easy sociological exercise to explain faltering societal stability in terms of the social disorganization that has been brought about by suburbanization, assimilation, secularization, and occupational and residential mobility. But if we press too hard, are we not overlooking the fact that societies are and always have been dynamic? The changes of the past were of different variety, but constant change there has always been. There is not now, and there never was a static society. So it might not be altogether fair to explain things in terms of the aforementioned sociological phenomena. Instead of explaining and understanding the situation, we may simply be explaining the situation <u>away</u>. As time moves along, we continue to make our adjustments in terms of the social change that confronts us. Our mass adjustment mechanisms are always in process.

But whatever the changes in the mass society, where does the rabbi <u>qua</u> rabbi stand? What is <u>his</u> focus? What is <u>his</u> function? <u>It is the rabbi, not the congregant who spells out what Reform Judaism is,</u> and to date it has never yet been spelled out. Although each individual rabbi may spell out <u>his</u> interpretation of Reform Judaism to <u>his</u> congregation, a <u>systematic code</u> for the <u>Movement</u> does not appear to exist. Without a uniform prayerbook, would there be any rallying point at all? As for the congregations themselves, we seem to have a <u>Shulchan Aruch</u> in reverse, <u>viz.</u>, complete congregational autonomy. The Constitution and By-Laws of the UAHC makes this explicity clear:

> Nothing contained in this Constitution or the By-Laws shall be construed so as to interfere in any manner whatsoever with the mode of worship, the school, the freedom of expression and opinion, or any of the congregational activities of the constitutent congregations of the Union.

It would appear, therefore, that <u>unless Reform Judaism is a rabbinical responsibility, it is no one's</u>. The whole Movement then, revolves around the person of the rabbi. If it is a strong, viable Movement, the rabbis have made it so. If it is a faltering Movement, if there is a crisis, the rabbis have made it so. If there <u>is</u> a crisis, and if this crisis is to be overcome, the rabbis will do that too.

In terms of what this study tells us about our contemporary American Reform rabbinate, it is not easy to say in what direction change might be expected. It is quite possible that <u>directions</u>, rather than any single direction, might be a more accurate view of what the future holds in store for Reform Judaism.

Let us look at what confronts us. Concerning the present study, here is how two rabbis reacted to it after they were first informed of its objectives:

> The major areas of inquiry to be studied ... leave me rather dismayed. Here we already have the answers. (What we need are answers to the following:)
> 1) Has the rabbinate a future?
> 2) Is religion disappearing?
> 3) Should the synagogue survive?

The second rabbi put it this way:

> If we think about it soberly, there is no question that Judaism will survive. Entrenched as integral parts of Judaism are the rabbi and the synagogue. We (the rabbis) and our synagogues will therefore also survive. But what does survival mean? This is where we need to take stock of ourselves. We must know <u>what</u> we are doing and <u>where</u> we are at, or we dare not talk about what is yet to be done. I look forward to this study to serve us as a mirror. Without this mirror - which should reflect honest answers from all of us - we can only rely on what we are telling ourselves. We must <u>see</u> ourselves as we are.

We see, then, where to one rabbi there is serious concern that perhaps all is about to crumble. Emotion abounds. To the other rabbi, such mass disintegration isn't even questioned. For him, it is a matter of rational self-evaluation. For the first rabbi, a crystal ball is needed. The second calls for a body of knowledge (a mirror).

One of the big questions in the minds of some rabbis is, "What does the congregation expect of me?" One experienced Reform rabbi attacks this as an improper question. He states as follows:

> We must be leaders, not followers, and no small part of the rabbi's mission is educating the congregations not to expect the impossible. Actually . . . the question should be . . . "What does the congregation have a <u>right</u> to expect of the rabbi?"

Again we see how there seem to be two completely different sides to the same coin. To some rabbis there is an earnest desire for the congregation to tell them what to do. To other rabbis, it is the rabbi who should do the telling (or possibly be told off).

Much of what is happening to the Synagogue today is little different from what started to happen to the University a few years ago. Chancellor Samuel B. Gould of the State University of New York described the situation as follows:

> I want to talk about only one thing today: the step-by-step elimination of reason or rationality from the education scene and perhaps from our whole society. This is a phenomenon evident for some time but only now beginning to be understood as it should be. It represents the single most fundamental value change of our time. Some pople find it exhilarating and liberating; some find it disquieting and even frightening; all find it fascinating both as to its present and its future. To me it is a fearful sort of fascination.*

Throughout his address, Dr. Gould tells us that faculty as well as students are equal contributors to this retreat from reason. Could this be what is happening in some of our Reform Synagogues? It appears to be so.

Since the objective was to identify the malaise, if any, that now exists in the Reform Movement, let us highlight some attitudes and behaviors of Reform constituencies that may be identified as such by some, perhaps not by others.

Concerning the Rabbinate

1) There is dissatisfaction in the whole area of rabbinical economics:

---

* "Retreat from Reason," Commencement Address, University of Pittsburgh, April 26, 1970.

1. Salaries
2. Increments
3. Vacations
4. Insurance benefits
5. Tenure
6. Pension benefits
7. Sabbaticals

Not only do many rabbis not understand what is going on, they aren't even clear what should be going on. Here the UAHC and/or the CCAR is clearly unclear, or possibly remiss. It is the system, the arrangements, the procedures that distress the rabbis more than the actual dollars involved.

2) Rabbis are discontent with what they call the non-rabbinical demands that congregations are making of them.

3) There are many rabbis who enter the seminary who come from comparatively uninvolved Jewish backgrounds.

4) Rabbis, especially the more recently ordained, appear to be oriented in increasing numbers to the secular as opposed to the Jewish academic world.

5) Less than half the rabbis say they are "fully satisfied" with their careers.

6) Less than a third of our rabbinate look upon "presiding over ritual and worship" as a "most satisfying" component of their professional activities.

7) Only 53% of the rabbis say they would choose the rabbinate again if they had the chance.

8) There is an extremely high and positive relationship between lack of commitment to career and one's dissatisfaction with it.

9) Despite the fact that only a comparatively small number of rabbis complain strongly about their own careers, 42% say there is a crisis in the Reform rabbinate.

10) Over one-fourth of Reform rabbis do not believe in God in "the traditional Judaic sense" or as modified "in terms of my own views of what God is and what He stands for."

11) In terms of religiosity, Reform rabbis can be categorized as 10% traditionalists, 62% moderates, and 28% radicals.

12) Some 41% of Reform rabbis officiate at mixed marriages (no prior conversion). Of those who do not, over half refer couples to rabbis who do.

13) The biggest single complaint that Reform rabbis have against their congregations is the "Jewish distance" between rabbi and congregation.

14) The majority of Reform rabbis feel that the use of the chuppa and the breaking of the glass in the wedding ritual should be at the discretion of the bride and groom.

15) Almost half the rabbinate agree with the statement, "The CCAR promulgates the values of success and competitiveness among its members to the point that it pits one man against another." The younger rabbis are more often those who register the most vitriolic complaints against their parent organization.

16) There are no marked uniformities to describe any majority complaints against the CCAR. Many individual objections are expressed by many different rabbis, but the objections differ from rabbi to rabbi. The CCAR often seems to serve as an overall scapegoat for most of its detractors.

17) Reform rabbis are asking for effectively functional CCAR _Regional_ organizations. They ask of these Regional mechanisms opportunities for study and sociability, as well as guidance and assistance with their business and administrative needs vis-à-vis their respective congregations.

18) Reform rabbis do not feel that the UAHC Regions are structurally or functionally suited to meet the individual _rabbi's_ needs vis-à-vis his congregation.

19) Reform rabbis from all age groups express mild to harsh criticism concerning the performance of HUC-JIR as a rabbinical seminary. The criticisms are often that the seminary 1) does not produce or even motivate Jewish _scholarship_ 2) does not adequately prepare for the _pulpit_ rabbinate, and 3) does not provide sufficient _personalized_ assistance and guidance to its students and their needs (especially the married ones).

20) Reform rabbis are suggesting that HUC-JIR ought to develop cooperative programs with other academic institutions. Some 69% of the rabbis and 85% of the seminarians would like to see the seminaries located in major academic centers.

21) The overwhelming majority of rabbis and seminarians agree that a Reform multi-university comprehending several different schools, in addition to a rabbinical seminary, would provide for a more enriched preparation in rabbinics, as well as a course of study in Jewish scholarship for those who do not seek ordination.

22) Less than one-fifth of Reform rabbis identify a crisis concerning <u>themselves</u> or <u>their</u> congregations, but some 42% say that it applies to the <u>rest</u> of the entire <u>rabbinate</u>. Almost two-thirds say it applies to most Reform <u>congregations</u>.

23) Reform rabbis, while they <u>prefer</u> to go it alone, are showing an increasingly receptive attitude toward a merger with the Conservative Movement with the understanding that this means becoming more traditional in the process.

24) Over half of Reform rabbis oppose the idea of a community team rabbinate (involving a combined structure with Conservative and Orthodox personnel), but those who favor such an innovation are very articulate in their position.

25) Regarding any merger procedures, on national and/or local levels, it appears that those rabbis who perceive Reform to be in crisis are those who are most willing to do something, although in one case it involves greater separation from the rest of Judaism, and in the other it involves greater cooperation.

Concerning Reform Congregants:

1) More than one in three congregants, ages 20 to 24, is now married to a spouse who was born non-Jewish. One in four of this age group is married to a spouse who has not converted.

2) Reform congregants rate "being an ethical person," and "Jewish identification" above "belief in God" as basic components of their Jewish consciousness.

3) Two-thirds of Reform congregants say, "I remain a Jew because it is simply the most convenient thing to do."

4) Over half of Reform congregants are strongly universalistic; 10% are strongly particularistic.

5) Less than one-fifth of Reform congregants believe in God "in the more or less traditional Judaic sense." Another 50% add "as modified in terms of my own views of what God is, and what he stands for."

6) Based on response patterns regarding "belief in God" and "being an ethical person," 48% of Reform congregants can be identified as religious, and 28% as non-religious.

7) It is the parents who are least religious who tend to be most critical of the rabbi's role in the religious school, and are also most critical of the rabbi's leadership of youth group activities.

396

8) Reform congregants who are married to converts are themselves more religious than those married to fellow-Jews. Based on our small sample, those whose spouses are <u>not</u> converted tend to be even more religious than those with converted spouses.

9) Of those congregants identified in this study as religious, most come from Orthodox-affiliated backgrounds, the second largest group comes from Reform-affiliated homes, next in number are those from Conservative-affiliated homes, and almost a third come from "other" backgrounds.

10) Generally speaking, there seems to be a negative relationship among congregants between religiosity and income, and between religiosity and formal secular education.

11) Most congregants affiliate with synagogues when the time comes to enroll children in the religious school.

12) The vast majority of Reform congregants <u>do not consider themselves religious</u>.

13) A little over one-tenth of Reform congregants are (or have been), active leaders in their congregations. They are usually fathers, and the more affluent but not the highest formally educated. Most often they are from either Orthodox or Reform backgrounds.

14) The most active lay synagogue leaders are those who usually blame poor rabbinical leadership for what is wrong with Reform Judaism.

15) The most active lay synagogue leaders tend to be much more concerned with Jewish affairs, the Jewish community, the general community, and with Israel than the rest of the Reform membership.

16) More than anything else, reform congregants expect their rabbis to be a good <u>pastor</u> (counseling, visitations, officiating at life-cycle events). The performances of most rabbis in this field tends to <u>exceed</u> their congregants' expectations.

17) Those congregants who are usually least satisfied with their rabbis are the ones who report that their rabbis do <u>more</u> than they expect of him.

18) In terms of general platitudes, congregants <u>say</u> they like their rabbis. In answer to specific questions, all sorts of qualifications are voiced.

<u>Concerning the Seminary Student</u>:

1) Many seminarians are disenchanted with many aspects of Reform Judaism. The CCAR is their chief target. They are reticent in revealing their sources of information. Many particularly suspect this study as a CCAR device to undermine the HUC-JIR. On the other hand, many vehemently criticize their seminary.

2) Some 44% of Reform seminarians identify themselves as agnostic. This is more than twice as many as amongst those who have been ordained since 1967. (For rabbis as a whole, the figure is 13%).

3) Only 4% of seminarians believe in God "in the more or less traditional Judaic sense." Belief in a qualified version of God is much lower than for rabbis, much lower even than among rabbis who were ordained in the last five years.

4) Of many reasons given for choosing the rabbinate as a career less than half say that it is because of "my intense belief in God and in Judaism and my desire to continue one of its major traditions, - to be a teacher unto my people." (Rabbis scored this same reason somewhat lower than the seminarians.)

5) Of several reasons given for choosing the rabbinate as a career, the largest number of seminarians (74%) say it is because "as an occupation it offered me the most opportunity to 'do my thing' in terms of my interests, needs, and general fulfillment."

6) Less than half our present seminary students plan to enter the pulpit rabbinate. Some 17% plan to enter teaching immediately after ordination. Another 20% intend to pursue graduate studies.

8) Seminarians tend to be more critical of the Union Prayer Book than are the rabbis.

9) Many wives of seminarians (based on interviews with wives of most recently ordained rabbis), indicate displeasure with HUC-JIR because of the latter's disregard for their welfare during their "student days." Some brand-new rebbetzins describe their days at the seminary with such words as "demeaning" and "dehumanizing."

Concerning Reform Youth:

1) Although virtually all Reform youth (97%) have been or plan to be confirmed, there is much displeasure with this ritual. Many are asking for a good religious high school program instead.

2) Over half of Reform youth say they never hear Zionism as a subject of discussion in their homes, despite the fact that 66% say that contributing to the United Jewish Appeal is the most important element in establishing their Jewish identities.

3) Only two out of three Reform youngsters are solidly pro-Israel. Many express strong anti-Israeli positions.

4) One-third of Reform youth attend services for Festivals and/or Holy Days only; 14% say they rarely or never attend services.

5) Some 50% of Reform youth believe in God "in the more or less traditional sense;" 32% are agnostics, and 4% are atheists.

400

6) One-fifth of Reform youth indicate the older they get they "become less and less satisfied with synagogue services."

7) Less than one-fifth of Reform youth feel that their "rabbi is intensely interested in the school and gives it the maximum attention that he can."

8) Only 13% of Reform youth say "it is easy for young people to approach and talk with our rabbi."

9) Reform youth feel that their Temple Youth Group should have professional leaders, not parents as leaders.

10) Reform youth view positively UAHC summer camp, but are critical of the ways things are run at these camps.

11) With regard to various components of Jewish identity, many Reform youth do not seem to know what their parents stand for.

12) On every issue of Jewish identity on which they were queried, Reform youth seem to be more detached from Judaism and Jewishness than their parents.

13) Only in anti-semitism do a number of Reform youth (37%) see a possible threat to Jewish survival. Issues such as mixed marriage and weak religious education are seen as threats by small numbers of Reform youngsters.

Concerning the Rebbetzins:

1) Rebbetzins tend to be ambivalent about the rabbinical way of life. Only 41% would want their husbands to be rabbis if they had it to do all over again. Some 21% would want them to be professors instead.

2) Only about 40% of the rebbetzins would say that they are living "fulfilling" lives; about one-third say they are "lonely," another one-third say it's been "generally good, but nothing exciting."

3) About half the rebbetzins feel "the need for developing (their) potentialities outside of home and synagogue."

4) While most rebbetzins would approve of their daughter marrying a Reform rabbi if that was what the daughter wanted, only 4% of the rebbetzins _preferred_ such a choice for their child. Only 2% preferred _any_ rabbi as the _ideal_ mate for their daughter.

So much for some of the more blatant highlights concerning potential crisis, even if viewed by the most traditional criteria. Let us now use a medical model to identify _crisis_. This provides conceptual as well as empirical insights.

Psychosomatic medicine identifies an ulcer as a _psychosomatic_ illness. This means that the _psyche_ (mind) had been exposed to such stress and strain that it had gone beyond a certain threshold of endurance at which point the psyche then "takes it out" on the _soma_ (body). To argue that "it's all in the patient's mind," is folly. The _psyche_ may still be in a stressful condition, but

the psyche is compensating by its new outlet. The body is now
carrying some of the burden of pain. And now the pain isn't just
in the person's head. It is now based on organic, physical malfunction.

But the best medical tests may reveal no ulcer. The patient may be
convinced he has an ulcer. The empirical diagnosis reveals no ulcer.
This is hypochondria. But the patient is ill. However, the diagnosis
calls for treating anxiety, a mental condition, not an ulcer, which is
an organic illness.

The medical definition of crisis is as follows:

> The point in the course of a serious disease at which
> a decisive change occurs, leading either to recovery or
> death.

Without arguing whether we are in a true state of crisis or merely
in an anxiety state, there is no question Reform Judaism is in a
state of some malaise. If so, we have problems, but all forms of
illness are not automatically to be labelled as crises. Not if
diagnostic data are to be used honestly and responsibly.

Based on the overall findings from this study, Reform Judaism is
not in a seriously painful and malfunctioning state. This statement
is not made on the basis of an evaluation of all the positive things
that are happening in Reform Judaism. On the contrary, the statement
is made on the basis of an intensive quantitative and qualitative inquiry into the aches and pains of the patient, a sample of which has
just been noted.

Aches and pains there are. The stresses and strains are diagnosable.
Are they hypochondria or organic breakdown? It is very possible, however,

that without treatment, <u>the Movement may have within it the potential for organic breakdown.</u>

But what is the case history of the patient? We mean here the whole organism, - the whole of Judaism. Based on the social change that is now evidencing itself throughout the whole of Judaism, and throughout Reform Judaism in particular, does the case history project a diagnosis of death? The most important thing is the diagnosis. What <u>has</u> <u>been</u> the case history? What is it now?

The case history:

1) Judaism is a case history of Inquisitions, Pogroms, Holocausts, and chronic anti-Semitism even under the best of socio-cultural conditions, and it <u>lives</u>.

2) With all its desecrations from without, with all its self-hatred from within, it <u>lives</u>.

3) From <u>within</u>, we have moved from the Pharisees/Sadducees/Essenes to Orthodox/Conservative/Reform. The case history is a history of argumentation and debate, and Judaism <u>lives</u>.

4) From <u>without</u>, we have confronted an Ethical Culture Society, an American Council on Judaism, and the Bahai and the Unitarians. Judaism <u>lives</u>.

<u>It is a case history of argumentation and debate.</u> Possibly there have been somatic-type stresses and strains that <u>could</u> <u>have</u> produced organic breakdown that <u>might have</u> led to demise. But it didn't!

In a moribund state we never were, and we are not now.

404

<u>Are we in a seriously painful state</u>? At times very seriously painful. And we may still have before us more painful days and years of our lives. But we continue "to be fruitful and to multiply."

Our "adjustment mechanisms" have taken us through years of wandering to years in Ghettos to Diaspora to the Secular City, Suburbia, and to Statehood, and the mind and the body have stayed <u>alive</u>, - still arguing, still debating, and thriving.

Nowhere has the writer seen it expressed more beautifully and with such poignant realism than in a sermon by Rabbi Abraham J. Feldman, Rabbi Emeritus, Temple Beth Israel, West Hartford, Connecticut:

> Ours is the romance of a people inspired ... of a people whose soul is on fire with the flame which played about the crags of Sinai as Moses proclaimed the moral law! Ours is a soul on fire with the charge and fervor of the prophets! Ours is a soul that harbors the flame that consumed the Temple but spared the Torah! Ours is a soul purified in the flames of the Inquisition, a soul undaunted by the brutalities of nations and ages ... Ours is a soul which in spite of all that it has witnessed and endured ... still dares to face the future with hope and confidence and trust... Ours is the romance of a people convenanted with God ... Individuals among us ... have failed to grasp the significance of the ... ideal glory of our Jewishness. There are dead branches on every tree ... but the trunk is sturdy.
> ... and even whilst we suffer ... Hamans go and Hitlers come--and go, (and) the Jew opens his book and reads his (own) tale. Tears glisten in his eyes ...*

So much for the case history. There simply is no hard evidence of

---

*Rabbi Abraham J. Feldman, "The Romance of a People," <u>Sources of Jewish Inspiration</u>, 1934, pp. 206-209.

any state or condition ever having existed, when Judaism, the whole corpus, was in the throes of a life and death crisis period.

Are we now in crisis, or are we at another time in the continuum of history where once again a crescendo of argumentation and debate is causing some of us to press the panic button?

First of all, even if Reform Judaism, as an organized Movement were to close its doors, there is no hard evidence that <u>Judaism</u>, the totality, would die. And what of Reform Judaism? This study has certainly revealed evidences of stress and strain. <u>Can these stresses and strains be diagnosed as being psychosomatically conducive to subsequent organic breakdown</u>? Yes and no. Very possibly yes, if the aches and pains, and the infections, if any, are allowed to fester without self-examination, without honest diagnostic <u>acceptance of what is</u>. Possibly yes, if no treatment or remedial processes are honestly formulated, honestly invoked, and honestly pursued.

<u>Can these stresses and strains be diagnosed as hypochondria</u>? To the extent that there are rabbis, congregants, and rabbinical students, whose emotional needs (regarding their own personal and/or professional lives), are lacking fulfillment, so that they consciously or unconsciously project their own discomfort on the system as a whole, and label the system as sick and dying (<u>sic</u> crisis), - to that extent there is a state of hypochondria. Can mass hypochondria lead to mass hysteria to mass organic breakdown? Nothing in the history of social systems of this ever happening is known to us. An example is the counter-culture movement in America today. But <u>the culture lives</u>, and by its very being makes possible the existence of the counter-culture. We are simply in a state of cultural change.

The heart of the whole question is this: What are the actual changes that are now taking place in Reform Judaism, and what are the assumed changes that many believe are taking place? An assumption, no matter how honestly perceived, may still be only an assumption, and not a fact. If an unverified assumption is then used as though it were a fact, the results may bring forth many unwarranted "conclusions." Such "conclusions" may induce subsequent behavior that may or may not be justified. Furthermore, such a situation may actually bring forth rejection of all problems.

Here is how one Board member at a UAHC Regional Biennial Convention reacted to the question of crisis when the interviewer discussed the matter with him:

> I think our rabbis are building up anxiety in us. Look at this (pointing to the program): Five of the six topics listed . . . we're told they are all crisis . . . Look at this . . . (He read the following titles:)
>
> 1) The Social Justice Crisis . . .
> 2) The Crisis in Reform Jewish Worship.
> 3) The Crisis in Reform Jewish Education.
> 4) The Crisis in Reform Jewish Youth . . .
> 5) The Crisis in Temple Budgeting.
>
> To me, all this is demoralizing. You know, you can always make a crisis. I used to have a foreman who always made a crisis of everything. I had to let him go. Now we don't have a crisis every day. Sure, things go wrong, - all the time . . . (but) you make changes . . . adjustments.

To the extent that the rabbinate itself, individually, in small groups, and in convention assembled will examine the data meticulously, to that extent will they unravel their own structure and process. A thorough-going diagnosis may be 90% of the "solution." Honest and knowledgeable confrontation with any problem is the minimum requirement for dealing with it constructively and effectively.

The findings that have been presented in this study provide data for diagnostic purposes.

And thus comes the end to this study, but as the poet T.S. Elliot put it so plaintively,

> " - the end is where we start from . . ."

The Changing Rabbinate: A Search for Definition

RABBI STANLEY RABINOWITZ
Adas Israel, Washington, D.C.

A birthday invites introspection; an anniversary, retrospection. The last time The Rabbinical Assembly engaged in introspective retrospection was in 1960. It is again time to look inward retrospectively, as it is written in the Haggadah: *b'khol dor vador chayav adam lirot et atzmo....*

Jack Shechter's invitation to discuss this subject came at the precise moment that I was searching for a sermon text for *parashat vayetze.* I had just reached the passage, "And he took from the stones of the place." Rashi suggests: "The stones began to quarrel for the privilege of providing the pillow for the head of the patriarchal *tzadik,* each one saying: 'Let the *tzadik* rest his head on *me.*' A later *darshan* added his comment that "this is the way it is when a *tzadik* dies among the *chasidim.* The *yorshim* compete for the loyalty of their father's followers."

"Look how times have changed," he continued. "In ancient times the stones competed for the privilege of serving the *tzadik.* Today the *tzadikkim* compete for the privilege of serving the stones!"

The *nimshal* is not that Rabbi Hertzberg and I are competing for the attention of stones, but rather that the conflict between the spiritual leader and the spiritually led is of ancient vintage, its tension going as far back as Moshe Rabbeinu, for even now there are those who ask, "Who has set *you* as a ruler among us?"

Criticism of the authority figure is not unique to the rabbinate, nor is a blurred self-image, nor is discontent.

There is, however, a special kind of sensitivity to criticism that is unique to the rabbinate. The pulpit may be defined as an elevation four feet above contradiction. It is not rabbinic paranoia that makes the rabbi feel threatened by critics. After all, even a paranoid has his enemies.

K'neged arba'ah banim dibrah torah. Crudely translated, we could read: Four kinds of critics challenge expositors of Torah. *Echad chakham.* We suffer the derision of the wise. Louis Ginzberg, of blessed memory, was heart-sick when he was forced to be part of a system which trained a rabbinate that had so little time to study. He had contempt for the superficiality of contemporary rabbinic scholarship. In a lighter moment he derided the rabbinate: "What point is there in revising Jewish theology for those who preach to pants-makers?" It's difficult for students of scholars to become saints.

Echad rasha: A recent article in a popular Jewish quarterly referred to rabbis as "*brakhah* brokers who invoke God's name for every cause from clean streets to Israel bonds; who are hired for their competence but who function at their lowest level of efficiency; who are expected to know much but who impart little." A community which selects its man of the year and its leaders according to the version of Torah authored by Dun & Bradstreet usually discounts what the rabbi has to offer. They force the rabbi to sit *mi-chutz lamachaneh*, the seat at the end of the dais.

Echad tam. Out of simple integrity we tear ourselves, and each other, apart as we measure the distance between what we are and what we should be, and as we measure the distance between the image we have of ourselves and the expectations that others have of us. Few criticisms are sharper than those levelled by rabbis at their chosen calling. One rabbi has referred to his profession as "a group of medicine men made obsolete by penicillin."

V'echad sheh-eino yodeia lishol. Congregations seldom ask the questions which rabbis have studied so long to answer. Congregations who expect their rabbis to be finished products compel their rabbis to steal time in order to study, much less to prepare their sermons. I won't give you the expected example of the rabbinic neophyte who cries out for someone to ask him a question because he has so many wonderful answers, but rather the tale of the rabbi who attends a congregational dance with his wife. A young man asks, "Would it be all right for me to dance with your wife?" "Thank you," responds the rabbi. "Forty years in the rabbinate, and this is the first time that anyone has ever asked me a *sh'eilah!*"

Salo Baron observed that some congregations in America have been resentful if a rabbi allotted two or three hours a day to study. They expected him to perform his duties rather than waste time over books.

Because no one asks the right questions, the rabbi is overworked. But he is overworked in a multitude of tasks that have little connection with his inner-defined goals. He is overly occupied in what is peripheral so that he has little time or energy left for what he once regarded as his primary function.

It is difficult enough to be a guide to the perplexed. It is infinitely more difficult to be a guide to the unperplexed, the unconcerned, the uninvolved, and the unlearned.

Tsey ul'mad. Anniversaries bring out the historian in us. We know that the *rav* did not officiate at *brit milah*, at unveilings of tombstones, or at affixing the *mezzuzah* to his congregants' doorposts. And he preached only twice a year, though in sermons so long in their duration that the one delivered before Passover made it *Shabbat Hagadol* in length as well as in name.

The expectations of the rabbi have changed. The rabbinic calling has not only been reshaped and restructured; it has been trivialized. A massive horde of ribbon-cutting ceremonies devours the rabbi's leisure moments even as it consumes his professional hours.

The image of the rabbi has changed. The pre-modern Jewish world defined the rabbi as a civil servant, who was a teacher and a sage. The contemporary synagogue defines him as an employee, who is preacher and pastor.

The role of the rabbi has changed. We are no longer the only, or even the best, educated personality in the community. We are no longer automatically part of the inner circle where decisions are made for the community. We share and even vie for influence with secular organizations whose professional executives and whose presidents, if they are rabbis, speak their minds with considerable authority and authenticity.

The Silver-tongued disciples of the Wise are no longer suited to the needs of the American Jewish pulpit, and those who ape them are caricatures.

Judge Simon Rifkind once observed that in Europe the rabbi was the product of his community, while in America the community was the product of the rabbi. And indeed, the history of the early American Jewish community discloses that where there were strong rabbis, there were strong communities. The rabbi shaped the Jewish community which he led. Today we are reverting to the European pattern. The community is shaping the rabbi and is defining his role.

The communities we serve have also changed since the last time we subjected our calling to *cheshbon hanefesh*. The question is, are we adapted to the new challenges or are we maladjusted to them?

What are the areas of maladjustment?

Maladjustment of training. Though we are heir to the mantle of the spiritual leaders of the past—*rav, rebbe* and *magid*, and sometimes *tzadik*—preacher and teacher is what our diplomas state. But the implications of the phrase hardly exhaust the expectations of us.

If we are confused about the blurred image of the rabbi, so is the institution which produced us. Up to recent times, rabbinic seminaries (and ours was no exception) felt that the text was the brick with which we could construct the rabbinic edifice.

It was assumed that the rabbi would know the classical text—its emendations, its deductions, its allegories and perhaps its secrets—

and that he would somehow absorb some basic skills in preaching and officiating. (For that purpose, there was a delightful course called Practical Theology.) There was minimal concern for counselling or any recognition of the serious psychological problems of the congregation.

Although our Seminary defined our role as rabbi and teacher, we were more like an encyclopaedia sitting on a shelf, waiting to be consulted.

Every rabbi was expected to be able to answer elementary questions of religious law about kashrut or death or marriage, or at least to know when a serious question had been asked of him so that he could ask somebody else for the answer which he couldn't answer himself.

Older graduates soon discovered that Torah is far more than a scroll. But the pressure of routine denied him the strength or the opportunity to be its *magbeah*.

The ring of the telephone, the knock on the door, the wisdom of the Sabbath receiving line: "So and so is in the hospital, so and so is having an operation, so and so lost his mother, so and so is a grandmother." This is the Torah that the children of Moses reveal to us, and we must respond, almost as did our ancestors: "We will do, we will do." We are fragmentized. What is worse, we are trivialized. Where shall we find assistance? (Assistants?) Our training did not prepare us for our role.

It must be stated that even as we are searching for a fresh definition of the rabbinate, so is our Seminary.

Maladjustment of authority. The traditional rabbi derived his authority and his status from his knowledge of *halakhah*, for his role was essentially that of a teacher and interpreter of Torah.

The rabbi today derives little authority from the Law because there is little Law to be authoritative about. The need for an expert in Jewish law no longer exists for most Jews.

Other professionals—the caterer, the undertaker, the florist and the wedding consultant—define the *halakhah* of sacred moments. We only officiate.

I am convinced that the primary reason that some people get married is to give them a chance to have their photographs taken.

All of us, I am sure, have had the painful experience of trying to resist making funeral arrangements when a death occurs on Shabbat. Try to explain why a wedding cannot take place Saturday evening at 7:00 P.M. during the Daylight Savings Time season, or that God did not ordain the Sabbath so that there could be a Bar Mitzvah.

Try to explain to people who refuse to submit to the discipline of Jewish law why they have not found comfort from the laws of *aveilut*.

In the voluntary Jewish community of today, Jews decide for themselves the extent and nature of their ritual observances. The rabbi may be consulted, but he soon discovers that it is seldom useful to devote long hours of study to master laws which his people do not observe. Few of us will be consulted on whether it is permitted or not permitted to have an abortion or to practice birth control, even though our opinion may be solicited in evaluating the court verdict on the issue after the jury has rendered its decision.

The rabbi's authority in the synagogue today is only as strong as his hold upon the people's affection. Only if they trust him and like him will they listen to him and accept his suggestions. The rabbi may be successful as a guide. He will not be successful as an authority figure.

Maladjustment to the new spirit of individualism. The rabbi's image as authority figure is maladjusted not only to a repudiation of *halakhah*, but by a return to *halakhah*, the *halakhah* of *The Jewish Catalogue*, a remarkable, delightfully sophisticated, sensitive and useful guide which belongs in every home. Its popularity, however, is a symptom of the new age of individualism and privatism.

The Jewish Catalogue puts Jewish ritual back on the living agenda, but it speaks the language of personal faith which offers salvation without affiliation. It reflects alienation and dissatisfaction with the establishment.

As much as the rabbi may want to reach out to touch those who respond to the *Catalogue*, though the rabbi may change his hair style from clipper cut to razor cut, rabbis are ordained by the establishment, the same establishment that gave us Watergate, Vietnam, racism, pollution, high rises, empty calories and freeways.

And if we successfully contact the counterculture, we are apt to be repudiated by the culture to which it is counter, the culture which produced most of us.

It takes more than a *gartel* to make a Hassidic *rebbe*.

That our self-image is blurred and that we are pulled in so many conflicting directions is the result of a tension far older than our calling. While we are heir to the mantle of the *rav*, the *rebbe* and the *magid*, it is far more accurate to say that we are heir to the robed priest and the sackclothed prophet. And these two roles, except, or even when they are combined in Ezekiel, have always been in conflict. The struggle, the tension, the paradox and the maladjustment within us and the rabbinate is, in my opinion, a contemporary replay of the ancient contest between priest and prophet.

Moses may have hoped that all the children of Israel would be prophets, but we serve a kingdom of priests. There is the conflict.

The classic prophet could not avoid controversy, confrontation and challenge. He was stoned, imprisoned, crucified, a man of sorrows. The prophet was never content with what he saw and with what he was. He disturbed the peace. Wherever he walked, people pointed at him with derision: Get thee hence. *Meshugah ish haruach.*

The priest was patient. The priest who mediated between the demands of God and the needs of man felt that the best way to achieve an important goal was by conciliation, by not going too far beyond the desires of the people whom he would lead. Sometimes it would be necessary to compromise with the principle in order to gain support and to preserve the domestic tranquility.

To the prophet, any compromise with principle was abhorrent; to the priest, anything that disturbed the peace was to be avoided.

The prophet pursued the truth with uncompromising integrity while the priest pursued peace with the same commitment. It is difficult for truth and peace to live together, for if one seeks peace, he must compromise with principle. With truth, there can be no compromise. Because he loved peace, Aaron was led to make the golden calf. Moses could not restrain himself from smashing the tablets.

In times of stress and tension, the prophets among us would sacrifice their people for the sake of the universal goal which they seek. The priests among us would sacrifice the future for the sake of not rippling the waters of domestic tranquility.

The conflict between priest and prophet is discernible in the streets and in the synagogues. There are those who want the pulpit to cry out against the evils of our society, and there are others who resent the pulpit's disrupting their Sabbath tranquility. They want the rabbi to bring them hope and comfort.

In his classic essay, *Priest and Prophet*, Achad HaAm compared the classic struggle between priest and prophet to the tension between the constellations of the heavens.

In the tension of the heavens, no one star has its own way. Compromise in the heavens is not a middle course so much as a totally new course. Similarly in the conflict between the priest and the prophet, what has emerged is not a compromise between the two, but a totally new element. So today, unable to decide what it should be, the rabbinate has created something new: the rabbi-counselor and the rabbi-teacher.

Indeed, many of our colleagues have resolved the conflict by institutionalizing their choice. Some have entered the field of education; others have become professional counselors.

In the pulpit, however, the contest has yet to be resolved. The rabbi may want to be a prophet, but the congregation wants him to be a priest. The rabbi may want to be an inspiration; he turns out to be a functionary.

The priest-rabbi, eager to please, will eventually be led into building the golden calf of vulgarity. He will seek to avoid controversy.

The prophet-rabbi runs the risk of being overwhelmed by the magnitude and multiplicity of evils that assail his conscience and which give him no rest. In his anguish, he will eventually shatter the tablets.

The new pastor-rabbi may discover that, unlike a psychiatrist, he cannot limit his practice. He can control neither the size of his clientele nor the demands upon his time. No matter how many times he may visit the sick or the bereaved, it may not be enough. No matter how many times he may visit the hospital, it may not be sufficient. No matter how soon he may visit the bereaved, it's seldom prompt enough. Few can satisfy the acute demands of the bedridden, the bereaved, or the betrothed.

Every profession may eventually accept defined limits in its scope of operation. There are few defined limits in the pulpit rabbinate, so that the sensitive rabbi eventually feels as though he is a pie with not enough pieces to go around.

The traditional *rav* was like a pot of simmering tea on a slow-burning fire, always available at the hour of *minyan*. He had little else to do. The contemporary synagogue has developed a new instant brew rabbi.

How can we resolve the inherent contradictions and tensions in our calling?

There are inherent tensions between leader and led, professional and volunteer, that are not limited to the rabbinate. Even in secular organizations, the professional may become impatient with the inexperienced or poorly qualified volunteer leader who has power over the professionals. The volunteer member or leader may be insensitive to pressures on the harassed professional.

According to a B'nai B'rith staff survey, some volunteers are unhappy when the professional cannot be reached at his office, and equally unhappy when they think the professional is spending too much time in the study when he should be outside, participating in various activities.

Tensions between the volunteer and the professional are as

normal as tensions in a partnership or marriage. They keep all parties alert. Even amongst the spiritual leaders of old there was tension between the desire of the scholar to study and his responsibilities to the community. Even when he was paid, the *rav* was paid for the amount of time he lost from study. In the long run, the scholar, the community leader and the pastor were each respected for what they had to offer.

Not all tensions can be resolved. Neither prophet nor priest has won the day in Jewish history. Each found his place in a tradition which was wise enough to endure the tension between them rather than to falsely choose one in preference to the other.

Some of us will look with derision upon the priest, yet one cannot live under the constant taunting of the prophet, and he himself cannot live under the constant anguish which he inflicts on himself, or with the constant reminder of his inadequacy.

Our congregations need the reassurance of the priest as well as the prompting of the prophet. Life requires a skillful politician as well as an uncompromising idealist.

There are blessings in the priesthood. People still need the priest to say the right words in the right way at the right time. The effective performance of the priestly function provides security and comfort to the anguished.

As one critic of the rabbinic calling admitted in describing the rabbi's services at the time of death, "I was more consoled by his simple presence than by anything anyone said or did. The fact that he was there was sufficient."

At a hospital the presence of a rabbi indicates to the patient that he is neither abandoned nor unloved. At times of personal crisis the tender hand of friendship becomes extremely important, and its absence painful.

It is self-flagellating to refer contemptuously to priestly functions or to the need to attend cocktail parties, Bar Mitzvah receptions, or invocation assignments, for these bestow status and self-esteem upon the people who invite us. If we refuse to attend social gatherings, Bar Mitzvah parties, we miss an opportunity to make contact with people and to communicate with them, if only by befriending them. The effective performance of the priestly function provides us with the opportunity and the freedom to perform the prophetic function. Perhaps the congregation pays us for being the priest, and if we perform the role well we will be allowed to be a prophet.

The blurred image of the rabbi is an opportunity for redefinition. The expanding role of the rabbinate and respect for individual freedom are liberating. There are broader opportunities of expression and more options for service in the rabbinate than ever before. We can address ourselves to sensitive subjects that would have been considered inappropriate ten years ago. There are alternatives to the pulpit in organizational, civic and educational fields that did not exist before. The blurred image allows us the opportunity to refine our own focus.

The contemporary generation, like the immigrant generation, has once again made the rabbi a respected authority figure, if only as a target at which it can fling its rebellion. Eventually most people will need authority figures, if only as a point of reference, or as a standard and example for the next generation.

The many demands which are made upon the rabbi are real: teaching, pastoral work, public relations, community improvement, social causes, administration—all have a place in our calendar. But it is the effectiveness of the pulpit which, if granted the first order of priority, will enable us to perform in other areas as well, because it is through the pulpit that we win a response to our effort. The sermon can be mass education, mass dynamics. It is the pulpit that is unique to the rabbinate. It is the starting point of our effectiveness.

In defining his own self-image and in resolving the tensions inherent in the rabbi's role, each person must ponder the changes that have occurred without and the changes that have occurred within himself. In the course of his own career, each of us will recapitulate the historic changes in the rabbinic role.

In sequence, we may experiment with each of the historic functions of the rabbi, all the while resisting the role the community forces upon us. Each of us must ponder the changes that have occurred in the community and the changes that we experience in our growth and maturation. Above all, we must rediscover and redefine the motives that led us to choose the rabbinate as a calling in the first instance.

Periodically each of us should write a letter to himself on why I wanted to become a rabbi. But don't mail it.

There is no need for us to feel insecure. At least we shall be the last profession to be replaced by the computer.

Of course we are maladjusted to the contemporary scene. Perhaps maladjustment is inherent in the nature of our calling. What we stand for runs counter to the prevailing idolatries. This has not changed. The rabbinate is a lonely profession.

Jacob sent angels to meet his brother Esau, rather than ordinary folk, because only angels could withstand the contamination of a vulgar environment. We must try to be angels even if we can't be scholars.

In an era of public hypocrisy, with so many scandals and disasters, with the decline of values, and with materialism, in an era when the light at the end of the tunnel appears to be flickering, sons of prophets and sensitive priests must verify Pascal's thought: not to be mad would be another form of madness.

Which, translated into Heschel, gives us the story of the distant kingdom whose grain crop had become contaminated with a poison fungus. It was discovered that anyone who ate of it went insane. Not enough food was available to sustain the population. There was no choice but to eat the grain. "Very well," the king said, "let us eat it. But at the same time we must feed a few people on a different diet so that there will be among us some who remember sanity."

The direction in which the American rabbinate is going is not entirely within our hands. In the final analysis, it is the community that will determine what the rabbi will be: teacher, religious authority, preacher, pastor or social engineer. It is pointless to argue which is the most important.

The stones will always quarrel for the right to provide the resting place, i.e. the foundation principle. Said Rabbi Nehemiah: "Three stones were involved in the dispute. The three stones were the pillars of Jewish life: *Torah, avodah, g'milut hassadim*. Each one said, 'I am the indispensable principle.' Whereupon the Holy One, blessed be He, made them into one." All three are essential.

In our being what we are, we shall resolve the conflict. With the tensions, we must learn to live.

The Changing Rabbinate

RABBI ARTHUR HERTZBERG
Temple Emanuel, Englewood, New Jersey

RABBI ISAAC KLEIN, CHAIRMAN: I come from Munkach. There people speak Yiddish, but they write what we call *deitschmerish*. There was a sign in a synagogue, in Yiddish naturally: *Hier viert nicht politiziren*. One Shabbes morning a gentleman walked in and sat down and gave a *krechtz* that went through the whole synagogue. So the *shamus* pointed to the sign that said, "No politics."

I listened to Stanley Rabinowitz, and I wanted to give a *krechtz*, but the Convention chairman said to me: "No comments from the chair."

I have a few things to say about our next speaker. One is that he is *bnon shel kedoshim*. I knew his father, a *tayrer yid*—but that's not *his* fault. I watched Arthur. The respect and the love that he gave to his father was *kibbud av* in the fullest sense of the word. I saw him do that, and it was heartwarming.

Another thing I want to mention about Rabbi Hertzberg. He should have been a member of *anshei knesset Hagedolah*. They were *machzirin atara leyoshna*. Those people who are my age remember the founding of the American Jewish Congress. I remember one time somebody came and asked me to join the Congress, and I said I already belonged to the American Civil Liberties Union. Recently, as you know, a change has taken place in the American Jewish Congress. The *Jewish* has become emphasized again. We know who's responsible for that, and some of us know a little bit about what's going on know how difficult it was, and we appreciate that.

Another thing I want to mention about Rabbi Hertzberg is that he does not practice what he preaches. He has spoken and written about the failure of the rabbinate, the failure of the sermon, the failure of everything that is associated with the Synagogue. In his practical life he has proven just the opposite—the functions that the rabbi has, the functions that the Synagogue has, and the self-fulfillment you can find in the rabbinate and the strength of Jewish life, everything exactly opposite of what he tried to make us believe in print, and we appreciate it very much.

I think this is one of the reasons why we feel that he can speak with authority on the changing rabbinate.

I am very deeply moved by that introduction, and I am deeply moved by the kind of things that you said about my father, and I find it an especial *zekhus* for myself, being named after the *rosh ha-yoshvim* in Belz (my father grew up in Belz) that a Munkacher should be capable of understanding!

Let me explain for those who do not understand that one of the great Hassidic quarrels of the twentieth century was between Munkach and Belz, so great a quarrel that even though the Munkacher is a cousin of ours, nonetheless the family relationship did not prevail over the allegiance and adherence of my family tradition to Belz. (Klein: "If I knew that, I wouldn't have given you that introduction!")

But Isaac, that is a great *zekhus* that you gave me in your introduction because it elicits a wonderful story.

It happened in Jerusalem six or seven weeks ago. It was one of the nights when everything was locked up at the King David because Allon was giving a formal state dinner for Kissinger and literally nobody could get in. At 8:45 P.M. a Hassidic type, *caftan* and all, one of the *gabboim* of the Belzer rebbe, one of the heads of the Belzer Yeshivah, found his way in, and told me that they had a car waiting outside. The Belzer Yeshivah had decided they were giving a small *messibah* in honor of Rosh Chodesh, and they had decided I was to come. Their emissary fought his way past the *shinbet* of Israel and the Secret Service of the United States. So I went. When I arrived at this little *messibah*, I found that I was the only person there without a beard or a *gartel*, not to speak of a *caftan*. After the third *l'chaim*, the Belzer Rosh Yeshivah arose to say something in honor of their guest from America. And what he said I continue to cherish. The Belzer Rosh Yeshivah said that if he would fall into the trap of saying something that might be interpreted by me or anyone else as being in praise of me, he wanted me to understand in advance that he did not mean it, and that he was only saying it out of respect for my father and the family name. That, insofar as I am concerned, was one of the high points of my life, the best introduction I have ever gotten. You repeated it in your own way, Isaac, and I am very grateful.

I would like to share with you today some reflections that I have been asked to prepare on the rabbinate. You will remember that the rebbe Alexander was the kind of gentleman who davvened with great passion and personally carried through the tradition which good Hassidim called *chavayess*. Behind him stood a Hassid. Every time the rebbe made a gesture, he instantly made the same gesture. After a while, the rebbe Alexander was very tired of the whole business and he looked back upon his Hassid and said, "Stop!" The Hassid said, "Why stop? I'm following directly after you, my teacher and master." The rebbe answered, "When I have made the gesture, it is finished; when you repeat it, it is no longer authentic."

I wrote a piece on the rabbinate back in 1966. On re-reading it in preparation for this morning, I find that I did learn from our teacher and master, Mordecai Kaplan. I did learn from him when one day, in order to save myself a good thrashing, I gave as the outline for a sermon to be given at the Seminary synagogue a verbatim account of what he had said on the subject the preceding Thursday. On Monday morning, after I delivered this sermon in class, he proceeded to demolish me totally. I turned to him and said with great passion and considerable anger, "Dr. Kaplan, I don't believe in all this either, but this is what you said last Thursday." He looked at me with a typical Kaplan smile and said, "But Arthur, I've *grown* since Thursday!"

There are one or two things that I think I have learned about the rabbinate, not by reflection nor by theorizing, but simply perhaps by living it out a few more years, simply perhaps by watching for seven or eight more years what's happening in the congregation in which I am not a tourist. I think part of our problem is that we are sometimes tourists in our congregations. You have to stay in one place for a generation and then ask yourself honestly what you have written large within a generation, within your own congregation. If you are in a place three or four or five or eight years, and then go on, you can say to yourself, "I've tried to serve them, I've done it well —or, I've done it badly—the rabbi-congregation relationship has been good, bad or indifferent." But if you're finishing nineteen years, you cannot say that anymore. You've been there long enough, so *you* are responsible for what is around you. Not the theologians, not *chakhmei hador*, not the symposiasts at Grossinger's, but you. Once it really comes home to you that it is not really others who cast you in roles or define your function for you, then it is possible to construct an intellectual and historical analysis.

I would like to begin by breaking one small lance. What little I know about Jewish history teaches me that the notion that the rabbi's role has become busier or radically different, is really not true. I want to deny that proposition. This common coinage that we are now pastoral psychiatrists, group therapists and hospital visitors and therefore we should appoint visiting committees and therapists to help us, does not impress me.

How many of you have read, either in Yiddish or in English, Isaac Bashevis Singer's *In My Father's Court?* Read it. You will discover that Singer's father was a rov and a *shtikel moyre hora'ah* in one of

153

the poorer neighborhoods of Warsaw. He was terribly busy all day, every day, not writing *chiddushei Torah*. He studied Torah and he was busy with *almones* and *yosoynem* and people who got into lots of trouble. He was, after all, an *avi yetomim v'dayan almanot*. As a matter of fact, so were the *zades* of some of us here.

In the days before I became a politician, I wrote a book on the eighteenth century Jews in France. In our own Seminary library, we have one of the great eighteenth century documents: the *pinkas* of the Jewish Kehillah in Metz from the second half of the eighteenth century. That *pinkas* contains a rabbinic contract for a rabbi much greater than anyone in this room, a gentleman known to us as *Sha'agas Aryeh* (in the French sources he is called Asser Léon). In that contract, his *ballabatim* defined for him a much busier set of roles than those you and I have. Furthermore, they asked him by contract to agree that there are a certain number of things that he will not touch with a barge pole, because they are left for the *parnassim*. Very soon there comes a battle over a *minhag* in the great synagogue of Metz. And the *Sha'agas Aryeh* establishes a personal *minyan* in his own home where he *davvens* for the last twelve years of his life, never darkening the door of the main *shul* in Metz because the *parnassim* had the *chutzpah* not to allow him to eliminate a certain *piyyut* on the second day of Shavuot. I submit that this is a greater *narrishkeit* than any of those that you and I have ever faced from a Board and, *mutatis mutandis, die selbe chaleria*. I think that we really have *cancanim chadashim malei yashan*.

As one who spends whatever time he can find on research in late medieval and modern Jewish history, I am thoroughly persuaded that Abrabanel in the fifteenth and sixteenth centuries, a banker and a politician and a representative before the government who wrote *peirushim* and dealt with reconstructing a community, was no less split into eighty-seven pieces than you or I. And I am thoroughly persuaded that the *Rambam* before him, the head of a community involved in innumerable things, deplored the fact that he was not a *baal melakhah achat*. Were he Stanley Rabinowitz or Arthur Hertzberg standing here, he would list, in the accents of our own time, a comparable set of complaints, in English rather than in Arabic or impeccable Hebrew. I don't believe that the situation has changed. We are not busier than our ancestors, or split into more pieces.

Some things, however, indeed have changed. Beginning with the end of the eighteenth century, two very radical things happened. The ghetto ended, at least in theory, and the *halakhah* ended for many Jews, at least in theory. I don't have to expand on this. Read a book you all know, Mordecai Kaplan's *Judaism as a Civilization*. Or read a book with more footnotes, available in both German and Hebrew (alas, not in English)—Max Weiner's *The Jewish Religion in the Period of Emancipation*. There you will see a brilliant description of what we are living with: post-halakhic Judaism. We are living it, whether it is the life Samson Raphael Hirsch, or Geiger, or Frankel, or Schechter. We are living in a situation within which the power of the Jewish community to compel religious uniformity no longer exists. I can put it very simply. There are still in some smaller towns here represented some Jewish country clubs which will not admit you if you don't give to the UJA. There is no organization which will expel you for eating *chazer* on Yom Kippur. So it is very clear that the Jewish community has decided *yehareg ve'al yaavor* applies to its sense of *Judennot*, the needs of the Jewish people, and not to its sense of what is halakhically enjoined in the ritual tradition.

We are essentially in an eclectic religious situation, whether it be Joseph Brenner's eclecticism, or Petuchowsky's eclecticism, or the eclecticism of Stanley and myself, or the eclecticism of all of us, or Solomon Schechter's eclecticism. As a matter of fact, this was already predicted in the very genesis of Hassidism.

Hassidism arose in the middle of the eighteenth century. It is a very strange interweaving of *kabbalah* and *halakhah*. It is *kabbalah* tamed by *hàlakhah*. Within Hassidism the notion is created that *tzadikim*, who are role models, can in the very nature of their lives decide *vus me meg and vus me turnisht*. It is halakhically inconceivable to *davven shachris* at one o'clock in the afternoon. Those people who decided to *davven shachris* at one o'clock in the afternoon certainly knew the *halakhah*. Nonetheless, they permitted themselves as role models to live it out differently, within what they regarded as acceptable limits of choice.

Let's get down to *tachlis*. Solomon Schechter has been so bathed in an aura of mythology that we no longer read him. He's become a kind of totem; we no longer know what the man said. What did he mean when he talked about "Catholic Israel"? Every one of us owns a copy of his *Studies in Judaism*. Do me a favor; go home and read it. You will find that every time he says "Catholic Israel" he means those Jews living within a contemporary situation who care, who have some sense of what the limits are and who make their choices by what they highlight or what they do not highlight. Schechter is most revealing in an essay in which he wrote about the Bible as read in the Synagogue. He makes the point very consciously that the portions of the Bible which the Synagogue chooses to read reflect its own set of choices, how much it wants to keep alive; and what, without making an ideology of it, the Synagogue decently in practice wants to inter.

155

Ahad Ha'am, whom Schechter argued with and loved and tried to invite to the United States, said the same thing in a rather more secular way. "We choose within the Jewish tradition," he said. "We live it out with a sense of what is authentic and what is not, and our choices become the new authenticity."

Ahad Ha'am confronted Claude Montefiore on the Synoptic Gospels. Montefiore had found some ideological Judeo-Christian set of ethical principles which would unite Jews and Christians. Ahad Ha'am, the secularist, the non-absolutist in theory, loses his temper: "Any authentic Jew knows that some things won't go, some things just won't be, and he who does not know this in the very marrow of his bones is already gone from us." Berdichevsky, Brenner and Klatskin very logically counter-attacked him: "On your principles, you can't reach your conclusions." Nevertheless, Ahad Ha'am did reach those conclusions.

Let me talk to you about what I would call the immanent theology of the Conservative rabbinate, about what we say, not about our theories on *halakhah*. Anybody in his right mind knows that a halakhic case cannot be made for eating *milchiks* out on *tref* dishes. As a matter of fact, the majority of us do. We make choices; not all of us, but a majority of us.

Once and for all let's ask ourselves not what we usually ask ourselves, in bad conscience, what we have chosen to disregard, but let us also ask ourselves about what we have chosen to emphasize. Let us not construct a theoretical, ideological case, because the young in my congregation are not convinceable by ideology, and neither are the young in your congregation. All of the young, including those who live in our own homes, know very well what we care about and what we don't care about. I very often hear of college students from my congregation who make the Pesach *sedarim* at their various schools. I have even heard of them constructing a *succah*. I have seen hundreds of them come home for Rosh Hashanah and Yom Kippur. I have seen dozens of them, when visiting home, come to *shul* on Shabbes. I have not seen very many go to early morning *minyan*! Do you know what they're telling me? They're telling me that they've been observing me very closely. There is no point of my saying that their parents have been casting me in the roles of hospital visitor, chaplain, psychiatrist, etc. The truth is that the young have been looking at me and, God love us, at you, saying *kazeh r'eh v'kadesh*.

We tend to discuss our problems in externalities because it is much easier to avoid the *atah ha-ish* when you write an article such as

I wrote for *Midstream* back in 1966. We say the world around us hems us in. As a matter of fact, the way we can tell that this is not so is not by asking what the Jews do not observe, because we do not. Let me ask about the things which the Conservative movement and, for that matter, the American Jewish community, have positively learned from us.

Jacob Schiff was a much tougher chairman of the Board than you or I ever faced, and Schecter was his *rov*. The Board of the Seminary could have fired Schechter just as easily as a Board could fire any of us. In 1906, in spite of the positions maintained by Schiff and all of his Board, Schechter announced that he was a Zionist, and the world did not fall in. As a matter of fact, I remember a Seminary graduation back in the 1940s when we wanted to sing *Hatikvah* at graduation and some people in high authority at the Jewish Theological Seminary said, "That's a national hymn in the middle of a political argument." We did not prevail at that graduation, but it did not take very long for us to prevail. Why did we prevail? Because *that* we really meant: our Zionism, our passion for *klal Yisrael*, our religious tremor for every Jew. To my knowledge, there is no rabbi in the Conservative movement who has ever put up with a notion that even approaches the Council for Judaism.

We have fought hard for Hebrew. That choice was made a long time ago by Zachariah Frankel who, if you read him carefully, did not believe a lot more than Abraham Geiger. He did not leave the Reform Synod because suddenly on the high road to Frankfurt the *ribono shel olam* appeared to him and said, "Don't do it." He walked out in the 1840s because he looked at the end of Hebrew. That was halakhically possible, but nevertheless totally repugnant. Out he went because he said, "That breaks the unity of the Jewish people." And he fought for Hebrew, as we have fought for it.

We have fought, oddly enough, or not so oddly enough, for *aliyah*. Why do we as a Conservative movement have the beginnings of a leg to stand on in *Eretz Yisrael*? Because the intellectual migration to Israel from the United States, beginning in the days when Dr. Simon Greenberg was the first American student at the Hebrew University, has consisted substantially of Conservative Jews. It is not accidental that Henrietta Szold came from within our polity, down to Moshe Greenberg, to Seymour Fox and to all kinds of others, because we have really cared about Israel.

We have affirmed something concerning intermarriage. If we should find a rabbi within the Conservative movement nowadays using a swimming pool for a *mikvah*, we'll allow it in the framework of a minority halakhic decision. (Personally, I think that is nonsense, but I have a right to dissent from such opinion within the rules of our movement). But find that same rabbi co-officiating at an intermarriage, and the liberals among us will conduct a battle in which no quarter will be given. Out he will go—and The Rabbinical Assembly does not easily throw people out, not even for the infraction of union rules.

We have indeed defined a *persona,* an identity, and we have defined it precisely as Solomon Schechter expected we would define it. In seventy-five years, in three or four generations, Conservative rabbis have effectively decided that they will live out certain things with passion, some with medium passion, and some not at all. If one of my *ballabatim,* or one of yours, was in Hong Kong on a Shabbes and heard that his rabbi was also there, quite as a matter of course the said *ballabos,* wanting to find his *rov,* would go to the *shul* in Hong Kong. But for most of us, unless we were saying Kaddish, neither that *ballabos* nor most of us would expect to find each other there on Tuesday morning at the seven o'clock *minyan.* So what have we really said? We have really said that, in terms of going to the synagogue, we are role models even on vacation. The degree to which we believe *me daf gehn davvenen in de vochen* is generally a matter of negotiation with the pulpit committee, not a matter of burning personal necessity.

Many of us have been role models for the notion that Jews should not be ignorant. We have taught, and we continue increasingly to teach. We are increasingly involved in education. We used to say, "We don't want to be Hebrew School principals." In my lifetime as a rabbi, increasingly you cannot keep us away from our teenagers or our adults, or from the notion that as role models we have to suggest that Jews ought to know more.

I could go on trying to define the *persona,* but I think Bob Gordis made an excellent suggestion yesterday, when we were debating Wolfe's remarks and Marshall Sklare's remarks on the Synagogue, that we have a self-study of Conservative Judaism. If we construct such a questionnaire, I hope we are not going to ask ourselves questions such as "Do you believe in the divinity of the *halakhah?"* I hope we *are* going to ask ourselves some very precise questions about our order of caring, about our emphasis and priorities in actual practice.

We are indeed role models in Jewish life, in competition with other role models: the fundraiser, the *tummeler,* the sociologist. Indeed, in my grandmother's generation, when *tsuris* came upon the Jews, they went to the rebbe, gave him a *kvitel* and asked him to intercede in heaven. Nowadays, when *tsuris* comes upon the Jews, one of the national Jewish organizations hires three sociologists to do a questionnarie, a quantitative analysis.

There are other role models floating around. There are role models of Jewish ethnicities, other than rabbis and in competition with them. But the worst thing is that we are in competition with ourselves. We are really trying to say to ourselves that we don't want these burdens. We would like to imagine, as we confront ourselves, that we don't really carry the whole burden of the continuity of the Jewish tradition, that it is carried by objective factors which are being burrowed under by contemporary disbelief, or that somebody else will carry it now, and therefore we let ourselves off the hook. We forgive ourselves as we see that what is around is failing.

Let me give you what I think is the ultimate example of what our choices mean in the terms of the creation of the *persona* of the Conservative movement. Solomon Schechter was right when he fought against the Board to get Mordecai Kaplan appointed as Dean of the Teacher's Institute. I've seen the correspondence; it makes very interesting reading. I've seen some of the Schechter-Adler correspondence, and some of the Ginzberg-Schechter correspondence. Schechter insisted that Kaplan understood him perfectly well. Kaplan's Reconstructionism, after all, is a pragmatic definition of what we are really about. So why has it failed to conquer the Conservative movement?

Why don't we behave according to the prescriptions of "Jewish civilization," having picked and chosen among "Jewish folkways"? Because in the very midst of our eclecticism we refuse to let go of the notion that the Jewish people and the *ribono shel olam* have a direct relationship with each other. We have recognized that unless we stand by that and live with it, then the central and transcendent importance of what we are doing is gone. Then what we are doing is as good as what somebody else is doing, and therefore also as bad, and therefore also as expendable.

These choices leave us with one simple proposition: In the contemporary situation, the rabbi has only his biography, nothing else. He no longer has anti-Semitism to "keep the Jews down on the farm," he does not have an organized community; he has competition. With only himself, and what he is, he feels terribly cold and terribly lonely, and he would like to be able to say like Moses, the very first rabbi and the greatest of them all, "Go send somebody else." But here *we* are. *We* are sent. We cannot avoid it. And the same thing has been going on before our eyes in the last generation in Orthodoxy. Liberal Orthodoxy has now been replaced by something else. It's been replaced because Rabbi Moishe Feinstein and the Lubavitcher rebbe are a different kettle of fish than the people who were here in the 1930s for Orthodoxy. Orthodoxy has gone to the right because the kind of people who are leading it have gone to the right. Reform has gone in different directions because the kind of people who are leading it have gone in different directions.

We have chosen some values to affirm and to fight for and some to ignore. We will kill ourselves for *klal Yisrael*, for the importance of the Jewish enterprise, for Hebrew, for Israel, for a decent traditionalism, as we will not kill ourselves for *shatnes*, as our ancestors did not kill themselves for the *ben sorrer umorre*, as we will not kill ourselves for the *mikvah*, as our ancestors did not kill themselves for equally important *mitzvot* which they decently interred.

And so we are, if we are honest with ourselves, in the most difficult and the loneliest situation in Jewish history. We are rabbis who have nothing going for us except our own passion, our own conviction, our own lives, and what we are willing to put them on the line for.

THE INNER LIFE OF THE RABBI

THE INTELLECTUAL

Victor E. Reichert

Dr. Leo Baeck once said to me with great concern: "The American rabbi is terribly overworked." Surely the multitudinous demands upon our time create a serious problem if we are in earnest about preserving our inner intellectual life. Amid the many distractions of our varied duties we may lose sight of the essential nature of our calling. The first step in preserving the integrity of the rabbinic office is to make a clear and firm decision that the rabbi is first, last and always a teacher of Judaism. Two thousand years of Jewish tradition validate that supreme rabbinic task. In 1871 Isaac M. Wise said: "The rabbi is the teacher in Israel, no more and no less."

Once a rabbi sees this truth clearly he will not shape his life according to the ignorance or the caprice of members of his congregation who might wish to turn him into something else. Fortunately, in Cincinnati, in Congregation K. K. Bene Israel, the tradition of rabbi as scholar and teacher is a century old, starting with Max Lilienthal and carried on by David Philipson. It will probably be harder in other communities where no such tradition exists to impress upon the minds and hearts of congregants that the essential vocation of the rabbi is still that of teacher of Judaism.

It is axiomatic that one cannot teach who is not a student. Our sermons, therefore, since the pulpit is the frequent spot in which we teach, should be certainly more concerned with enlightenment than with abuse and scolding. A good sermon will always reflect some real learning rather than the easy sound of the jingling of a few paltry coins of unreflecting emotion.

The rabbi must invent some effective strategy for daily study. A good wife here can be of immense help. Any rabbi who really wants to enrich the intellectual content of his life will have the originality and enterprise to find the kind of strategy that will fit his particular situation. If he wills it he can work it, but he must set a fixed time for the study of the Torah.

The *what* of the rabbi's intellectual life is more elusive. There are many mansions of wisdom and beauty in the vast domain of Judaism and each rabbi should select the spot that best suits his temperament, talent and taste. Nevertheless, all rabbis must be grounded in the Hebrew Bible. The Sedra of the week studied out of a rabbinic Bible with attention to the Targum, Rashi, and Ibn Ezra, as well as to the Midrash Rabbah pursued over a number of years, will give a rabbi possession of the basic and enduring attitudes of Judaism. Moreover, all rabbis must know the traditional Prayer Book, the Siddur and the Mahzor. Beyond that there is need for familiarity in the following three domains:

(1) Talmudic-Rabbinic
(2) History and Literature
(3) Philosophy, Theology, and Liturgy

I recommend the reestablishment of a rabbinic summer school for graduates of the College-Institute leading to the doctorate degree.

The rebirth of the State of Israel as a reality and the attendant tremendous renaissance of Hebrew literature in our time makes an imperative demand upon the modern rabbi for familiarity with this Jewish creativity. The American Reform rabbi certainly possesses better than did his immediate predecessors the golden key of Hebrew to unlock these treasures. No modern rabbi can be ignorant of the great outpouring of Hebrew literature that today is part of the glory of the undying Jewish spirit. All rabbis must give time and study to this literature and continue to build upon the excellent courses given at the College in modern and contemporary Hebrew literature.

THE DEVOTIONAL LIFE OF THE RABBI

Marcus Kramer

Formulations about devotional life present many difficulties, and some perils. Private prayers and meditations of aloneness are a man's most sacrosanct experience. Therein, his soul widens for maturity, for spiritual perfection. This quest, as we know, is not always serene. The religious individual who conducts himself with conventional piety is often torn within himself by a fateful struggle, a war without mercy between faith and anarchy, good and evil, spiritual uplift and the waning of physical health. Often, all that can be maintained is a precarious balance between belief and doubt, between hope and frustration. Peace of mind and peace of soul are elevating concepts, but there are too few among us who can maintain them amidst the multitudinous activities that constitute the daily round of a rabbi's responsibility. Faith and spiritual high-mindedness are crucially tried in a materialistic society.

The rabbi is a member of a select group. His education, training, and practice afford him a tremendous spiritual advantage. His is a sublimated service that sets him at the opposite pole of those who are alienated from society and from self. His is a loyal link with reality, confirmed by the emotional richness of his everyday experience.

Reality never escapes him. He knows people and the substance of their ways. With greater knowledge and greater experience, reality becomes more burdensome. The axiom מרבה נכסים מרבה דאגה is also true of the religious field. Responsibilities and increasing knowledge are the rabbi's accumulation of property.

The burden and the distress with it will be effaced by the chief recourse that a rabbi has to fill the cracks in his spiritual structure — his devotional life. Out of his meditations will come forth many deep convictions. Among them are a tolerance, an understanding, and, I am impelled to submit, a love for Israel far more luminous than anything he had experienced before. For these, indeed, are the children of Israel, a stiff-necked nation, a scattered lamb, a righteous people. They need leadership and inspiration, they merit compassion, and beneath the cover of their worldliness is a basic idealism that is the wonder of the world.

The rabbi's calling demands a depth of character beyond that of any other profession. His multitudinous duties exact a fearful expenditure of physical powers and emotional content. He cannot long endure unless he sees the needed strength and emotional fullness of his own life in proper relationship to his consecrated work.

The rabbi's health, his family welfare, his portion in this world, are a crucial element of his personal happiness. Yet, there is no approbation for material aggrandizement. Many are the dilemmas, many the temptations, many the bouts with conscience, that abound in this area. Blessed, indeed, is the rabbi who, out of his devotional life, rises above them, whose inner wholesomeness gives him the fortitude to deal with them wisely and tranquilly.

The devotional life all adds up to the spiritual independence which is the essence of the rabbi's role. No more extensive tradition exists in Judaism than man's independence of mind in relationship to the moral truth. This independence includes the freedom to speak out, the freedom to protest.

As never before, humanity looks to its spiritual elite to do the protesting, to build the divine tenets inwardly, and to pronounce them outwardly. There is a cry in the land for depth of spiritual understanding that shall burst forth in the light of the day as faith, and as the emotions it generates — love, hope, trust and compassion.

The general community accepts the rabbi, and gives him an amazingly respectful hearing. Here his opportunity is great, here his articulated spirituality and learning illumine the community, widen the awareness of the willing and bring vision to the unseeing.

The devotional life is not a withdrawal from the problems of the physical world. Only as the rabbi brings religion to use into affairs of man is he satisfied in soul. But his inwardness is the abode of his heightened spiritual moods in preparation for the duties awaiting him. What a store of riches does he see there! Not only the replenishment of his powers, his renewal of emotional resource, but a promise of wholeness; if he will, a nearness to God that is possible only for the elect and the pure! A hint of the Divine is to be found in every period of prayer, in every moment of meditation.

There are no precise prescriptions for devotions. Quietude is an indispensable boon, a few snatched moments between activities, a period of contemplation in the study, a walk in the park, an hour of silence in the night. Meditation and prayer are not comfortable in the turbulence of the mind. Quietude is an ancient tradition. The "still, small voice" has a greater chance in the silence of solitude.

The still small voice, the communings with his soul, are the rabbi's hidden life. This hidden life is his true story, truest to his accepted vocation. His prayers and meditations give him the key to his stature before God and man. Therein he may roam from the simple to the sublime, through the whole range and variegated facets of his activities to attain the wide perspective so essential to him. Therein, he may gather the finite fractions of his experience and mold them into a unity.

RECORDER'S REPORT

In the discussion following the presentation of the papers Rabbi Joseph Utschen said the problem is that of the rabbi in a small community which does not have a learned layman. Under the circumstances the rabbi has no intellectual companionship. The result is that ויותר יעקב לבדו. His one compensation in his lonely isolation might be his yearning for a union with the אין סוף. The Placement Committee should take into consideration the rabbi's need for study and opportunity to use his potential ability in a given field.

Rabbi Theodore H. Gordon expressed surprise at the fact that recent graduates were not present at this seminar. He claimed that there must be something wrong with rabbinical training if the rabbi does not become aware of the problems of his inner life until so late in his career.

Rabbi Martin B. Ryback suggested that the Conference open with a worship service which will reflect the principle of daily הכנה. He stressed

THE INNER LIFE OF THE RABBI 181

the need for אהבת ישראל and reminded his listeners that the Lubovitcher Rebbe, contrary to David Max Eichhorn, also accepts sinners. He added that William Rosenwald, with a strong Reform background, spent six hours with the Lubovitcher Rebbe.

Rabbi Albert S. Goldstein said he sets a specific time for his studies and lists it in his appointment book. He then does all in his power to keep a date with his studies in exactly the same manner as he would keep a date with his family or friends. Buber, he recalled, tells the story of the man who is about to leave for another city and asks his Tsadik to recommend a Tsadik in his new community. The Tsadik replies, "I do not know anyone there but I have a rule of thumb. Ask the Tsadik this question: 'How can I think about God even while praying?' If his reply is, 'Sit down and I will tell you,' then he is not the right man. But if he replies, 'I have been trying all my life to find the way,' then you may rest assured that he is the right man."

Rabbi Joshua O. Haberman advised that we should concentrate on one or two individuals. Both rabbis and laymen appear to have lost their "private religion." He told of visiting recently a very active lady member of his congregation in the hospital. She wondered why he did not pray with her. "The priest," she said, "always does." He asked himself the question why did prayer not come naturally to him and the answer which came to him was that it is due to the fact that prayer has always been a public matter. The rabbi should not spend so much time on secular matters but should retreat and attempt to concentrate on a few individuals. He said that he used to spend a Shabbat afternoon in his home with five people and had to give it up because of Bar Mitzvah and other social affairs. "Let us follow Professor Samuel Cohon's advice, 'Stay at home every day until one or two in the afternoon for study — עשה תורתך קבע.'"

Rabbi Beryl D. Cohon asked: How do we stay alive spiritually and intellectually? His answer was: 1. Having a manuscript always in the typewriter. We should have a sense of direction. When one drives a car one knows the destination. Lay people are not familiar with the vocabulary of the Bible. We should try to speak like them. 2. Taking even the most humble assignments seriously. I organized a Bible class for just a few people and prepared myself. An assignment to address a church group should be taken seriously. This method helps one to stay alive, and also builds one up. 3. Reading the Sedra regularly. 4. Reading the Haggadah. 5. Reading the Mahzor on all holidays.

Rabbi Jerome R. Malino claimed that the rabbi will not have an inner life unless there is a practical program for the official life of the rabbi. Rabbis, he said, are challenged by the secular form of life in America which has made Jewish life secular too. Congregations constantly try to reduce rabbis to their level and call upon them to be "one of the boys." The invitation to play golf and tennis with them is a perfect example. "If you wish to pick up a man from the ground do not get down on your belly." "If you go further than your knees you will lose leverage." People will not pray unless they are taught how to pray. Just as one cannot play the piano without being taught, so one cannot pray without being taught. People must be taught what prayer will do for them. הכנה is important. A distinguished Rebbe said, "I pray that I may pray well." Effective prayer is like Jacob's ladder.

Rabbi Max Kaufman said that rabbis must apply the formula of the past to the present. They must mold the people. Being alone should not frighten us.

Rabbi Lawrence A. Block added that rabbis must never stop growing intellectually and spiritually.

EPHRAIM F. EINHORN, *Recorder*

The American Rabbi in Transition

RABBI MAX J. ROUTTENBERG

Inasmuch as this is the first Canadian convention in the history of The Rabbinical Assembly, I want to assure our Canadian friends and neighbors that this is not part of any strategy on the part of the United States for the annexation of the Dominion of Canada. Lately, there has been voiced growing concern by some leading Canadians about the expansionist tendencies of its great neighbor. Mr. James Reston of *The New York Times,* in his column of last week, entitled, "Washington: Too Damn Big and Rich," noted that the editor of the Toronto Star had said last year in an address to American newspaper associates, "We like you, but we are worried about you. American cultural, economic and political influence so pervade our way of life that we have begun to wonder if our relatively small nation can retain its independence in face of the strong pressures generated by our giant neighbor to the south." He further quoted the Canadian Minister of Finance, Mitchell Sharp, who in a recent manifesto called for the reversal of the trend towards United States domination of the Canadian economy.

Whether this concern is justified or not I am not prepared to say. I can tell you, however, that the exact opposite worry obtains in The Rabbinical Assembly, namely, the apparent domination of this overwhelmingly American body of rabbis by Canadians and former Canadians. Two of my illustrious predecessors in the office of the presidency, Rabbi Louis Levitsky and Rabbi Aaron Blumenthal, as well as myself, are products of Montreal. Toronto, not to be outdone, has given us our vice-president, Rabbi Eli Bohnen, our treasurer, Rabbi Gershon Levi, and of course our distinguished Executive Vice-President, Rabbi Wolfe Kelman. Many other native-born Canadians have held important posts of leadership in our organization and they will be properly recognized during the course of this Convention. I take it as a great tribute to the Canadian Jewish community that it has been so richly productive of rabbinic leadership, not only in our

[1]

"denomination," but in the Orthdox and Reform groups as well. However, I do seem to hear a growing chorus of protest against this brand of domination and I would not be surprised to see some banners flying here with the legend: "Canadians go home." At any rate, I simply want to indicate to my Canadian friends that we, your native sons, have adequately taken care of restoring the international "balance of power" to this continent.

I am departing from traditional practice which requires the president to give a report of his office during his incumbency. I am afraid that would be both dull and unproductive. I would simply be repeating many of the things that have come to your notice through the proceedings of the Executive Council, reports of our various committees, news releases and newsletters, as well as the usual grapevine communications which, though not always reliable, are far more interesting than our routine communiques. Instead, I want to share some thoughts with you on a subject that is very close to my heart, as I am sure it is to yours, namely the changing role of the rabbi in the American Jewish community —and here I use "American" in its geographic, continental connotation. This is not a new subject. The rabbi has not gone unnoticed in recent years. We may bemoan the fact that we are terribly misunderstood, unjustly maligned, but we cannot complain of being neglected. If anything, we are being over-exposed to public view and discussion.

For at least a decade now, the American rabbi has been the subject of serious study by our sociologists, the hero or protagonist in current novels and movies, a case study for a number of psychiatrists, and a "whipping boy" for a motley group of observers of Jewish life, including some active participants in the rabbinic experience. It is not my intention to answer our critics, for the very nature of their criticism disqualifies most of them from being taken seriously. Their snide remarks, their superficial knowledge, their tiresome cliches, reveal a basic hostility which blurs their judgment and renders them incapable of making any constructive contribution to this subject. There is a body of literature dealing with the American rabbi, unfortunately not yet available to the general public, which presents a true and accurate picture of his various roles, his strengths and weaknesses, his failures, his hopes and frustrations, told with sympathy, with understanding and with utter candor. I refer to the annual conferences of the Herbert H. Lehman Institute of Ethics which, for

[2]

the past few years, have explored every phase of the rabbinic life and have produced a remarkable series of studies contributed by a number of our colleagues. If you want genuine criticism of the rabbinate, if you want an honest estimate of the rabbinic function, if you want a true insight into the very soul, the core of being, of the rabbi, you must read these papers. I am hopeful that the Institute will publish them in the near future.

In the meantime, let me summarize for you my own conclusions on the rabbinic role, based on more than three decades of personal experience and of shared discussion with my colleagues. I am limiting myself to an appraisal of the congregational rabbi, though I do not intend thereby to derogate the importance of the work of the rabbi-scholar, rabbi-educator, rabbi-administrator, or of those rabbis serving in specialized fields of Jewish life, in Hillel, in the chaplaincy, in social welfare, and the like. I speak of the congregational rabbi because I know him best, love him most, and happen to believe that he, above all others, holds the key to the future of Judaism. He is the Jewish spiritual leader *par excellence,* serving directly the masses of Jews, living in their midst, serving their various and multiple needs, and sharing their weal and their woe. It is he who carries the major burden of preserving, transmitting and adapting the legacy of our people for our day and for posterity.

Mah tivo shel ubar zeh? What is this American rabbi of which we speak? It is well to understand that he is a unique phenomenon in Jewish history. There has never been any one quite like him in the whole record of Jewish spiritual leadership. It is fruitless either to compare or contrast him with any of our past models. He is neither priest nor prophet, neither scholar nor judge, neither *Rov* nor *Rebbe.* But he does partake of all of them; he is, in effect, a synthesis of all the sources of creative Jewish leadership of the past. He is unique in another sense, in that he has fused into his pattern of leadership the multiplicity of religious trends and modes and *nushaot* which Jewish life has bequeathed. Except for rare exceptions, he is not an Ashkenazi or a Sephardi, he is not a Mitnaged or a Hassid, he is not an East-European Yeshiva *bochur* or a West-European Germanic Seminarian—but he is all of them. He has been influenced by all of them and has absorbed all their flavors and nuances, their traditions and customs, and blending them with the colors and patterns of his American environment has emerged *sui generis,* an American rabbi.

[3]

There is, however, one central strand of continuity which binds the twentieth century American rabbi with all the spiritual leaders of the past, and that is his essential role as teacher. Like all his predecessors, in all ages, he recognizes and accepts the teaching function as his *raison d'etre* and it is his fondest hope that he may be the kind of priest that Malachi envisioned:

"For the priest's lips should keep knowledge and they shall seek Torah from his mouth; for he is the messenger of the Lord of Hosts." Interestingly, among the many charges leveled against the rabbi, the main criticism is that he has abandoned the traditional function of being the rabbi-teacher, that the people no longer see Torah from his mouth because he is too busy with his many peripheral activities. This simply is not true of the vast majority of rabbis and only confirms what I have said about the hasty and superficial judgments of our critics.

The truth is that the American rabbi finds himself in a totally different, unprecedented type of Jewish community which has forced upon him not a change in role but a change in technique and procedure in the teaching process. The historic rabbi functioned in a community that took the existence of Judaism and the Jewish people for granted. They may have asked their rabbis, why do we suffer, why are we in *golus,* when will *mashiah* come? They never asked the question, "Why should we be Jews?" Their questions turned on the problem of how to be Jews, how to live in accordance with the Halakhah or, at rare times, how to reconcile the tradition with certain philosophical and theological issues that were disturbing the intellectual elite of the day. The rabbi, as teacher, was the expert in Jewish law, the head of the court and of the academy, and the guide to proper Jewish conduct and thought. Appropriately, when he was summoned to occupy a rabbinical post, it was designated as the *Kisei Harabbanut,* a kind of professorial chair in the university of Judaism. He sat in that chair, not only because it was a good place in which to study, but because the people came to him and they knew where they could find him. Many of the rabbis were noted for their depth of learning, for their complete mastery of the classical texts; by their teaching and writing they strengthened and deepened the love and loyalty of the people for the Torah and its way of life.

The American rabbi finds himself functioning in a totally different set of circumstances and conditions; it is almost as if he were functioning in a void. The Jewish community which he

[4]

is called upon to serve is made up of Jews who, increasingly, are asking not *how* to be Jews but *why* be Jews altogether. Certainly this is true of a great proportion of our college-trained generation which is virtually denuded of all Jewish practices and innocent of Jewish knowledge. Alas, many of our people have received their Jewish training in the congregational schools which we head, and we must confess that we have produced the greatest all-American *amei ha-aratzim* to be found in Jewish history. The rabbi, then, faces a congregation of Jews which, to use the picturesque phrase of the Haggadah, *does not know how to ask* the right questions; the rabbi's function as a teacher becomes, *at p'tah lo,* open his mouth and put the questions there.

But there is another side to this American Jew whom the rabbi must teach. He is, by and large, probably the most cultured, the most educated human being the Jewish people has ever produced. To-day, our congregations are filled with a preponderance of college graduates, many of them professional people, university professors, artists, teachers and highly cultivated men and women who occupy important positions in our society. The rabbi is confronted with the challenge of making Judaism meaningful and relevant to these people who have no ritualistic-halakhic question to ask but who, by the very conduct of their lives, are profoundly questioning the whole basis of the Jewish way of life. This challenge to the rabbi comes not by way of confrontation or dialogue but by the simple expedient of staying away. How shall the rabbi teach such a generation of Jews? In this connection, I would interpret for you one of the "dayenus" in the Haggadah. It is said, "If He had only brought us near Mount Sinai, and had not given us the Torah, that would have been sufficient blessing." What kind of blessing is this: no Torah, just drawing near Sinai? The American rabbi understands this blessing very well. If only he could get his people near the Synagogue, if only they would expose themselves to him and to his teaching, *dayenu,* what a blessing that would be!

It is impossible, therefore, for the American rabbi to be *yoshev al kisei harabbanut,* a professor in a rabbinic chair. He must go out to his people and frequently on a person-to-person basis win them over, or persuade them to give him a hearing. Furthermore, to be able to speak to his people, he must have a much broader education than his predecessors. He must be at home in the general culture of western civilization, as well as in Jewish letters. He must be able to transpose the teachings and values of

[5]

the classical heritage into the modern idiom of science and philosophy, of ethics and psychology, else he could never communicate with them. In this sense, he is a product of the culture and conditions of the times in which he lives. He is responding to the needs of his people in his day, just as the rabbis of another age dealt with the needs of their people. The rabbi remains the teacher that he always was. His pupils, however, are different than those of former years and he has had to devise a new curriculum for them and new methods and techniques of teaching. This is a very difficult and strenuous task and no doubt there are times when the modern rabbi longs for that *kisei harabbanut,* where he can sit and study the livelong day, and night. If there is any consolation, it is in the certain knowledge that our rabbinic predecessors undoubtedly had plenty of *tzores,* the kind that we would not trade for our own. Long ago, some unhappy rabbi said that there is no rest or serenity for rabbis, neither in this world nor in the ideal world of tomorrow. *Talmidei hakhamim ein lahem menuhah, lo ba-olam hazeh v'lo ba-olam haba.*

Whatever one may think of the rabbi's role as preacher, it has become today his most effective teaching tool. I know there are those who regard it as fruitless and a monumental waste of time. Let us remind ourselves that, in spite of poor attendance at our religious services, more people are exposed to our message from the pulpit than anywhere else. Whether we like it or not, the preaching of sermons has become one of our major functions and it can become one of our most important techniques in transmitting the heritage and arousing deep and lasting commitments to Judaism. It is encouraging to note that there is a marked trend away from oratorical pronouncements and emotional harangues from the pulpit in the direction of solid Jewish teaching. It was happy to note that Dr. Trude Weiss-Rosmarin, editor of the *Jewish Spectator,* in her excellent editorial on the new American rabbi, makes this very point. She writes:

> Book reviewing and sensational themes are no longer popular. With the exception of some larger city (not large suburban) congregations which expect their rabbis to preach for quotation in the newspapers, especially *The New York Times,* the American pulpit is reverting to the traditional-type sermon of Jewish teaching, based either on the portion of the week or in the form of a continuous course of "lecture-sermons" in an area of Jewish thought and history.... Al-

[6]

though eloquence remains an asset in the rabbinate, the rabbi-orator has become a relic of the past. While their parents loved nothing better than a dramatic preacher, today's typical suburbanites, better educated, better read, and much more worldly, scoff at the few lecturers who still follow the obsolete style of dramatic-histrionic oratory.

The Synagogue, then, is the rabbi's classroom and the pulpit his teaching lectern.

In addition, the American rabbi is responsible for developing both the formal and informal educational program for all the age groups in the congregation. He may or may not teach in the religious school, but he may never surrender his responsibility for the development and implementation of the curriculum and the religious and educational standards of his school. His congregation looks to him, as the spiritual leader, for the proper supervision and conduct of the education of their children. This will include concern for the educational content of the youth program and the rabbi's personal leadership in special seminars and discussion groups for his young people. The rabbi's role in developing a program of adult education is central and decisive. If there are signs of a more Jewishly committed leadership in our communities, of an increasing number of men and women growing in Jewish knowledge and sensitivity, it is largely due to the rabbi's prodigious efforts in the field of adult education. There is a general consensus that it is here that the rabbi feels a great sense of achievement and is deeply rewarded for his efforts. More and more, the rabbi is staying away from the seductive public forum type of programming, so fashionable a decade ago, and turning to the far more nourishing fare provided by classroom instruction in texts and by home study groups. These may not attract the crowds that come to hear name lecturers, but they produce the kind of Jewishly-oriented men and women who are the glory of our congregational life.

I am sure that the rabbi of former days was both pastor and counsellor to his people. What Jew did not visit the sick and console the mourner? Why not the rabbi? What Jew did not come to the rabbi for counsel and advice in his personal problems? Certainly, no rabbi ever turned him away. To speak of these functions as aping the Christian minister is to miss the point completely. The pastoral-counselling work of the modern rabbi, which occupies so

[7]

much of his time, is different only in degree, not in kind, from that of his predecessors. It seems clear that Jews of today are beset with many problems which rarely, if ever, existed in pre-modern Jewish life. The deterioration of Jewish family life, the growth in the Jewish divorce rate, the increasing tensions between parents and children, the rise of intermarriage, the breakdown in traditional morality with its concomitants of juvenile delinquency and crime, pre-marital pregnancies and illegitimate children—all these and so many more, are problems that are frequently brought to the rabbi for advice and help. I believe these are all legitimate areas of the rabbi's concern and he must perforce deal with them. But he must deal with them as a rabbi, not as a marriage counsellor, psychiatrist, psychologist or social worker. Except for a few rabbis who have engaged in special study and qualify as professionals, when such professional help is needed the rabbi should refer his congregant to the qualified practitioner. What the rabbi has to offer in the pastoral-counselling relationship no other professional can give. The rabbi brings a great moral-spiritual tradition to bear on his encounter with his people and helps them reach decisions through the wisdom, the insights and the values of the tradition which he represents and for which he is the spokesman. He does this in the sick room, in the house of mourning and in the privacy of his study. His very presence is a lesson in Jewish compassion and service. His replies to questions, his participation in discussion can become an educational experience for those whose lives he touches. Above all, he brings to the encounter the warmth of his love and friendship, his concern and personal identification with the human beings involved, and this alone is a powerful lesson in the love of one's fellow man, *ahavat habriyot*.

In a very real sense, the rabbi is a public servant, or to use the term first coined by Professor Mordecai Kaplan, he is a social engineer. While the rabbi's first duty is to his congregation, he is not exempt from serving the needs of the larger community, both Jewish and general, of which he is a part. After all, he was ordained a rabbi in Israel, not in Temple Israel or Temple Beth-El, or what have you. No congregation has a moral right to limit the activities of the rabbi to the congregation alone. It is the best part of wisdom, however, for the rabbi to impose limitations upon himself. He need not be at the beck-and-call of every organization that invites him to give an invocation, address a meeting, or serve as window-dressing on the dais. He must have a special function

[8]

to perform in his role as rabbi which no one else can do; and his public work must flow out of his commitments and interests as a spiritual leader. He need not be a fund-raiser for U.J.A. or Israel Bonds or the Jewish National Fund to make his contribution to the State of Israel. He will make it by preaching and encouraging his fellow-Jews to give moral and financial support to Israel, urging them to make frequent pilgrimages to *Eretz Yisrael,* to send their sons and daughters to study and work there, to give serious thought to settling there. He will keep *ahavat tzion* alive in the hearts of his people in a multitude of ways, by stimulating the study of Hebrew and Jewish history, especially the glorious chapter of Zionism in the last five decades, by arranging programs in the school, the youth program and in the adult program which center on Israel observances and achievements. A rabbi does not have to be a Zionist leader today to make a maximum and significant contribution to the cause of Israel. He is much more effective and, in the long run, achieves more enduring results when he is the preacher and teacher and inspirer of his people, leading them to an understanding of the centrality of Israel in Jewish life and prodding them into whole-hearted fulfillment of their responsibilities to the State of Israel.

I would apply the same yardstick in determining the rabbi's role in the field of social action. No rabbi may declare himself exempt from participation in the great moral-social issues of our day. The battle for civil rights, the war against poverty and the war against war, the protection of our civil liberties, all of these and others, are legitimate concerns of religious leaders who take their prophetic legacy seriously. Yet, here, too, I believe the rabbi must place certain limitations upon his time and effort. To be sure, he has a great contribution to make to the reconstruction of our society, but he must do so as a religious leader, not as a politician, an organization man or as a party activist. His specific role, as well as the area of his special competence and effectiveness, is to sensitize his people to their social responsibilities, to make them aware of the moral issues of the day and to stir them into active participation in the affairs of the community. He can do this from the pulpit, the classroom and in his pastoral and social relationships. Above all, since action and not preachment is of the essence, he must create and work through a Social Actions Committee of his congregation. Here he has a channel through which he can take his stand and make clear his view on the social problems of the day and galvanize his people into a program of direct action in the community. It is here that he can make his greatest contribution in behalf of human rights and dignity and not necessarily through dramatic participation in protest marches and demonstrations—though there are times when this form of action becomes mandatory. Similarly, in all his communal responsibilities, in philanthropy, in social welfare, in inter-faith work, the rabbi should confine himself to his essential function, as the moral guide and teacher, who speaks out of the Jewish tradition and demonstrates its relevancy and cogency in contemporary society.

These are the basic, inescapable functions of the American rabbi in the congregation and the community: he is preacher, teacher, pastor-counsellor and social engineer. Obviously, he cannot be an expert in all these fields and this is often a source of discontent and frustration, even breeding a sense of guilt that he is not measuring up to his responsibilities. Yet, it is fair to say that, given the dedication to the task and the sense of worthwhileness in what one is doing, the rabbi can develop a useful competence in all of these fields. He must know his limitations and ever be mindful of the admonition that he who undertakes to meet all the demands that are made upon him, will soon enough discover that his accomplishments are slight indeed; *tafasta merubah, lo tafasta*. Let him not be beguiled by the thought that in order to be "successful," in the Madison Avenue sense of the term, he must project his image everywhere, that he must be seen and known by the entire community. The day of the "star" rabbi is over and done with. As Jewish life in America matures and stabilizes itself, our people are looking for and demanding rabbis who will serve their real and pressing needs. They are becoming disaffected with pulpit pyrotechnics, with glamor boys who scintillate at cocktail parties and in country clubs, with publicity seekers and office holders who measure their success by the number of times they appear on television, are quoted in the press, or the number of national and international boards on which they serve. They realize, increasingly, that the important work of Jewish life is being carried on in the congregational sphere, in the pulpit, in the school, in the youth program, in the adult education classes, and they want rabbis who can function devotedly and effectively in these activities. They are turning their backs on those who glitter and radiate their light on the stage of national affairs, and

[10]

rather seek the services of the dedicated rabbi-teachers whose laboratory is the Synagogue and whose stage is the Jewish heart and spirit. This may not be a very glamorous vocation, indeed it is a most burdensome one, but it is infinitely rewarding and soul-satisfying for the rabbi, as well as providing solid Jewish nourishment for our people.

Of course, in the fulfillment of these roles there is a price that the rabbi—and the community—must pay. It is virtually impossible for the rabbi to achieve the depth of learning, the mastery of the texts, the profound scholarship of the historic rabbi. This does not mean, however, that he cannot become a very learned man, with a broad and comprehensive knowledge of many disciplines. This qualifies him to fulfill another important function in Jewish life, that of the *meturgeman*, the translator and interpreter of the heritage for the edification of his people. This the scholar cannot do—he is too far removed from the masses of people. When the rabbi performs this task ably, as so many do, he is serving the cause of Judaism at least as well as the scholar—and both the scholar and the rabbi should know this!

Even to be a good *meturgeman* a rabbi must have a good grounding in the classical texts. This requires constant study, a luxury in which, unfortunately, most rabbis cannot indulge extravagantly, in the active rabbinate. It becomes imperative, therefore, that rabbinical students be exposed to as much classical learning as possible during their seminary years. I am very much afraid that many of the new courses on so-called practical subjects which have invaded our seminaries are a sheer waste of time. The precious hours taken away from the study of Bible, Talmud and history have not been compensated for by learning some of the "tricks of the trade." These the rabbi will learn, willy-nilly, in the school of life where experience is still the best teacher. I would therefore urge our seminaries to intensify the curriculum by providing additional hours of study precisely in those subjects which the rabbi is likely to neglect when he is launched into a congregation. It is with joy and gratitude that we hail those of our colleagues in the rabbinate who, burdened like the rest of us, have enriched the heritage and the lives of all of us by their fine studies in so many fields of Jewish interest and concern. The time is long overdue to give proper recognition to these rabbis who have kept the tradition of Jewish learning alive and whose creative efforts have raised the intellectual and cultural standards of the American rabbinate.

[11]

It would only be fitting that we hold an annual *siyyum* at our conventions at which we would review their works and at the same time offer them our heartfelt tribute.

One final word. The Jewish community is growing, the number of congregations is increasing and the demand for congregational rabbis continues to be very pressing. Among all our other duties, let us accept the responsibility of encouraging our ablest and most receptive young men to enter the congregational rabbinate. Let us not be guilty of selling the rabbinate short; let us not contribute to the myth that this is no profession for a Jewish boy. We must shatter the cliches and canards about the shallowness and purposelessness of the American rabbinate. In my book, as I am sure in yours, there is no more meaningful and spiritually rewarding work in our entire society. The congregational rabbi, as teacher and preacher, as pastor-counsellor and social engineer, stands at the very heart of the human experience and serves his fellow men in all the crucial and sensitive areas of their beings. Unless all idealism and altruism are myths; unless life is solely a struggle for that great American syndrome of success, power and prestige; unless man is doomed to a mechanistic and materialistic existence, then I say that there is no more daring, more challenging, more adventurous life than that of the religious leader of his people. There is a sense in which we are all failures, in which we can never succeed in our work—in the sense that no man is ever able to reach his goals, to fulfill the ideal life which he envisions, to perfect the society in which he lives. But we have been told that this does not really matter; what matters is that man must only turn his heart heavenward, he must reach for the stars, *ubilvad she-y'kavein et libo lashamayim*. If not in his lifetime then some day, the children of men will stand on earth with heaven in their hands. For the joy is in the journey, the exhilaration is in the quest, the reward is in the certain knowledge that having made His will ours, He will some day make our will His. *Asei r'tzono kirtzonkha k'dei she-ya-aseh r'tzonkha kirtzono.*

A Rabbi Dies
Richard L. Rubenstein

It would be a gross error to interpret the rabbi as a holy man bereft of his holiness. The following paper by Richard L. Rubenstein does not, according to the author, "describe an actual case history; it is a composite picture of various facets of the perplexities and problems, internal as well as external, which color the rabbi's life and work. These observations apply to no one rabbi, though parts reflect the inner turmoil of many rabbis, including myself. I have used this fictional portrait as a device wherein I can best communicate opinions and conclusions which I have drawn from my visits with rabbis in many communities and my studies in the area of the psychoanalytic interpretation of religion." Rubenstein, in "A Rabbi Dies," describes the role of the rabbi and the psychological realities that explain that role.

He was a good man and he was dead. We expected it. Still, it was a shock. He had had a series of heart attacks. I don't remember how many. He puzzled us. The doctors warned him that they could not be responsible if he resumed work too soon, but he insisted on returning to his desk after each attack. He broke bread at the Men's Club brunch; he reviewed the latest novels for the Sisterhood; people died and he was there; he officiated at a Bar Mitzvah every Saturday; he made the hospital rounds; no committees of the congregation felt entirely adequate without him. He should have taken six months off to recuperate. Instead, the heart attacks recurred. He couldn't rest until his body gave out.

Why did he keep going? Was he so insecure after a lifetime of rabbinic service? There were men in his congregation who could have helped him with the preaching and the pastoral work. He must have known that no man is indispensable. Today another man does what he did. Life goes on—rabbis die; congregations have a way of surviving.

Did he want to die? There are kinds of suicides. There are the big suicides like jumping out of a window or cutting one's throat. They are untidy. Society doesn't approve because the victim confesses his sense of failure too loudly. There are also little suicides, an ulcer, chronic overweight, hypertension, perhaps cancer, and the biggest little suicide of them all, the coronary. Not every coronary is a little suicide. Nevertheless, some coronaries are the body's final consent to the soul's craving for rest after a bitterly disappointing life.

He seemed to have everything to live for. His children were married. He had a large congregation, one of the largest and most affluent in the country. He had a beautiful home, the one the new rabbi now lives in. He had a respected position in his community and in the Conservative Movement.

Was he afraid they'd fire him? It wasn't very likely. One doesn't fire a rabbi for getting heart attacks. Yet, he had no sense of personal security. He kept a phone at his bedside, hardly a wise thing in a heart case. At first people were thoughtful about calling him. They inquired about his health. Within a short time his hospital room became his office. All the currents of human emotion in the congregation swept to him over the phone.

There was the subtle pressure to get back to work: "Keep away as long as you need to, Rabbi. We want you to get well, but as soon as you get back, we'll have to discuss..."

"We always hoped that you'd officiate at Jack's Bar Mitzvah. Of course we understand..."

"They're sitting *shivah* for Abe Frank. Maybe you'll send a card from your bedside..."

"The holidays won't seem the same without you..."

Perhaps it wasn't insecurity that kept pulling him back to his work. There may have been a deeper threat he couldn't tolerate, a threat more devastating to him than death, the threat of free time for self-examination and self-confrontation. Perhaps he wasn't afraid to face himself; perhaps his satisfactions were genuine. Nevertheless, he seemed to have preferred busy-ness and death to insight. He may have realized that he had worked his entire life for a kind of recognition which ultimately meant nothing to him. Nothing others said or did could change the way our rabbi felt about himself. Actually, he probably didn't feel very good about himself and, in all likelihood, his death was not entirely accidental. He may have at least consented to it. I suspect that something within him yearned for it.

He had succeeded in the rabbinate but, in his own eyes, he had failed. He revealed himself more than he realized. Everybody knew that his life was his work. There should have been more to it but there wasn't. Like Jeremiah, he was too early destined for his role. His father had been a rabbi, as had his father before him. When our rabbi died, I remembered that he had mentioned his father on the Sabbath before Passover. He spoke of the importance of *Ta'anith Bechor,* the fast of the first born, which immediately precedes Passover. Our rabbi was a first born. He told us how his father had often impressed upon him the importance of honoring this little known but awesome fast by completing the study of a Talmudic tractate on the occasion or, failing that, by actually keeping the fast. As this fifty-year-old man spoke, I could feel the power and the presence of the long-dead father who had given him both his fundamental identity and the values he lived by. Deeply, more deeply than most men, our rabbi had spent his life seeking the approval and commendation of his dead father. As he neared the end of his own life, he still sought it and was convinced that he would never be worthy of it. Thousands of years ago the first born of our people were doomed to be the sacrificial victims of their fathers and their God. By fasting, redemption money and animal substitutes Judaism has succeeded in muting the conflict between the fathers and the sons. Nevertheless, the curse of the first born had never entirely departed from the men of Israel. We shall never know what nameless fear bound him to it. The son-rabbi never failed to observe the fast. There was something awesome about the way he spoke to us of *Ta'anith Bechor.* Nevertheless, he probably never understood the archaic fears within him which furthered his resolve to keep it.

His father had been a well-known Talmudist, born and trained in Lithuania. American Jews hardly set a premium on such men. We honor the exceptional few who are needed as professors in our seminaries. We regard the rest as impractical anachronisms. Who would be foolish enough to become a Talmudist when he could become a used-car dealer or a dress manufacturer? Our rabbi knew this. He knew all too well the enormous practical disadvantages involved in his father's career. There was as little point in becoming a Talmudic scholar as there was in starving. America needed rabbis, not *luftmenschen.* Our rabbi's grasp on reality sent him into the practical rabbinate, but, like most of his fellow alumni at the Jewish Theological Seminary, *he never regarded himself as a real rabbi.* His father had been a *real rabbi* and his family had barely squeaked by. Our rabbi did far "better" for his family than his father, but he never had his father's sense of the authenticity and authority of his role. His professional prosperity only aggravated his sense of having cheated himself of his inner dignity.

His father spoke English with a pronounced Yiddish accent. His marital life had been drab. Life had been exceedingly difficult for him, but he had a sense of dignity the son was never to know. The

Jewish Theological Seminary in New York hadn't added to the son's sense of dignity or authority. His teachers were men not very different from his father, save for their PhD's and their greater exposure to German scholarship. They lived in their own hermetically sealed world, isolated from the vulgarities, but also the realities, of American Jewish life. They were an elite group and they knew it. Many of the real estate offices, bakery shops, and dry goods stores of Main Street, America, were run by former Talmudic scholars from the Yeshivoth of Slobotka and Volozhin who hadn't made it. The Seminary professors had made it in their own eyes. Some of their success had been luck, most incomparable ability. They were very special and so they regarded themselves. They did not respect rabbis. On the contrary, they had contempt for them. They mocked their ignorance of the Talmud and their prosperity. The Seminary diploma did not carry the historic formula of rabbinic ordination. It read *rav yitkareh v'haham yitkareh*, "he shall be called rabbi and he shall be called wise." When our rabbi was a student at the Seminary, a very distinguished Seminary Talmud professor mocked the Seminary ordination: "Let them be *called* rabbis. After all, what's the harm? Someone has to do the dirty work."

The famous professor constantly implied to his students that no self-respecting man would take such a job. He told them that the Rabbinical Assembly was just a trade union for hired professionals. Really able men became professors; the others were second-class men at best. The bureaucratic structure of the Seminary and the Conservative movement emphasized the elite's disdain for the congregational rabbinate. The Conservative movement was hierarchical and episcopal in structure without having any official bishops. It didn't matter. Everybody knew that the faculty members were the cardinals and bishops; the congregational rabbis were at best parish priests. There was even a Curia and a Holy Office to deal with troublesome dissenters.

All his life our rabbi wanted to demonstrate to the Seminary professors that he really wasn't second-rate. He had a dream. He'd write the book which would show his teachers how much he really knew. Someday he'd prove to his dead father and to the living men like his father on the Seminary faculty that his mother was right, that he was the beloved wonder child who could do anything he set his mind to. Someday he would amaze them.

It was only a dream. It flickered and grew dim as the years passed. He enrolled in the Seminary's doctoral program but never completed it. He thought he'd finish his dissertation during vacations. He never did. The years passed. One day he realized it was too late. He was a washout. He'd never be half the man his father was. He'd always be a mediocrity. That year his raise was bigger than ever. It should have filled him with a sense of pride. The congregation had expressed its confidence in him in the most tangible way they knew. On the surface he was pleased, but somewhere within he hated himself for his raise. It seemed unearned and undeserved. He couldn't let the world know the truth, but he knew: He was a fake-rabbi, a fraud, in his own eyes.

He never got to know himself. He was a driven man and he paid a terrible price. When he was a very small boy he thought he caught a rare glimpse of his mother's woman-need for her man. It was a terrible shock. The next day he had forgotten the glimpse. It was as though nothing had happened, but everything had changed in that instant. He'd never be as good as his father. His mother would never express her woman-need for him. He became second-rate in a moment he could never remember but which never left him. His first reaction was murderous, uncomprehending rage. He'd kill his father. The thought was hideous, so hideous that he could never acknowledge to himself that he had it. There was only one way out. If he couldn't kill his father, he'd become like him. He, too, would be a rabbi. He'd never succeed in really being like him, but, if he came close enough, he might someday possess a woman like his mother. He'd never be as good as his father and his woman would never be as good as his mother, but what could a second-rater hope for? He'd always be mediocre. His father would always be the bigger and better man. Still, the hope never left him. If he could only find his way back to mother and her woman-love, he'd never be a second-rater again. She had been dead for years, but he never gave up hope. And, he never knew what it was he hoped for. It was the book, the doctorate, the love he thought his congregation withheld from him, but behind all the proofs of worth which always evaded him, he continued to seek an assurance he never understood.

The rabbi and his wife seemed like a perfect couple. She came from a rabbinical family, as did his mother. Truth to tell, the resemblance was there. Of course, he didn't think much of those new psychological theories which saw incest in every decent feeling. Life in the congregation was difficult. The world had never expended much love on Jews. Jews couldn't easily hit back at those who treated them harshly. Like the blind man who instinctively smiles when he feels his anger rising, Jews are afraid of their anger. A two thousand year old crime poisoned their relationships with Christians. Even two thousand bishops couldn't really change things. There were times when they had to hit back at someone. The rabbi was a perfect target. He did not dare to retaliate. It could have been at a committee meeting. An objection was raised, not for the sake of the objection, but for the sake of wounding the rabbi. It could have been at a social occasion. Humor can be vicious. The occasions were legion. The rabbi quickly learned the lesson. He could as little afford to return his congregants' hostility as they could afford to retaliate against gentile aggression. He was the congregation's Jew. Subtly, often unconsciously, they treated their rabbi the way gentiles treated them.

He winched, but he had to take it. "It was a rotten life," people said. "It was no job for a Jewish boy," they laughed, but he had to take it . . . and smile.

Things might have been easier if he had been able to come home and find comfort there. She was a good wife. She provided his meals. She kept the house clean. The furniture was always in good shape. People liked her as a hostess, but something was missing. She had her own reasons for thinking she too was second-rate. Her parents wanted a boy. Every Jewish mother wants boys, not girls. Every Jewish mother is under the illusion that their daughters do not understand their mother's disappointment. In her household, boys became rabbis. All that she could do would be to marry a rabbi. That wasn't nearly good enough. As she grew up, she saw the difference between the way her parents treated her and the way they treated her brothers. Her brothers' Bar Mitzvahs made her angry. Unaccountably, she became hostile at these celebrations. Nobody could understand it, least of all herself. Her brothers went off to the Seminary to become rabbis. The family talk was about them and their accomplishments. Little was said about her. Sometimes she thought she had to atone for some nameless sin. Sometimes, she thought the nameless sin was the crime of being a woman. She never wanted to be a woman. She never learned how to enjoy a woman's feelings.

As a girl she wasn't bad looking, but her body infused her with stirrings which made her afraid. She knew that she was supposed to be a "good" Jewish girl and that she had to be careful. She knew girls who were pretty loose but she was determined to be a "good" Jewish girl. She watched herself and she kept her body in check. She never really gave in to her feelings. And, she became ever angrier, an anger she never dared to show. Their courtship wasn't very long. Their lives had been predestined for each other. The marriage was inevitable. She came from the "right" kind of family. She knew what was required of a rabbi's wife. She was the logical choice. He was already ordained. He was a friend of her older brother. He had a promising career before him. Theirs would be an excellent *partnership*.

The match had logic, but I am not sure it ever had much love. Nobody ever really knows what goes on between two people, but there are a number of things about their lives about which I have often wondered: They both had such unfulfilled faces. Did they get any real pleasure of life? Was their bed a place where they found release or were they tortured by an intimacy which was in fact a terrible wall forever separating them? His life was difficult outside. Did he find the warmth and comfort in sexual union which would have given him the confidence to face a difficult and problematic vocation or were the frustrations of his role multiplied by the more devastating frustrations of his intimate life? Could a clean house and a good salary compensate for a fundamental lack of deep sexual gratification?

People regarded him as a successful man, but his life was different from that of the other successful men in his community. There were a lot of unhappy marriages in his congregation. Several of his board members had taken mistresses, often from among their gentile employees. The rabbi unknowingly envied these men their out-of-town trips and their greater sexual freedom. Occasionally, a woman in his congregation would consult him about her inner discontents. Sometimes, these women stirred him. They wanted a man; they wanted him. His wife never seemed to value him *as a man*. She never experienced any pleasure in their intimacy. A favorite theme of his wife's conversation was "If only they knew you as I do. . . ."

The temptation to have an affair was there but nothing ever happened. He was impressed by the old rabbinic legend that Joseph was prevented from accepting the invitation of Potiphar's wife because the image of Jacob, his father, appeared before him in the moment of temptation. The image of our rabbi's father was always there. It made him feel continually mediocre. It infused him with guilt for the longings of his unfulfilled body. It made him hate himself for lusting after women he'd never touch.

He was desperately afraid someone would find him out. The rabbinic image had to be preserved at all costs, but sometimes the strain between his own image of himself and what he hoped his congregants would think of him was too great to bear. He experienced moments of anger and fury born of his inner frustrations. He could not look at his wife in the bed without a measure of disgust. Was this the reward of an observant Jewish life or was this the prison to which he had condemned himself without hope of escape? She looked so unappealing lying there. Age had not improved her looks. He never realized it but there were times when he wanted to kill her. He was a rabbi, but he was also a man with body yearnings. As he grew older and death became, not something that happened to others but something that would soon happen to him, his sense of desperation grew ever greater. He insisted on middle-aged, unattractive secretaries in his office. He could not bear to have attractive young women around him although he could never admit this to himself.

I always used to wonder why he spoke continually of the beauty of Jewish life in Eastern Europe before Hitler in his sermons. There was an incredible nostalgia in his preaching. I came to realize that *he was not urging his congregants to live his kind of life but his father's.* He called upon his congregants to return to a lost world as his way of expiating his own guilt at having left it.

Preaching was difficult. He seemed convinced that the ills of the Jewish community derived from their having forsaken his father's kind of Judaism. His basic message was always the same: "Return to the life of Torah; don't be taken in by the rootless, vulgar commercialism of the world of buying and selling; in Judaism you'll find the sense of worth, assurance, and dignity your lives no longer possess."

It was not an easy message for him to deliver because he was closer to the life he preached against than the one he urged upon his congregants. He hardly wished his life on anybody. He told his people to give up the externals, but he wanted the very externals he belittled. He was more like his congregants than he was like his father, and he despised himself for it.

There were times when all his anger and frustration were condensed into passionate sermons of moral condemnation. He berated American Jews for their shallowness and their materialism. When he became angry, he could make us squirm with intense discomfort. One day I realized that he was furious at us as he spoke, that he hated our being like him. I also saw that there was something sadistic about his condemnations. Nevertheless, I was surprised by the reaction of the congregation. *The people never appreciated him more than when he lacerated them.* They felt guilty and they wanted to be punished, provided that they did not have to take the punishment seriously. They often came to the synagogue just to be scolded. They too had fathers whom they could never appease; they too despised themselves; they hated themselves for the tawdriness of their lives.

They also hated themselves for being Jewish; they hated themselves for their money and for the way they earned it. They possessed more than their fair share of anxiety and guilt. If their fathers were no longer alive to whip their bare behinds for stealing the cookies of life, they had to set a father over them to do it for them. Our rabbi's anger at his own unfulfilled life harmonized with their need to be punished. They were tied to each other by bonds deeper than they could ever understand.

I never had much to say to him. We were both Jews, but we lived in such totally different worlds. I loved our services, largely because of the cantor and the music. I came regularly but found his preaching boring. I saw life as somewhat more complicated than simply learning how to become like his father. Still, I remember him with affection in spite of all that separated us. When my father died, he called on us. I was more consoled by his simple presence than by anything anyone else said or did. The fact that he was there was sufficient. In a way, it was just as well that we didn't have much in common. What would have been the point of our discussing Buber, whom he couldn't understand, Sartre, whom he regarded as a sick nihilist, or Freud, whom he saw as sex-obsessed?

He visited me at the local hospital during my brief illness. Hospitals are never pleasant places. Their antiseptic sights and smells are hardly conducive to good cheer. Without knowing it I had become depressed and felt abandoned—until his visit. We talked small talk. I suppose he wasn't exactly pleased that he spent so much of his time in chatter, but it was the only kind of conversation which worked in the hospital room. By his visit he told me, "You are neither abandoned nor unloved. I come to you on behalf of your friends and your community." Of course, he didn't say this explicitly, but that was what his visit meant to me. I was totally unaware of it before his visit, but I needed him and I was grateful. His dull, pedestrian sermons hardly mattered. What did matter was that he was there.

At times he had to be a magic helper. I had no doubt he had conflicts about being both priest and witch-doctor. I saw his magic work one time in a way I'll never forget. A friend of mine had a ninety-four-year old grandmother who had just lost her sixty-four-year old son. When I came to pay a condolence call, she was in a horrible condition. She was cursed with an alert mind and felt the loss of her eldest son more acutely than most younger women. She hadn't eaten for three days and kept on moaning, "Why didn't God take me first?"

The rabbi came in. She managed a brief word. He tried to say the right things, but it was obviously difficult. I didn't envy him the task. He asked her whether he could pray for her. She nodded. He read psalms which praised God for his righteousness and truth. The old woman nodded agreement. She joined him in praising the righteousness of God. The effect was unbelievable. Ritual had helped both the rabbi and the woman. Her only hope lay in accepting reality so that she might turn from the loss to finding some happiness with her other children, grandchildren and great-grandchildren. Nobody could have helped her by simply telling her, "You must accept reality." That would have been too verbal and too intellectual. His prayers and his reading of the psalms brought her to acceptance and consolation. As she followed him in affirming the righteousness of God, she reminded herself that, though the world did not conform to her wishes, all was by no means lost.

He promised her he would be mindful of her son when he recited the *Kaddish* before the congregation. His promise probably made him feel uncomfortable and slightly guilty. After all, he was not a medicine man and the *Kaddish* was a doxology, not a prayer for the dead. For the old woman, our rabbi's promise was almost like the assurance of eternal life for her son. She knew her son was dead, but she also knew that someone cared, that the inevitability of eternal forgetfulness would be delayed. Neither she nor the rabbi really knew what had transpired between them. When he left, she ate heartily for the first time since her son's death. At that moment, he seemed to us like a *wunderrebbe*. I know he added time to that womans' life. She is now ninety-six. I am sure that if I had asked him how he helped her, he could not have given an adequate answer, but he had bestowed the gift of life on a woman who otherwise would have wasted away in misery.

His officers were a rough, tough, hardened group. They were all self-made men. They had fought their way up the hard way. Nobody had given them anything. They had started out penniless. Many of them were now millionaires. To the gentile world, they were still just pushy, overly clever Jews, to be watched and never to be trusted. They made their money in jewelry and dry-goods, real estate and small banking. As they prospered, they realized that they were still regarded as second-class by the people who really counted in our city. They were ignored by the leading charity drives. They never acquired any social standing among the WASP elite. To the ruling WASPs they were just rich Jews, and that wasn't much.

They hadn't had it any easier with the old monied German-Jewish families who were the town's so-called Jewish elite. Actually, the German-Jewish elite had none of the characteristics of a real aristocracy. They were too busy trying to be imitation WASPs. Our board members were invited to take part in the fund-raising drives of our Jewish Charities Federation, the JCF, but they were seldom invited to sit on the board with the old German-Jewish families. The only time they saw the inside of the German-Jewish homes was at parlor meetings to raise money.

Our officers were never invited to join the Harmony Club, the Jewish city club, or the Westminster Country Club. It rankled them that they had to build their own country club, Whispering Pines. It was bigger, better equipped and more expensive than Westminster, but everybody knew it was second-class. Only the Reform rabbis were members of Harmony Club and Westminster. They made our rabbi an honorary member of Whispering Pines. He liked golf. He and his wife used to come out during the golf season, but once I heard him say, "I feel like a kept woman every time I come to this place."

The officers were rich, bitter, opinionated men. A whole life of work had brought them neither recognition nor contentment. *There was one place where their word was absolute law.* They ruled the synagogue with an iron determination. They finally found in the synagogue all the recognition they craved from the outside world. Here they were absolute masters. What did it matter that the Reform Congregation was more fashionable? They were more Jewish! Maybe the Germans had a real country club. They had a real *shule!*

The younger men in our congregation complained that the leadership never sought new blood. Why should they? They had worked hard to build what they had. They were used to buying things. In our synagogue their success was recognized, their money counted, and if they were rich enough, they could buy even greater prestige with their contributions to the Jewish Theological Seminary and the United Synagogue of America.

They had a peculiarly ambivalent attitude towards our rabbi. They recognized his importance and his authority, yet he was their hired hand. Many of the trustees contributed more money to the synagogue and its three million dollar building fund than our rabbi received in salary. The trustees' attitude toward our rabbi vacillated between inordinate respect for someone who took the place of their fathers and contempt for the valet. Sometimes both attitudes were intermingled. Inevitably, our rabbi missed a few sick calls. There was no greater wrath than the fury of an officer whose sickness had gone unnoticed. The rabbi's neglect triggered their deepest fears of their own irrelevance and lack of worth. They were threatened by the thought that perhaps the gentiles and the German-Jews were right in putting them down. Surely a lifetime of work was not to be repaid by such a slight!

In reality, he was always their hired hand. He depended upon their generosity and they expected their hireling to give them the prestige the world had denied them. If they had received it from the larger world, they would have been less interested in the synagogue. The world's contempt had done more than Jewish loyalty to drive them back to the synagogue whose values their lives had denied. They did not want our rabbi at their board meetings. They liked to *tell* him what to do, but they were always stopped by the fact that he was the rabbi. They could never quite make up their mind, hired hand or revered father. They never knew. When their contempt was too openly expressed they felt guilty and ashamed. They turned to reverence, but they couldn't remain respectful very long. They also knew the difference between our rabbi and a *real rabbi*. There was something almost schizophrenic in their attitude toward him. It was never consistent. He was condemned to be a man apart, a lonely man who could never forget his lonely role.

Morris Levy had been the Honorary President of the congregation for years. He had seen rabbis and presidents come and go. He had buried several. He had been the real power in the congregation for fifty years. Everybody wanted to unseat him. Nobody dared. Our rabbi quickly learned that Morris Levy was the one man in the congregation who could destroy him. Morris always maintained a surface politeness toward him, but Morris was a man of unbending will. He knew only one emotion, dominance. There had been neither love nor children in his life. Morris Levy had only one world, our congregation. He ruled it more absolutely than any eighteenth-century monarch ever ruled his kingdom.

There never was an open confrontation between Morris and the rabbi. They hated each other, but were condemned to live with each other. The rabbi never expressed an opinion on administrative policy. He could assert his authority on ritual matters, but he knew that questions involving real power were handled by Morris. He made it clear to Morris that he had no intention of fighting him. This only heightened Morris' disdain. Our rabbi was not a real rabbi in Morris' eyes. Our rabbi was not like the men Morris had met in his father's house. "What kind of a rabbi would take orders from somebody like me?" Morris asked himself. Morris' self-contempt made it impossible for him to respect those who recognized his power. As a result, Morris was never satisfied. To accept Morris' dominance was *ipso facto* proof of worthlessness. For the rabbi not to accept it would have meant loss of his job. By submitting to Morris, our rabbi degraded himself in his own and Morris' eyes, but he had no choice. He knew that his father could have handled Morris. He had watched Morris with men like his father. They had a hold over Morris our rabbi never possessed. His surrender to Morris preserved his livelihood, but it deprived him of all dignity.

I shall never forget the reaction of the trustees to the news of our rabbi's death. They were horrified and inordinately guilt-stricken. One man told me he could not eat because he was so sick at our rabbi's "sudden passing," as if his heart attacks had no relation to his death. They draped our rabbi's chair in the synagogue with black ribbon. It became a sacred place no man could approach. Everything he used became taboo. The officers were depressed and anxious. They spoke of him in tones of sincere but utterly exaggerated respect. Was this their hired hand, the man they had told to come to early morning *minyan* more often, whose sermons they ordered shortened to twenty minutes? As I listened to their comments and to the tributes at the various memorial ceremonies, our rabbi seemed to become another Moses, a saintly genius, an irreplaceable treasure. I asked myself, "Do they really mean what they are saying? Do they believe all this after everything that has transpired?" It didn't take me long to concluded that *they meant every word*. As he lay dead before us, he had become the most important person in the world to the Yom Kippur-size congregation which gathered for his funeral. The grief was real; the tributes sincere; the guilt unbounded.

Our congregation experienced the same sort of shock in reduced dimensions which the nation had experienced when President Kennedy died. Just as there had been people who had said we had all killed President Kennedy, there were people who said we had killed our rabbi. I dismissed the thought when somebody confessed to me that he felt a little responsible for the rabbi's death, but, as I thought about it later that day the idea made sense. We were all living through the archaic ritual death of the king. He was our primitive offering just as President Kennedy became the nation's. The King must die and we had killed him— long live the King. Shortly after our rabbi died, an insane young man arose during Sabbath services and murdered Rabbi Morris Adler of Detroit. At the time I remember wondering whether this insane young man had acted out a temptation "normal" people experience and then repress.

Did we wish for the death of our rabbi? I know I did if I am honest. I was glad every time he preached a mediocre sermon. It made me feel superior. I loved his failures. I was delighted with the gossip I heard about his trouble with the board. I wanted to see him levelled to the position of unexceptional anonymity in which I found myself. His sermons on the Torah angered me. I am free of that stuff. I eat as I please. I live as I please, but he still had the power to make me feel guilty for my freedom. If only I could get rid of him, I might be rid of my guilt.

I resented the fact that he always received attention that I never got. After all I was smarter than he, but that didn't make any difference. He was the rabbi. I never had the opportunity for the kind of sexual high life of a few men in the congregation. I wonder how guilty he must have made them feel. We all felt guilty and we all wanted somebody to die for our sins.

He was very observant. More than once I heard a great devotee of Chinese food in the congregation observe that while he didn't keep kosher, he couldn't respect a non-observant rabbi. There was never the slightest suspicion about our rabbi's conformity in ritual matters. He was encased in it and couldn't get out, though I doubt that he ever wanted to. Whether he did or not, *I wanted him encased in it.* I wanted to know that someone in the congregation lived according to the Law. He was doing it for me as well as for himself. I took a secret delight in the restrictions that hemmed him in. I laughed at him. It was in part my revenge for the special attention he received. He was somewhat like a king whose people revenged themselves upon him because of his preeminent position by insisting that he observe all sorts of enclosing, limiting rituals. I could understand the risks President Kennedy took with his life. He must have gotten sick at looking at Secret Service men forever disturbing his privacy. Finally, he decided that safety was too high a price to pay for their intrusive presence. Our rabbi never had to worry about Secret Service men, but he did have to worry about where he ate and what, about whether to wear a hat or not, about when to be himself, if he ever knew how, and when to retain his mask. It was our way of killing him bit by bit.

You see we wanted him dead and when he died we were frightened and guilty because he had given us what we wanted. We had fathers too and they never ceased to make us feel second-rate. If only we could get rid of our fathers.... He had taken the place of our fathers. He had become the voice of conscience they had been. He had some of the magic they had had. He was the symbol of everything that kept us in check and we hated him for it. And so, we wanted him dead.

We didn't know it. How could we? If a pollster had asked us whether we wanted to murder our rabbi we would have done violence to him. Murder our rabbi? Impossible. We loved and respected him. Look at the fine home we gave him. We just gave him the raise he asked for. We wanted him to live a long life and always be with us. We... we wanted him dead. We only understood it when he was dead and we couldn't eat, when we turned him into the saint he never was, when out of our unnamed and uncomprehended guilt, we pledged ourselves to projects in his memory.

We wished him dead and it got through to him. There was an unspoken covenant between us. We wanted him dead because he had been the exception in our midst. He yearned for death because he regarded his life as worthless and unjustified. Why did the priest of Diana of the woods cut the golden bough and murder his predecessor? He murdered only to be murdered. He became priest to die the death of kings. Our rabbi died the death of kings. Thousands of years had passed since the first king was murdered and eaten and it had happened again.

We said we had killed him, but that was not the whole story. We killed him but *he consented. He let us do it. He was with us all the way.* We were all accomplices. Abraham could not offer Isaac without Isaac's *"Hineni,"* "Here am I." *Our rabbi intuitively knew we wanted him dead and he gave himself.* Ironically, he never knew the real truth about himself, that he was a good man, a decent man, a man who by his deeds, the only test that really counts, had made an important difference in our lives. Because he was a good man we wanted him dead. Because he could never believe in his own goodness, he wanted to die. He was our victim. He consented.

I watched them lower his coffin into the ground. I paid my final homage as a Jew, I who had wanted him dead, I poured earth upon his grave and passed the shovel to the next in line. He had returned. He had found his peace. The rains of springtime were gently falling. Earth had claimed her child. Soon, she would give us of her fruits once again. She would give us other priests, other kings, other victims, but our rabbi was gone. He was a good man and he was dead.[4]

---

[4] Richard L. Rubenstein, "A Rabbi Dies," unpublished, © 1971 by Richard L. Rubenstein, pp. 1–17.

STUDYING AT HEBREW UNION COLLEGE, 1942-1945

By RICHARD RUBENSTEIN

This article consists of excerpts from Chapter IV of Richard Rubenstein's forthcoming book, Power Struggle, *to be published by Scribner's this summer.*

MY YEARS OF STUDY at the Hebrew Union College in Cincinnati, the seminary for the training of Reform rabbis, coincided almost exactly with the period during which Hitler's "final solution of the Jewish problem" was being carried out. Over one million Jews had been slaughtered by the time I entered the college in September 1942. When I left in June 1945, six million had perished. Hitler was dead, but he was victorious in the one war that really mattered to him.

Jean-Paul Sartre has observed that things happen in one way, we tell them in another. Happenings are transformed into stories with plot and meaning, a beginning and an end, by memory and hindsight. My memories of the college are highly selective. They tend to focus on my reactions to the great events that were taking place in the wider world rather than vignettes of student life. It is only in retrospect that the bizarre character of those years in Cincinnati has become apparent. Perhaps the most indecent aspect of our rabbinic studies in the years the death camps were operating at full capacity was the banal normality of our lives. We knew that mass slaughter was taking place. We had heard Hitler promise the extermination of the Jews, but somehow the catastrophe had little reality in our daily lives. The events had almost no impact on the way we lived or on our hopes for the future.

When I first arrived at the college, I was struck by the luxury of the place. Things changed somewhat as the war went on, but in 1942 the college was more like a country club than a school. We ate exceedingly well, far better in fact than most of us had eaten at home. Seconds were always available. The dining room was staffed by white-jacketed Negro waiters who also took care of our rooms. The College was situated in a pleasantly wooded area off Clifton Avenue, not far from the University of Cincinnati campus. We had an indoor swimming pool, a gymnasium and excellent tennis courts. Images get mixed up retrospectively. I can still see the mounds of sweet butter, the lemon sole, the Friday evening roast chicken and the steaks, but I cannot recall these images without en-

---

Copyright © Richard L. Rubenstein, 1974.

visioning our contemporaries, the starving Jews with burnt out, hollow eyes, caught in a limbo between life and death, dressed in the striped pajama uniforms of the concentration camps. We were truly innocent, not-knowing. We suppressed whatever knowledge we had of the European tragedy. We were primarily interested in living well, getting to know the local girls at a time when most of the local men were in military service, and studying only when we had to.

It did not take me long to understand why we were encouraged to live as well as we did. In the early forties Reform Judaism was largely an upper-middle-class, German-Jewish movement. Its strength was greatest among the more assimilated Jews of the South and Middle West. However, very few sons of prosperous German-Jewish businessmen had any interest in the rabbinate as a career. It was necessary to recruit young men from Eastern European, traditional backgrounds. Although the boys from the traditional backgrounds were far more knowledgeable about Judaism than those with Reform backgrounds, they were usually somewhat deficient in social skills. Their speech, table manners, and dress needed polishing. The normal course of study lasted six years after the B.A. degree, far longer than the average Ph.D. The length of time could not have been justified by any learning acquired. Even after ordination, few Reform rabbis could match the knowledge of Jewish sources possessed by their Conservative and Orthodox colleagues. The unduly long apprenticeship was in reality an acculturation process. The college had to transform its student raw material into socially acceptable functionaries who could serve the religious needs of the rich and the nearly rich. The surroundings were part of that process. So too was the knowledge about proper dress the older students imparted to the novices. We speedily learned that J. Press and Brooks Brothers suits were more acceptable than the wide-brimmed, wide-lapelled styles then in fashion. The preferred manner of dress was imitation Ivy-Wasp. That was what the Reform congregations seemed to want, so much so that occasionally congregations would state their preference for blond graduates as candidates for their pulpits. The story may be apocryphal, but it is said that on at least one occasion, a request was made for an "Aryan-looking" rabbi.

I DID NOT COME to the college to become an imitation Wasp. I hardly knew what I wanted, save that my Jewish identity was a puzzle and a problem I was determined to unravel and I was intensely desirous of acquiring the priest's magic. Because of my limited knowledge of Judaism, there was much that was foreign to me when I first arrived. I was still woefully ignorant of both the Hebrew language and traditional religious practice. Because of the wartime emergency, I was one of a number of students who were admitted without proper preparation. The night before my first class in bible, I stayed up all night attempting to translate the first chapter of *Joshua* from Hebrew into English in order to give a decent account of myself in class. I also found the mealtime rituals strange. Meals were concluded with the *birkat ha-mazon*, a Hebrew blessing. I had never heard the blessing before and felt extremely uncomfortable when it was chanted. Eventually, I came to enjoy the chanting, but my first reaction was one of annoyance that both the blessings and the biblical texts studied in class were not in English. Initially, I found the college a very strange place and saw myself very much as an outsider.

During my three years at the college, the dominant issues among the students were Zionism and the observance of traditional ritual. The faculty was largely anti-Zionist. Despite the European catastrophe the majority saw no reason to alter their deep opposition to the establishment of a Jewish state or their conviction that Jewish identity rested primarily upon religious belief. I shared that opposition until I sorrowfully concluded that the survivors of the Holocaust dared not trust the postwar generosity or tolerance of any of the European host-nations for their survival.

Anti-Zionist convictions were espoused with especial force by the president of the college, Julian Morgenstern, a biblical scholar of considerable repute. He believed in "classical" Reform Judaism with its rejection of ceremonialism as well as of Jewish ethnicity. The year before I entered, he interviewed me at the Hotel Governor Clinton in New York. During the interview I told him that if being a rabbi meant being a Zionist, I could never be a rabbi.

Morgenstern smiled warmly as he replied, "That will be no obstacle."

Morgenstern had spent his entire life minimizing the difference between Reform Judaism and liberal Protestantism. His college had hired an elocution teacher to cleanse the students of the more obvious traces of Yiddish intonation. The Saturday morning chapel services were brief, uninspiring imitations of the services in the Protestant chapels of New England colleges and universities. Many years were to pass before the facts of ethnicity in American life were to be confronted with frankness by Reform Judaism. Zionism was fought because it implied that being Jewish was beyond both creed and free choice. Morgenstern's attitudes mirrored in the religious sphere the social aspirations of the German-Jewish group that dominated the college and the Union of American Hebrew Congregations at the time. Any attempt to suggest that there was an irreducible element of ethnicity in the Jewish experience was countered by the assertion that such thinking represented a capitulation to Nazi racial doctrines. The majority of the faculty believed that the war was being fought to realize the ideal of a truly democratic world and that, in the postwar period, Europe's Jews would have a share in that labor.

Most members of the faculty were apparently ignorant of the effect on European Jews of Europe's history and demography. They did not seem prepared to face the fact that Europe's Jews were everywhere regarded as a distinctive and unwanted national entity. They regarded anti-Semitism as an unhappy interlude which would diminish with the victory of the Allies and the resumption of mankind's march toward enlightenment and progress. They were convinced that the Jews of Europe had a responsibility to help to bring that fortunate time into being.

D<small>URING THE ENTIRE PERIOD</small> that I was at the college, I never heard a sober analysis of anti-Semitism as a *modern* phenomenon or as an expression of the concrete social, economic, and political disorders of the twentieth century. At the college, there was much mystifying talk about Israel's mission as a "light unto the nations." This was taken to mean that Reform Judaism was the most enlightened and rational of all religious movements. Both trinitarian Christianity and Orthodox Judaism were regarded as falling short because of the "irrational" and "superstitious" elements of their spiritual inheritance. In spite of the devastation of World War II, the fundamental goodness of mankind was constantly affirmed, as was the faith that proper education and social reconstruction would elicit that goodness from the majority of men. This "rational," "enlightened" faith was contrasted with the faith of those who believed in the doctrine of original sin and the depravity of Adam's progeny. At no time, for example, did I ever encounter a serious discussion at the college of the rise of nineteenth century racist thinking which divided the world into superior Nordics or Aryans and inferior Semites, Blacks and Asiatics. Nor was there any consideration of the impact of technology on western Europe with its creation of a surplus of both men and capital. These two surpluses led to the imperialist ventures in Africa and Asia which were a prelude to the Nazi policy of domination and mass extermination of Jews and other "enemies" of the Reich in the heart of Europe itself. Although I heard much about the enlightened character of liberal Judaism, I never heard a competent historical or sociological analysis of the social and economic forces that had led to the distinctive forms of marginal status experienced by European Jews and ultimately to the devastatingly successful assault upon them. We remained blissfully ignorant and utterly privileged in a world of death and dying. Only in the United States did Jewish institutions possess the security and the resources to attempt to comprehend scientifically what was taking place and to project realistic possibilities for the future. Yet there was a good deal of talk about the Hebrew Union College's role as a center of Jewish study in *preserving* knowledge of the *past*. There was pathetically little effort to understand the present. No attempt was made to utilize the intellectual tools of twentieth century social research to understand the desperate situation of our people.

The other major issue at the college was religious observance. Reform Judaism had arisen in large measure as a protest against the all-encompassing demands traditional ceremonial practice had made upon the individual Jew in every area of his private, public, and especially his commercial existence. Inevitably, a reaction against the more extreme forms of Reform anti-ceremonialism set in. The Nazi assault upon the Jews had caused a turning inward and a re-evaluation of Reform's attitude toward tradition; the influence of Franz Rosenzweig and Martin Buber was beginning to be felt, in part because of the influx of refugee rabbinical students from Germany.

THE ARRIVAL OF Professor Abraham Joshua Heschel in 1942 added impetus to the turn to tradition. Heschel came from a long and distinguished family of Hasidic rabbis. He was a product of the best traditions of Eastern European Jewish mysticism. He also had a Ph.D. from the University of Berlin. He was able to interpret to his students both the traditions of the Hasidic world and the insights of European existentialism and phenomenology. He had a powerful personality and was living proof of the vitality of the very traditions Reform Judaism claimed it had superseded. He was personally observant. By virtue of his knowledge, his strong personality, and the fact that he was far above the other faculty members as a thinker, writer, and creative spirit, he soon acquired a small but devoted following. Heschel satisfied the needs of a group of students for a leader who would be both a teacher and a spiritual guide.

When Heschel arrived, he was an impecunious bachelor. The college offered him a small stipend, far less than it offered other men who did not possess his gifts. He lived in the dormitory and took his meals with the students. People reacted very strongly to him. His disciples gathered together informally for prayer and study, and a group began to offer daily prayers every morning using the Orthodox prayer book. Some even took the seemingly radical step of praying with the traditional *tallith* and *tefillin,* the prayer shawl and phylacteries normally worn by religious Jews at morning services.

The appearance of a group under Heschel's influence devoted to traditional worship aroused great antagonism among some of the students. Heschel's disciples were referred to derisively as the "piety boys." Their newly found religiosity was regarded as somehow subversive of Reform Judaism. Undoubtedy, part of the antagonism toward the "piety boys" was hostility toward Heschel. People were seldom neutral about him. They were either devoted or took a strong dislike to him.

Another element in the turn toward tradition among the students was the impact of Reinhold Niebuhr and the rise of Protestant Neo-orthodoxy. Quite a number of students read Niebuhr's *The Nature and Destiny of Man* after its wartime publication with great appreciation. Niebuhr's stress upon the tragic and ironic elements in the human condition seemed to be a far more realistic appraisal of what we were experiencing than the more optimistic religious liberalism against which Niebuhr had reacted. The shift in Protestantism from liberalism to Neo-orthodoxy contributed to the reassessment of traditional Jewish modes of religious expression among an important group of students at the college. Neo-orthodoxy's protest against liberal religion's optimistic view of human nature and faith in historical progress was especially important. Few Protestant liberals were as naively optimistic on these issues as Reform Jewish spokesmen, in spite of the fact that Jews had far less justification for optimism than did their Protestant counterparts. The anthropological insights of Neo-orthodoxy seemed to be more realistic in the world of the death camps than Reform Judaism's faith in the progress of mankind to ever higher levels of moral and spiritual enlightenment.

As a mood of pessimism about human

potentialities set in, many of the students were disinclined to trust their own instincts in the area of personal and religious behavior. They sought guidance in the historically authenticated insights of the great rabbinic teachers of the past. They became more willing to let their lives be guided by the discipline of religious tradition rather than to assert the authority of their own moral insights. In view of the way in which totalitarian leaders were asserting the primacy of their own will, with such disastrous consequences for the Jewish community, it is not at all surprising that the freedom to decide for oneself was no longer regarded as the boon it once was. The disciplines of traditional Judaism were a welcome alternative to the moral chaos that was regnant on the European continent. Very few students were untouched by the change in atmosphere. Most saw no conflict between their newly discovered attachment to tradition and remaining liberal Jews. A few, however, saw a conflict so intense that it impelled them to leave the college.

THE FACULTY HAD an institution known as "roll call." Twice a year they reviewed the work of each student and decided who would be permitted to remain. My record as a student had been poor. Because of my limited Hebrew background, it was difficult for me to perform well in my studies. I was moved by a peculiar combination of unwarranted pride and an inordinate need for approval. Students from traditional Jewish backgrounds invariably did far better in their studies than I. This intensified my wounded sense of self-esteem.

From a professional point of view, it seemed as if I were a very poor prospect indeed. It was expected that students at the college would develop the personality traits necessary to function well as Reform rabbis. This included the ability to get along smoothly with people, and I was anything but smooth. The immediate test of how well we developed was how well we managed with our professors. I failed that test rather dismally.

The evening of the spring 1944 roll call some of us went down Clifton Avenue to get a hamburger. When we returned late in the evening, we noticed that roll call was still going on. There were only about a hundred students, but it took many hours to go down the list. I said, "I wonder who is being roasted tonight?"

I found out the next morning. I was summoned to the president's office where Dr. Morgenstern told me the faculty had come to the conclusion that I was not suitable as a candidate for the Reform rabbinate. He said that my relationship with the college would be terminated at the end of the term.

I was caught by surprise. I knew that I had not been getting on well, but I had no idea of just how bad things really were. Above all, I was unprepared for what I regarded as the disgrace of dismissal. I knew that, were the dismissal to stick, it would be a hard thing for me ever to live down in my own eyes.

I was one of three students whom the faculty voted to dismiss. Fortunately, when the other students learned about the decision they petitioned the faculty to give us another chance. After some deliberation, the faculty decided to put us on probation for a year. It is likely that the dismissals were really meant to shock us into shaping up. Whatever the faculty's real intentions, the incident served as a most effective warning.

Although I have since come to be grateful to the college faculty for expressing their doubts about my suitability as a candidate for the Reform rabbinate, I was bitter at the time. I felt that there were a few students who were using the college as a wartime hideout and who had no interest in anything more than finding a proper trade for themselves. They were left alone while I had almost been dismissed. I did not understand that no matter how cynical such men might be, they were far more likely to serve as well-functioning rabbinic professionals than I. They seemed to be a better investment of the college's resources.

MY LAST YEAR at the Hebrew Union College coincided with the final apocalyptic year of World War II. As the Allies moved closer to the heart of Germany, ever more death camps were discovered. I could not possibly harmonize the European horror with the smug, complacent atmosphere at the college. With each newly discovered death camp, it became less possible for me to find any credibility in Reform's liberal theology. The thought that I would spend my life ministering to an affluent American Jewish community seemed more like a life-sentence to immensely distasteful labor than the promise of a rewarding career.

The mood at both the college and in the congregations remained upbeat in spite of all that had happened. At the time, Rabbi Joshua Loth Liebman was one of the leading Reform rabbis. His *Peace of Mind* became a national best-seller shortly after I left the Hebrew Union College. Its pop-psychoanalysis and its faith in democracy, progress, and enlightenment were expressive of the dominant mood of Reform Judaism in the face of the worst disaster in over three thousand years of Jewish history. It was a mood I could not share.

Abraham Joshua Heschel, as a Polish Jew who had watched from a distance as his family, relatives, and friends were systematically exterminated, found the smugness and the optimism of Reform Judaism far more offensive than I. As the facts of the death camps became known, there was less opposition at the college to the establishment of a Jewish State than there had been at the beginning of the war, but in spite of all that had happened, opposition to a Jewish State remained strong among the faculty and some segments of Reform's lay leadership. Perhaps more than any man on the faculty, Heschel understood how urgent was the need for a homeland for the survivors. There was much about the college which offended Heschel deeply. With his strong sense of what was authentic in Jewish experience, he could not have had a high regard for the imitation-Wasp life style, which was almost unconsciously fostered upon the students. In the spring of 1945 he accepted an invitation to join the faculty of the more traditional Jewish Theological Seminary of America located in New York City.

Although I subsequently entered the Rabbinical School of the Jewish Theological Seminary myself, I had no intention of following Heschel in the spring of 1945. With my poor showing at the Hebrew Union College, I would undoubtedly have been rejected at the time.

I was, however, in great conflict about remaining at the college. Heschel urged me to quit and pursue work in philosophy. He knew that I had no desire to live a traditional Jewish life, but he was in sympathy with my rejection of the liberal optimism of the college. He warned me against remaining at the college simply because of the security it offered. I am permanently indebted to him for his counsel.

THINGS CAME TO A HEAD about the time the students tendered a farewell reception to Heschel. Although as I have mentioned, Heschel had many student admirers, there were some who resented him because he was going to a rival institution. Even those who disliked him, and there were many who did, resented his departure. I have never forgotten his remarks: "Gentlemen, it is often said that only students graduate. That is not true. It is also possible for professors to graduate."

Heschel made it clear that he had little regard for the college and was leaving for what he considered to be the superior institution. I heartily agreed with him then. After I came to know some of the other institutions of learning supported by American Jews, I revised my judgment. The college is certainly no worse than any of the other major institutions. It performs an indispensable function by training scholars and rabbis. Furthermore, the college has become a far more sophisticated institution today than it was thirty years ago.

Heschel's reception came shortly after the final collapse of the Third Reich. It was an apocalyptic time. Nineteen forty-five was the year of the apocalypse for those of us for whom World War II was the *war* of our lifetime. Apart from the discovery of ever more death camps, 1945 witnessed the demise of Hitler, Mussolini and Roosevelt, the collapse of Germany, the surrender of Japan, the exit of

Churchill from England's wartime leadership. A million Jews moved from death camps to displaced persons' camps. Jewish life and culture on the European continent had come to an end, yet it was by no means certain that the Jews of Palestine could overcome the dual obstacles of British opposition and Arab enmity to create a viable, self-governing community. It was a time of the catastrophic end of the old order and the infinitely painful beginnings of the new.

RICHARD L. RUBENSTEIN *is the author of* My Brother Paul; After Auschwitz; Morality and Eros; *and* The Religious Imagination. *He is Professor of Religion at Florida State University.*

The Future of Rabbinic Training In America

A Symposium

DANIEL JEREMY SILVER
EUGENE B. BOROWITZ EMANUEL RACKMAN
IRA EISENSTEIN SEYMOUR SIEGEL
ARTHUR GREEN EUGENE WEINER
CHARLES S. LIEBMAN ARNOLD JACOB WOLF
MARK LOEB SHELDON ZIMMERMAN

Introduction

ARNOLD JACOB WOLF

Rabbi Gilbert Klapperman, in his "The Story of Yeshiva University," reminds us that the current conflict in our rabbinical schools is really old-hat:

> In the space of a few short days, the quarrel between the students and administration of RIETS [Rabbi Isaac Elchanan Theological Seminary] had been transferred from the relative insignificance and obscurity of a local struggle to one of wider importance. It received national and international coverage in the Yiddish, Hebrew and Anglo-Jewish press as well as some prominence in the English press, which often completely confused the issues, places and people involved.
>
> This time the students did not surrender as easily as they had in 1906. The strike was well thought out, and the discipline among the students was rigid. No sooner was the strike declared than a prepared plan was immediately put into effect. The first news of the strike had appeared on May 5. Only three days later on Friday, May 8, the newspapers announced that a number of students would speak on the subject of the strike in various prominent Synagogues the following morning during the Sabbath Services. The purpose was "to explain their trouble with the directors of the Yeshiva."

This was in 1908!

Yet, it seems obvious there *is* something new under our sun, indeed that the sun herself is not unchanging. It is impossible any longer to pretend that our students are the compliant, careerist young seminar-

---

On May 25, 1969, JUDAISM *sponsored a symposium on the theme: "The Future of Rabbinic Training in America." The major presentation was made by* DANIEL JEREMY SILVER, *rabbi of The Temple, Cleveland and president of the National Foundation of Jewish Culture, who read a paper to which nine panelists were asked to give five-minute responses. The symposium, held before an invited audience who later participated in the general discussion, was chaired by* ARNOLD JACOB WOLF, *rabbi of Congregation Solel, Highland Park, Ill., who last year served on the faculty of Hebrew Union College—Jewish Institute of Religion in New York. What follows below is an edited transcript of the proceedings.*

ians that they once were—even if it turns out they never were. A few short years ago there were no new experimental rabbinical schools. A few years ago the drop-out rate was lower, and a student who left rabbinical school was likely to be less, not (as now) more competent than his fellows. A few years ago student strikes were not often threatened, faculties were not fearfully defensive, JUDAISM did not think to sponsor a symposium like this one.

What are the students so angry about? The *tallit* that a certain school requires to be of a certain size and shape? The "required elective" course in another place? Money spent on buildings or public relations but not on them? Stodgy, unimaginative faculties? An anti-anti-intellectualism which is, however, not quite intellectually respectable either? The freezing-out of alternative non-conformist views? The grades, the attendance-taking, the junior-high-school atmosphere incredible in a graduate school? The unwillingness to discuss, much less to help solve, real problems of real communities?

All these and more. Students *are* angry. And not only they. The graduate rabbinate itself is girding its loins to find out why the graduates of our schools want to be anything but rabbis or, alternatively, have so little notion of what a rabbi might be. The larger Jewish community has begun to respond to such studies as Professor Charles Liebman's pioneering "The Training of American Rabbis" (*American Jewish Yearbook*, 1968), in this case more sharply than the author seems to have intended. The enormous over-arching problem of higher education in America has finally come home to our own seminaries. Curriculum revision, heart-to-heart talks with students and a small number of strategic resignations are its first fruits. The cliché name of the new game is "relevance," as Herbert Blau tells us in an article with that title in the issue of *Daedalus* titled "The Future of the Humanities":

> If we really mean that we teach, there's no repose ahead for the university. Up to now, the initiative has come from the students, but it grows increasingly hard for us to insist on the disengagement necessary for sober thought. That's disturbing, but it's not too great a price to pay for a revival of faith in our best students, to whom no particular subject is, finally, more relevant than any other, though a man in needless pain or a man dying before his time, unjustly, is more relevant than any subject. Can we argue with that? I don't think even Milton would argue with that, who said as good kill a man as kill a good book, for that was prefaced by his refusal to praise a fugitive and cloistered virtue, unexercised and unbreathed. The greatest blessing of our educational system is the refusal of our students to be cloistered, in systems, departments, requirements, or ratiocinative meditativeness that can destroy. For the time being, we have to be where they are, or we are, for the sake of the future, no where at all.

I think Blau is right for us, too. Rabbinical students are not rebels without a cause, but radically traditional Jews who want to learn and to learn Judaism and to learn Judaism in a way that will build a Jewish community. They do not want simply to be penned in or ridiculed or ignored: those who have treated them unfairly must now read the handwriting on the wall. Too many good students and too many good books have been "killed" by schools that protected their own prerogatives instead of opening themselves to persons, both living and dead. There is really nowhere now to be Jewish unless we are where our students are, not that we might pander to their inclinations, but in order to confront their sacred selves.

The conflict in the schools of America is partly a disagreement between faculty and students about the relative importance of subjectivity and objectivity, analysis and engagement, making and being. Strangely enough, our rabbinical schools, where one would have thought the heart's reasons had advocates, have sold out to the objectivist ideal almost without qualification. If it is not the *Wissenschaft* of Reform and Conservative (and, to a considerable extent also, modern Orthodoxy), then it is the unmitigated *Mitnagdut* of the traditionalist which settles the issue before it is joined. It will seem important to know J from E but not what Jeremiah could mean to a young C.O. It is called romantic to care about the Jewish obligation to blacks but realistic to study "human relations" as the art of manipulation. Memorizing equals scholarship, while working through profoundly intellectual problems with emotional overtones is merely self-indulgent. Professors are to lecture, to grade, to admit or reject, to ordain or dismiss. They are not obligated to discern, to care, to debate or to surrender. In our seminaries there are fewer professors of social ethics than ever before, while the century goes up in flames. Our students are compelled (there is no other word for it) to study texts that are systematically denied relevance for the sake of an ideology that is discredited if not downright anti-Semitic.

Why must Judaism, whose greatest art was always combining mind and heart, now perceive itself as witless objectivity? Why cannot our students' demands not for therapy but for therapeutics, for minds that can heal and texts that can transmute—why must these demands be persistently subverted? Why must we study Talmud as if it were a genetic code or pray as if the chapel belonged to somebody else? Why need we stop caring in order to find out? Writing in the same issue of *Daedalus* we have already quoted, Professor James Ackerman of Harvard proposes a synthesis of feeling and knowing which might heal the hurt in all our schools:

> If the personality of the educational community is split in this way, it cannot be reintegrated simply by repressing its "id." A more promising therapy would be to encourage the articulation of deeply felt convictions by giving them rational as well as subconscious expression. This responsibility of the teacher and scholar cannot be assumed so long as feelings and values are exiled from the classroom.
>
> In trying to formulate goals for higher education in the coming years, we must preserve the best in both of the styles and find ways of arbitrating their differences. The Analytic Style gives the individual precision tools with which to manipulate his environment. From it, we should preserve the degree of objectivity and rational method required to support intercourse among individuals with different aims and talents, and we should retain the principle that knowledge of what happened in the past and in cultures different from ours is essential to our survival and must not be lost. The Engaged Style demands effective human contact between the individual and the object of his attention; it has shown us that a legitimate function of higher education can be to help people to formulate and actively observe ethical and aesthetic commitments.

"Ethical and aesthetic commitments" are what rabbinical training is all about. We can safely surrender to the universities a good deal of our technical responsibility if we work to realize our own uniquely significent potential. We are small, committed, fairly well-supported schools. There is nothing to prevent our revolutionizing American Jewry except our own timidity or our own smugness. In the symposium that follows, many issues are joined. The Establishment (identified by its denial that there is any such thing) dredges up the considerable successes of its own years of magisterial imperialism. The rebels, the critics, the students call for something very new and very much better, which will also be something very old.

With the barricades of the mind, it is always 1789. For the Jew, Sinai is wherever and whenever the commandment is heard at last.

Presentation

DANIEL JEREMY SILVER

> In the book of Elijah we read: Everyone of Israel is duty bound to say: "When will my works approach the works of my Fathers, Abraham, Isaac, and Jacob" How are we to understand this?
>
> "Just as our Fathers invented new ways of serving each a new service according to his character: one, the service of love; another of stern justice; a third of beauty; so each of us in his own way should devise something new in the light of the teaching and of service, and do what has not yet been done."
>
> MARTIN BUBER, *Ten Rungs*.

Biography I

I am the seventh in a direct line of *musmakhim*. Family history records that my forebears wrote commentaries, tutored the sons of the well-to-do, wrote legal opinions, manufactured and sold soap, spent their time studying on reasonably permanent scholarships, administered a *moshav zekenim*, and organized the Zionist movement.

Observation

The rabbinate is not in the first instance an occupation. The rabbinate is first and foremost the pleasure and mastery of Torah. The Torah-learned have always had a role to play in our community; though not always a full time professional role and not always be the same one. The *yeshiva* taught Torah because its mastery was redemptive.

This focus on the blessedness of Jewish learning has been blurred and largely forgotten. Today the rabbinate is seen as a definable occupation and a seminary's proper occupation obviously is to produce properly trained manpower. For the synagogue economics has hastened this process. The seminaries are supported almost entirely by and through congregations and congregational unions who send their money to sponsor a future assistant rabbi rather than *Torah lishmah*. Annual seminary fund drives depend so much on this "piece-goods" appeal that one wonders if the schools would dare alienate this support by shifting their training emphasis away from congregational manpower.

The urgent need for congregational rabbis has affected admission standards and curriculum. The seminaries admit the academically borderline and keep course requirements within their limited reach. This whole numbers game is of dubious value to the man, to the congregations, and to Judaism. The man is in a demanding profession, probably in over his depth. The congregation is encouraged to hire a less than adequate teacher of Torah and the alert Jew has living proof that Judaism has little to offer him. Moreover, the ordination of these men confirms some seminary faculty in their low opinion of the scholarly requirements of the pulpit and confirms their estimate that they need present to their classes only the patina of Jewish learning.

Quotation

"A faculty board will typically devote its energies to the potential scholars rather than to the future rabbis among the students." (Charles Liebman, "The Training of American Rabbis")

Paradox I

The rabbinic seminaries are the only professional schools in which some faculty habitually derogate their students' chosen profession.

Paradox II

As long as the seminaries see themselves as professional schools they will not teach Judaism professionally.

The Generation Gap I

"Do you really mean that there were synagogues that could afford rabbis but did not hire them?"

Biography II

Seventeen years after ordination, one-half of my graduating class does not now occupy a pulpit. Patently the congregational rabbinate that is mine, and that has given me profound satisfaction, is only one of many designs for rabbinic service within the American Jewish community.

Musings

Life has caught up with the romantic image of rabbi and congregation coexisting in an effective symbiosis. Any discussion of rabbinic training must begin with a judgment of the contemporary synagogue, its quarter-filled pews, its restless schools, its largely indifferent membership and the anti-institutional bias of the contemporary environment in which it must do its work. Seminary training must concern the renewal and radical reshaping of the synagogue, not simply the competent administration of the present structure.

Furthermore, the proliferation of congregational sub-specialties has phased out the rabbi as congregational *kol bo*. Educators take over the schools, administrators the office, cantors the music and to some degree the liturgy, group workers the youth group and case-workers the counseling. Some day soon a congregational president will ask: "Why do we need a rabbi?"—and no one, least of all the rabbi, will have a functional answer.

Further Musings

Despite pious presidential reports, the seminaries have long since accepted this state of things. A generation ago Hebrew Union College—Jewish Institute of Religion, the Jewish Theological Seminary and Yeshiva University existed primarily to train rabbis. Today they do almost everything else. The time is not far off when less than one-half of the funds of these institutions will be invested in the training of rabbis.

Puzzle

Find the rabbinic seminary in this self-description from the 1967 *American Jewish Yearbook*:

> Organized for the perpetuation of the tenets of the Jewish religion, the cultivation of Jewish literature, the pursuit of Biblical and archaeological research, the maintenance of a library, and the training of rabbis and teachers.

Paradox III

The Diaspora and the synagogue are one. The Diaspora and the synagogue 5728 model with built-in rabbi need not be one.

Question

What then is the role of the rabbi?

A Response

"The end of the matter all having been heard, the rabbi's task remains what it has long been: serve people, study and teach Torah. All else is treading water." (From a questionnaire on the rabbinic role)

A Further Response

To teach Torah, to reach the human soul, and to be a judgmental force does not preclude the familiar congregational role. On the other hand, it does not require it. Some of our most seminal rabbinic figures did not occupy pulpits or had signal accomplishments outside their congregations: Magnes, Wise, Silver, Heschel, Kaplan, Soloveitchik. One of the more attractive proposals for rabbinic effectiveness involve teams of rabbinic specialists in the larger congregations or at the communal level.

Rhetorical Question

Does a trade-school seminary have a trade to teach?

Department of Short-Sighted Realism

"Jewish philosophy and Jewish theology are perhaps essential for giving the rabbinical student or rabbi a sense of spiritual identity in the broad perspectives of Israel's religious development. It remains true nevertheless that in the practical rabbinate Jewish philosophy and theology are so much unnecessary baggage." (Edgar Siskin, "The Rabbinate and Curriculum")

Observation

In my university classroom, in the city and in The Temple, wherever I meet still questing and questioning minds, I find an explosion of vital questions, theological questions, a desperate search to handle life. "Rabbi, help me, at least, ask the right questions. I do not want your ritual mumbo jumbo or wax candles or a lecture on ethnic loyalty; I want some of that vaunted insight you rabbis are always talking about."

Three Questions

Does our vaunted Torah tradition have all the answers? Is it sufficient to revise curriculum so as to relate the tradition more immediately to the existential situation? What must be taught beyond texts?

Proposal

Let's reorganize the seminary curriculum to train men for possible new roles among the urban unaffiliated, the apartment alienated, and the campus disenchanted.

Second Thought

Let's not. Every proposal for a practical rabbinate presumes certain knowledge of a model. We lack such knowledge. Seminaries can arm the *eirev rav* only with an awareness of Judaism's existential possibilities and some realism about the make-up of Israel's mixed multitude. The community, the man, and opportunity must take it from there.

Question

Whence *parnasa?*
Congregations, colleges, communities, wherever. Some will continue

for a long time to "serve" congregations. Some can better "serve" the people by not living off the people. Robert Gordis once suggested that the social worker and youth leader become "lay rabbis." His proposal presumed a specific rabbinic model. If as I believe there is none, why should not some rabbis simply become social workers or youth leaders? They would be with *amkha* and be able to deal with many spiritual crises which do not come within the purview of our institutionalized lives.

Question

If there is no rabbinate only rabbis, what is a rabbi's claim on Israel's respect?

Response

Some rabbis teach the generation, and others teach *Tazriah-Metzorah* to twelve-year-olds. Some are functionaries, fund-raisers, front men. Others speak the living word and lead men into the larger life. Ordination *per se* establishes no claim on Israel's respect.

On Graduation and Ordination

The practice of the seminaries to ordain their seniors has them uptight, and forces them to be technical schools, that is, to be part of that unhappy pattern in American education which has transformed our schools into essentially apprentice-training agencies to some Establishment. Scholarship is sacrificed to courses in technique and the resulting mix is neither the meat of learning nor the milk of counseling.

On Purpose and Relevance

Today's seminary curriculum has two foci—both terribly limited—the congregational *kol bo* and the denominational scholar. The *kol bo* is a vulgarity, and the denominational scholar an anachronism. The issues today concern life-stance and value-system, not minor battles over forgotten nuances of doctrine.

In a time when men need bridges between faith and life, between Israel and the nations, the seminaries have raised their drawbridges and lower them only on highly publicized occasions when a pop-culture pundit is invited to speak or receive an honorary degree—a carefully orchestrated charade designed to convince benefactors whose sons balk at rejoining their parents' congregation that the seminary administration and faculty are with it.

The Generation Gap II

". . . If helping to create a more meaningful community were, indeed, the rabbi's function, he would need training that differs radically from the one he is now receiving. The seminaries would first have to explicate the goals of Jewish life, as they see it. At both YU and JTS, the goal, as implicitly understood, is the recreation of a romanticized notion of 19th-century East European Jewish life. It is a goal so patently absurd that no one really dares to voice it openly. If they were forced to give serious consideration to the problem, both YU and JTS would offer more meaningful goals. (HUC-JIR simply has no model or ideal of Jewish life.)" (Charles Liebman, "The Training of American Rabbis")

Question

Who will be a disciple of the aimless?

Rhetorical Question

Are we training morticians to embalm once vigorous institutions, or leaders who can challenge, change and revive?

Observation

The confusions of our age are pervasive and potentially fatal to the spiritual heart of the Jewish people. Yet the mood of the seminaries remains largely placid, past-oriented, and pedantic. Only a few teachers and students work up a sweat wrestling the long night with the living presence of God. Yet how else does one win the name of Israel?

Biography III

When I was at HUC, a registrar tried to stimulate my competitive drive by showing me the report record of my father. I was put down not by Dad's over-reach—I, too, was a dutiful student—but by the shock of realizing that there was something to compare. Even the course numbers hardly had changed in nearly 40 years.

Biography IV

I was being trained for the rabbinate of 1915, and he was trained, really, for an end-of-the-century rabbinate in which *Wissenschaft* was the cool faith of the day. *Wissenschaft* implied turning off, it was the way to turn off the voice of medievalism, so that men might hear an older and presumedly less cramped Judaism. *Wissenschaft* was a valid surgical procedure. But the seminaries never turned faith back on. For generations Bible and Talmud have been presented as intellectual puzzles, not as spiritual prizes. The student has been served a heavy diet of footnotes, which lie on the soul and give the neophyte a bad case of spiritual indigestion.

And beyond the deadlines of pedantry there was and is the dark shadow of mock scholarship, the closing of professorial eyes to more than occasional intellectual incompetence. Among the announced theses of our scholarly profession, this year as every year, such titles as these are included:

> A chronological survey of significant events of American Jewish History.
>
> Toward a teachers training program through visual techniques for a Reform religious school.
>
> The rabbi as perceived and idealized by members of the congregational board.

Question

To build anew or rebuild?

Suggestion

Both. The nineteenth century required *yeshiva* and *Hochshule*. The twentieth century requires established seminaries and experimental study programs. The existing seminaries have the merit of tradition, presumedly of careful standards and factually of excellent libraries. The new groups can plan without having to fight habit and can challenge the mediocrity, the tedium, and the absurd length of the rabbinic course.

Question

To build anew or rebuild?

Suggestion

Sectarianism is an intolerable scandal. The institutional separation of our traditional seminaries is an *averah* which compounds many *averot*. Each student needs courses, men, perspectives, ideas which no insulated seminary can provide him. Yet, almost all rabbinic training is carried out in splendid isolation, yes, even in the middle of New York.

Question

To build or rebuild?

Suggestion

The separation of the seminaries from meaningful affiliation with the university tradition only guarantees a meager curriculum. No seminary can have first-rate men in every possible discipline and no disguise of the traditional curriculum as a University of Judaism or an Institute for Advanced Studies in the Humanities changes the constricted reality.

A modern seminary must be part of a university system. Students should be able to take courses in Semitic languages, Eastern philosophy, abnormal psychology, cultural anthropology, etc., which no seminary possibly can provide, and the theological and historical resources of the seminary ought to be available to the campus. An active undergraduate

Jewish studies program can give Judaism exposure and authenticity at a critical time of decision in the lives of many young Jews. Research conducted by the National Foundation for Jewish Culture has shown that undergraduate courses in Jewish studies have stimulated interest in graduate Jewish studies and in the rabbinate. At Case-Western Reserve University there is already a move under foot to use inter-term next year for a month-long exploration of texts by those who are seriously contemplating the rabbinate.

Being part of a university atmosphere does not require a slavish aping of academic trappings, an all too familiar seminary weakness. Outside of the rabbinic program the seminaries have patterned their offerings after academe—full-blown, though not necessarily full-bodied, master and doctoral programs. All too little thought is directed to the occasional yet specific needs of graduates for summer institutes, short courses, retooling.

Question

To build anew or rebuild?

Suggestion

We need alternative curricula. My rabbinate is congregational-academic. Yours may be communal-institutional. Another may spend his days as a scholar-teacher. Other combinations are conceivable. Beyond Hebrew, a sense of *amkha*, Torah, and some personal spiritual guidance—which, by the way, no seminary now offers—each student should be able to pursue his special interests and there should be continuing education for those whose interests change.

Question

Why not one united *ulpan* for all first-year students in Jerusalem? An American rabbi without Hebrew is unplugged not only from the past but from the creative present.

Question

Why not an interdisciplinary approach which would permit an HUC-JIR student to take Codes or Talmud at JTS and a Yeshiva student to take Bible or hermeneutics at HUC? A faith which puts blinders between itself and other attitudes is intolerable and disqualifies itself from serious consideration, and a mind trained to parrot a sectarian party line can hardly teach Israel to love all Israel.

Question

Why must *semikha* come after a promised number of courses? With the varied needs and backgrounds of men and communities, why must the rabbinical degree be a four- or five-year graduate package? For some a year or two of exposure to texts and tradition may be enough to "rabbinize" their lives in social service, counselling or religious school teaching. To those who bring or who are completing a doctorate in some Jewish study at a secular university a year of spiritual training may be enough.

Question

Why not leave practical training to a separate year, a year which a rabbi could take whenever he felt the need to specialize? For some it might be a year in education, for others a year in congregational practice and counselling, for others a work-study program in the sociology of the Jewish community—always an optional year. Freed of the practical burden, the seminaries presumably could confront Torah and *amkha*, and become again places of high-voltage learning.

Question

Why alone among the faiths must Judaism remain tied to the imbecility of a womanless ministry? Why alone among the professions is the rabbinate in violation of the Fair Employment Practices Act? Can we afford any longer to keep half of our human talent in the rabbinic deep-freeze?

Question

Why not add competent spiritual tutors, father figures, to the seminary staff? All seminaries teach subject matter, none teach the man. Yet seminary, as Mordecai Kaplan has suggested, implies a seedbed, not a hot house.

In Place of a Conclusion

Our search is for a usable past. Both the long past of *lernen* and the more recently discovered past of *Wissenschaft* no longer provide an adequate perspective. It's no longer simply a choice between the Talmud and the prophets, but of confronting the deeper, more human, more demanding elements in the entire literature. We want to know more about the state of a prophet's soul and somewhat less about the state of his text, more about struggling people and less about pristine principles, more about the paradoxes of the human condition and less about disembodied truth, less about the known and more about the ineffable, less about *iluim* and more about that wisdom which may ultimately be revelation.

Conclusion

Today's seminaries must be as paradoxical as life.

Responses

SHELDON ZIMMERMAN

I should like to raise three points of issue, but first, let me say that I stand in awe of those who speak here. I certainly hope to learn from all of you.

One issue is that of "soul": the current concern with "soul" in America, generally, must, I submit, find its Jewish counterpart in a concern for the Jewish soul. Secondly, the curricula offered in all our schools of rabbinic training must be altered to reflect changes in pedagogy and, especially, must be integrated. Lastly, there is a need for the rabbinical schools of our day to be concerned with producing people—in Buber's sense of "person," as opposed to the mere individual.

Let me deal with the first point. The lack of concern with the Jewish soul is reflected on all levels of rabbinic training: I suggest you check Prof. Liebman's article on the religious atmosphere of the seminaries. In order to rectify this, we have to form a *havurah* (fellowship) and establish it as a basis and model of Jewish life in our day. Caring and concern will arise out of a living Judaism, not out of a merely talking or philosophizing one. Torah and *amkha* will develop out of this. You come to know God through the common Jewish experience, wrestling with God as a group, as a *havurah*. And I sense that this is lacking, certainly at my school, Hebrew Union College, where there is a distinct dearth of *havurah*. We should not, therefore, be so much concerned with the shortening of the period of seminary schooling, as Rabbi Silver has suggested; rather, we should see to it that our four or five years together be spent as a group living Judaism, sharing an existential experience.

Secondly, as for changes in the curriculum, we should have men from different departments and disciplines sharing the same classroom. This procedure, as you may recall, was suggested by Rabbi Wolf in his review of Prof. Liebman's article (JUDAISM, Winter 1969); but whereas Rabbi Wolf's proposals were topic-centered, I am inclined to a more text-centered approach. Take a page of Talmud, for instance. Have one teacher deal with the texts, with the concepts and logic of the arguments. Have an historian come in and deal with the historical background in both the general community and the particular Jewish community. Have a theologian deal with the theological problems raised by the *sugya* in question. Have a philosopher deal with the philosophy of law and its relevance to our day. Have a specialist in medieval commentaries deal with Rashi, the Tosafot, the Aggadic and Midrashic sections. And there must also be time left over for a practical consideration of what it means to be a Jew in our day. In sum, I do not think we need new topics as much as we need to return to the text. The texts, however, must be handled differently than heretofore; the approach must be integrated.

My final suggestion is for sensitivity training in our schools—how to be a *mensch;* what does it mean to a *mensch.* There are those who suggest that it is impossible to train a rabbinical student to be a person in Buber's sense. I would suggest

---

SHELDON ZIMMERMAN *is past president of the Student Association of the Hebrew Union College—Jewish Institute of Religion, New York. He teaches philosophy at the Hunter College of the City University of New York.*

that there are some guidelines in the Jewish tradition about what it means to be a person, and that our schools must concern themselves with this as one of the major items on their agenda for the future.

MARK LOEB

What Rabbi Silver has said about the image the seminaries have of themselves is not completely correct. I think he is giving us a Reform perspective. Of course, the image that the Jewish Theological Seminary has of itself is equaly absurd. The Seminary very frequently says—and I have recently observed this even at fund-raising affairs—that we have within our institutional four walls the capacity to interpret the Tradition and to bring forth its wisdom to solve modern problems for our young people. Last year one of the leaders of our Seminary offered, during the Columbia crisis (and with a straight face), to bring the Torah to bear to mediate between Mark Rudd and Grayson Kirk. All of this is obviously nonsense. If we are indeed a fountain-head of wisdom, we are doing a superb job of concealing this fact from the world.

The vision of Seminary education has traditionally been that of associating with great men. I would equate that with the star system at the opera. However, in the opera, if Franco Corelli gets sick, that doesn't mean *La Traviata* dies; *La Traviata* is still a great opera, and Verdi himself remains. The two critical problems at our seminary, as I see them, are curriculum and personnel; and, frankly, curriculum is a secondary problem, which can be solved by proper personnel. I

MARK LOEB *was vice president of the Student Association of the Jewish Theological Seminary, 1968–69.*

have had four Hebrew teachers in two years, three of whom were unmitigated disasters. We meet once a week, and in our second or third year people meet only for one semester, one half of a year. There is no language laboratory; some administrators have suggested we should perhaps go to Israel to improve our Hebrew. The problem in Bible and Talmud is even worse. Texts are taught on what must be, for the faculty, a high-school level. The faculty prepares very little; consequently, we prepare very little, since we emulate our teachers. We rush through the text, and, as Professor Liebman has suggested, ultimately we have no time to wonder about the state of Isaiah's soul because we're too busy wondering about his haplographies.

Rabbi Silver is also correct, I think, that these intellectual puzzles lose a great deal in spirituality. A Hasid told me in Israel recently that he had heard a whisper through his *payes* that at Hebrew Union College *Genesis* is now an elective. It is now the case, I am told, that at JTS two-thirds of our student body are taking, have taken, or will be taking courses outside of the Seminary in order to satisfy their intellectual needs—spiritual needs, I should call them. Professor Jacob Neusner spoke at the Seminary last week and mentioned that several of his students in his graduate program at Brown University, who have come from the Seminary, after being in special programs, had recently written a paper for him—and that this was the first paper they had written since they had left the university!

Standards in the Seminary curriculum are handled in the most blasé and narrow-minded way. Someone said we had to raise standards. So the solution was more accurately to define an A between 90 and 100, and a B between 80 and 90—a "solution" which is absurd. The whole question gets to be, whether we're doing this for the *yeshiva shel ma'alah* (the heavenly academy) or for ourselves. Ultimately the question remains one of individuals: whether we are going to be able to acquire faculties for whom *Wissenschaft* is not the end, philology is not the objective; whether we can create a theology that stimulates, not "somnolates"; whether we are permitted to learn from people who can assist in our theological and spiritual struggles.

I think the most telling point Rabbi Silver made in his paper is that we need someone like Rabbi Mordecai Kaplan (who recently spoke at the Seminary to great enthusiasm) to create a place which can be a seed-bed, not a hot-house. Sadly, it is inconceivable today that a man of Rabbi Kaplan's stature could even be hired at the Seminary. This is, to me, the greatest tragedy.

IRA EISENSTEIN

I must tell you at the very outset that I deeply resent having to be confined to five minutes to tell you what some of us have been working on for about two years, namely, the establishment of a rabbinical college which would meet the requirements that Rabbi Silver outlines in his paper.

Practically every one of his proposals has been incorporated into the new rabbinical college established by the Reconstructionist Foundation. We are in a combined program for a Ph.D. in religion with Temple University. The Ph.D. is a prerequisite for the ordination, which will offer a Doctor of Hebrew Letters and the title of "Rabbi" to those who complete the combined program. It is a postgraduate program running for five years; if dissertations are not completed, it may run to six, to seven, until the work is done.

Secondly, it is an integrated curriculum. For the first time we have tried to translate into curricular terms a conception of Judaism which you may accept or reject, a conception of an evolving religious civilization. In the first year everything is built around Biblical civilization; in the second year, Rabbinic civilization; in the third year, the medieval; in the fourth year, the modern; and in the fifth year, the contemporary. We don't drop the Bible after the first year, nor do we drop Rabbinics after the second. It is a truly cumulative curriculum, constantly interpreting Judaism in the light of the particular age that we happen to be involved with.

These courses are integrated with parallel courses at Temple University. For example, in the first year those of the students who are taking Biblical civilization must take those courses at Temple which are offered on the Biblical age. This year, all our students have to take Biblical theology with Robert Gordis, and in the second half year the *Book of Job* with Rabbi Gordis. Next year, in Rabbinic civilization they will be studying the whole year with a young, brilliant Orthodox scholar. They are exposed to a variety of viewpoints because both the Temple faculty and our own represent the whole spectrum of Jewish views.

In addition, they are exposed to the whole of world religions—Buddhism, Hinduism, Islam, all forms

---

IRA EISENSTEIN *is president of the new Reconstructionist Rabbinical College in Philadelphia. He has held pulpits in New York and Chicago, and is chairman of the editorial board of the* Reconstructionist.

402 : *Judaism*

of Protestant Christianity, Catholicism, and so on. They are working in an ecumenical atmosphere, both at Temple University and in our own school.

Thirdly, they are offered a variety of specialties. In the third and fourth years those who have demonstrated a talent for and an interest in other areas than the pulpit rabbinate specialize in those areas. Those who want to become pulpit rabbis will continue in homiletics, Midrash, synagogue administration, school, management, counseling. Those who want to go into teaching, for which they will be qualified with a Ph.D. when they graduate, will specialize in the scholarship of their chosen field. Those who want to go into adult education, Hillel work, into communal work, or bureaus of Jewish education and so on, will be offered the opportunity to do this. They will know the issues, so that they will be able to make an excellent choice.

The response to the establishment of our school, which is now completing its first year, has been quite extraordinary. We had forty applications for about fifteen admissions the first year, and we had over a hundred admissions for about the same number of admissions the second year. I am sorry to have to say that a number of students are going to be transferring from other institutions.

EMANUEL RACKMAN

I follow the pattern of the jottings and musings of Rabbi Silver, whose paper I enjoyed very much. It is hard to react to any particular proposals because his paper is, as

EMANUEL RACKMAN *is assistant to the president, Yeshiva University, and rabbi of the Fifth Avenue Synagogue in New York.*

he said, rather disjunctive: a lot of interesting insights, sometimes contradicting each other.

First, a biographical note of my own. My father was one of two instructors at Yeshiva Rabbi Isaac Elchanan in 1908 when the strike, to which Rabbi Wolf made reference, took place. So I know a little bit about student revolt from way back and who knows but that I've been a rebel too, ever since then, though unborn in 1908.

My great problem with Rabbi Silver's paper is that he has broadened the conception of the rabbi to such an extent that he's certainly no longer a rabbi in any historic sense. Take a physician. The practice of medicine has changed radically in 2500 years, but the basic meaning of a physician is the same: to heal a man who is ill, whether mentally or physically. While methods may change, that's still his principal role. Likewise, the lawyer, who remains essentially a man who is making a contribution either to the interpretation of the law, or to the enforcement of the law. While there may be frontiers of the law—and a school like Yale Law especially may concentrate on the frontiers of the law—we all know what the role of the lawyer is.

As for the rabbi, historically his role was simply to be the master of a special kind of learning, and no more than that. That is why George Foot Moore called him the doctor of the law. If we take the traditional definition, then in a way the rabbinical seminaries may not have failed too badly. I don't say they are producing scholars. But insofar as it is expected that they shall produce masters of the law, at least in our school we hope that most of our students will emerge with enough confidence to handle the materials of the Talmud, to study the Codes, to read the responsa literature and understand them. With experience, they may even be able to apply them to concrete situations.

With regard to other aspects of the rabbinical vocation, we have solved our problem at least in one way, and that is to provide other kinds of schools. Educators can study in our department of religious education at the Ferkauf graduate school. The rabbi who wants to go into social work can receive a master's degree or a doctorate in social work. He may at the same time choose to take a rabbinic degree, but he knows that his career area is either education or social work, or the like. If we think of the rabbi in our limited definition, we will not feel so sick about the situation.

On the other hand, perhaps the thing to do would be to change the name, to let the word "rabbi" or *rav* not apply to what some of our graduates will do. The real problem is, to get a new term, perhaps *parnas* (educated layman), to create some new terminology for the Jewish community, so that the different vocations of the different areas of activity within Jewish life could have a wide gamut of titles. And, who knows, in one situation the *parnas* may be far more important than the *rav*, and in another situation the *rav* will be more important than the *parnas*.

EUGENE WEINER

Taking my cue from the previous speakers, I, too, shall supply some

EUGENE WEINER, *who headed the Lehman Institute of Ethics of the Jewish Theological Seminary of America, will be teaching sociology of religion at the Hebrew University in Jerusalem, starting this fall.*

autobiography—relevant to the discussion, I trust.

As a fledgling rabbi, fresh out of the Jewish Theological Seminary, I assumed a pulpit, as the phrase goes, in Canada. Eagerly, I came to my first board meeting, prepared to exercise whatever rabbinic function the occasion would demand. The first item to be discussed—this after five years of Seminary schooling (on which $25,000 dollars, I'm told, was expended) and four years of pre-theological training—was the size of the garbage cans to be used outside the synagogue. That wouldn't have been so distressing but for the fact that the discussion took an hour and a half. Shortly thereafter, my president came up to me and brushed imaginary lint off my shoulders—which I somewhat resented—and said to me: "We like rabbis who wear ninety-dollar suits." Now this wouldn't have distressed me at all, except for the fact that that was exactly what I *had* paid.

So much for the rabbinic end of the stick. On the Seminary end, I've had the rather undistinguished but, I think, important job during these last few years of being a tranquilizer to rabbis in the field. We have a number of programs at the Seminary that really are designed as institutionalized group therapy, where we invite rabbis to write about the things that are on their minds; and they usually write the truth because they know that these papers are not going to be circulated. I had the underground job of being the sponsor for about seventy-five papers that rabbis have written about "the moral problems of their own rabbinate." These documents are available for perusal by people who are sympathetic. I think they demonstrate that we have a crisis on our hands.

How are we to meet this crisis

of role identity, of role strain within the rabbinate? The only instrument for change in the situation, at the present time, since all of the duly constituted bodies are rolling along in their own way, is for rabbis (the only group powerful enough to change the situation) to elect or appoint or convene a blue-ribbon commission that would spend two or three years studying theological education in the American Jewish community. The difficulty with rabbis is that they're so harrassed that in order to get them to do a responsible job it will be necessary to free them from their congregational duties for these two or three years. To get these men together over that period of time will require an enormous expenditure of funds on the part of the Jewish community. I do not know where the unity is going to come from, or the necessary impetus; but we need a group of people—sociologists, political scientists, social scientists, psychologists, rabbis, scholars—to engage in such a serious, in-depth study.

We all applaud the valiant efforts being made by the Reconstructionists and by the Boston group, the *chavurah,* who are dealing with some of these problems and are trying to evolve creative forms. While we are all indebted to Rabbi Silver, to Professor Liebman's article, and to this symposium, I am afraid that I agree very substantially with Rabbi Eisenstein that what we really need is much more time and much more seriousness, much more money, many more people, and a greater dedication to the idea behind what it will take to evolve creative forms in rabbinic education for the decades ahead.

EUGENE B. BOROWITZ

Rabbi Weiner will excuse me, I hope, for using his remarks as the basis of what now I know I want to say, namely, that a bureaucratic approach—more men, more money and a serious study—will not help us. Anyone who has read the studies of Protestant theological education in the United States will know that they generally come up with very little.

To take the bureaucratic approach and appoint a commission; or to propose that we rabbis who are already in the field and who are older and who know better should carry out the necessary revolution —both these suggestions are wrong. They are wrong because they suffer from the besetting sin of our seminaries now, namely, that they are paternalistic. Regardless of who we are, whether faculty members or rabbis in the field, it seems to me we all have our vested interests of one kind or another. The people who best know what is radically wrong with our congregations and our rabbis, the ones who have suffered from them most, are our incoming students. It seems to me, then, that the people who are most likely to know what needs to be done and in what direction we need to go are the students. If there is to be any hope for the kind of radical educational reform which I join Rabbi Silver in wanting, it needs to come not so much from above as from an understanding on the part of alumni and faculty and the boards of governors of our various institutions that our students can best lead us.

EUGENE B. BOROWITZ *is professor of education and Jewish religious thought at the Hebrew Union College—Jewish Institute of Religion in New York. His most recent book is* How Can a Jew Speak of Faith Today?

It seems to me that we face three problems. They are problems which Rabbi Silver has outlined. First, we need men who are masters of Judaism. Second, we need men who are deeply and knowledgeably involved in the contemporary culture. Finally, we need men who are spiritually competent and rooted and confirmed in faith. If there is a crisis in the contemporary rabbinical school it is not only that students come to us who do not know very much about Judaism. The big surprise is—and I have taught at more than one seminary—that they do not know very much about contemporary culture either. Further, they suffer from the general malaise of our time in that they do not come with a very deep faith.

We could use a saint-in-residence, who is also a poet-in-residence, who is also a *Gaon*-in-residence. It seems to be somewhat difficult at the moment to find that precise combination of qualities. However, if there is any hope, again, it is in our better students. They come to us today knowing that they need to become masters of contemporary culture, and on the basis of what they have done in their undergraduate work, they hope to continue learning it. We should encourage them. But they also come to us hoping that they will, through the possibilities open to them at their seminaries, become masters of the Jewish tradition. And there we ought to try to get out of their way as much as possible, to facilitate what I find is their increasing desire to study.

But the third problem—that of trying to help men grow in an inner way—is one about which I worry the most. There is, on the part of many young students today, a sense of incredible dependency upon us, the older generation. Regardless of what they say about being revolutionary or radical, they really do not want a teacher but a guru. Most of us in my generation consider ourselves lucky if we have been able to master a certain amount of knowledge and put together a certain kind of religious life. The demand made of rabbinical schools that they and their faculties be the exception to all the institutions of our time and of our culture is unreasonable. We cannot hope to give students injections of faith, nor can we hope very readily to set before them the necessary models of what their spirituality can be. But I do think we have an obligation to ask the men on our faculties and our instituitons to be concerned for *their own* spiritual welfare, and to help our students in their own ways to become meaningful men of the covenant in our time.

ARTHUR GREEN

I agree that the demands Rabbi Borowitz has just mentioned are unreasonable, but I think he would agree that the religious enterprise is, and has to remain, unreasonable.

I think Rabbi Silver has said most of it. I only want to add some general remarks. One of our real curses is the professionalization of the rabbinate. I was very upset by Rabbi Rackman's choice of analogies—doctor, lawyer, rabbi, each with his own kinds of specialization, each with his own kind of role in the community. As long as we see the rabbi in a professional role, I don't think we can talk about the kinds of spiritual personalities and maybe even prophetic personalities that the age calls for.

ARTHUR GREEN *heads the Chavurat Shalom Community Seminary, Cambridge, Mass., of which he was a co-founder.*

I am appalled by the concept of the rabbinic role as a professional role. It seems to me that the leading spirits of today's generation are not rabbis, and rabbinical education, as we would want to conceive it, has to reflect that fact very seriously. The term "rabbinic training" is somehow offensive. Training means professional training, technical training. I want to talk about rabbinic education as primarily the cultivation of the religious personality—*cultivation,* and not production nor creation, because I do not think such personalities are created or produced in seminaries. These things happen much earlier in life and have to be a much bigger factor in the criteria for choosing rabbinical candidates. The real goal of the seminary is to nurture the religious growth of the student as an individual. The prime goal has to be the student's own shaping of his spiritual and moral life through contact with real religious teachers and through contact with the texts of the tradition.

I would disagree with Rabbi Silver in formulation. I would not put the question, "What function does the rabbi have?," as the synagogue president might ask it. I would like to ask: What need does God have for rabbis in this world? To me that is a really important question, and if we are uncomfortable with that formulation I think it's because we are uncomfortable (and I include myself) asking religious questions in religious language. I think God has relatively little need for rabbis in His world to fill professional pulpit roles. But if His kingship is to be taken seriously, He has a need for the kinds of people who will bring about His *malkhut shamayim* (Kingdom of Heaven).

In the seminaries, we must begin with the overcoming of roles. We can no longer talk about faculty and students. As long as the teacher sees himself in a faculty role and hides behind faculty cover, as long as a student is seen as only a student and not a religious human being growing with the faculty as they "grow" to be religious human beings, there can be no religious learning. The legacy of the seminaries is inevitably carried over into the congregations. If the legacy of the seminary years is one of spiritual dryness, the congregation will be spiritually dry; and that cannot be covered up with homiletics courses. If the legacy of the seminary is the legacy of the pedestal, of authoritarianism, of respect for role rather than person, then that too will happen in our congregations, and that, too, will continue to alienate our most significant and important Jews. If the rabbi is to be—as Rabbi Silver says he is to be, and I agree—the creator of a more meaningful community, he must emerge from a meaningful community. If the congregation is to become a religious community, a community of people growing together, the seminary must be one. A man with no experience in what religious community means cannot go out and create it in a vacuum.

The religious life as I would want to see it in our day, perhaps more than in other days, requires revolution, requires radical commitment—within the individual, and in society. As an individual, I can only begin that revolution within myself; as a society, our community can begin the revolution within itself. The seminary as an institution must begin its religious commitment by a struggle for inner revolution. Anything short of that, anything that does not break down roles, that does not break down conventional distinctions, that does not break down the pattern of meaninglessness and dryness which we all know well and which has been described over and over today, will not meet the religious need of this hour.

SEYMOUR SIEGEL

I must confess I began reading Rabbi Silver's remarks with some trepidation. I was prepared for the usual tirade against the "Establishment," the irrelevance of the curricula of our seminaries, and a general jeremiad as to the state of our theological schools. These conventional calls for radical innovation are both unfair and unproductive. Luckily for us, Rabbi Silver does not fully join in the discordant chorus which sees anything "established" as corrupt and anything "traditional" as irrelevant. For this, I am grateful. I am not, frankly, quite certain just what Rabbi Silver does propose, but some of his suggestions, like the pooling of resources, the admission of women, etc. are well taken—as a matter of fact, some of them are even being implemented.

I do, however, wish to raise my voice against the current fad of anti-intellectualism which is curiously so popular in the center of intellectual activity—the academy. By anti-intellectualism I mean the consistent and by now boring putdown of efforts to correctly understand an ancient (or modern) text; of solid knowledge of material which is not absolutely and instantly "relevant." It is the kind of attitude which believes that occupy-

―――――――――
SEYMOUR SIEGEL *is professor of theology at the Jewish Theological Seminary of America. He was unable to attend the symposium in person, and his response was delivered in writing.*

ing a building in the name of some dispensation delivered by bearded revolutionaries is superior to figuring out a difficult Talmud commentary. One of my colleagues says that a person should preach with one eye on the Bible and the other on the *New York Times*. Many people, including good scholars, mistakenly believe that both eyes should be on the *New York Times*, or at least the *New York Review of Books*. You will recall the discussion in the Talmud whether Sinai was preferable to *oker harim*. The Rabbis decide that Sinai is better because "everyone is in need of the owner of the wheat." Dare we forget the tradition which glorified *torah lishma* and instructed *derosh v'kabel sakhar?* The teaching and the learning should make us better Jews and better human beings—and thus also better workers for justice. It is a grievous error to demean the painstaking work of scholarship and real study. Even Rabbi Silver falls into this trap, favoring a one-year rabbinical course for some people—concentrating on *amkha,* etc. Authentic theological education—in the Jewish mode at least—requires good hard study. What a wonder that this should have to be said! I have frequently heard rabbis who have been serving congregations for twenty-five years or more express their regret that they did not learn more Talmud when they were in seminary—and they do no refer to the "exciting" or the "relevant" parts either. Anyone who has heard a *shiur* of Rabbi Soloveitchik or Professor Lieberman knows that the study of texts can be exciting without invoking the new bitch-goddess "relevance."

Secondly, let me say a word about the "Establishment." It is fashionable—nay, practically a *mitzvah*—

to knock the Establishment. This *mitzvah* apparently is obligatory even on the members of the Establishment. The functional definition of "Establishment" seems to be anyone in authority I do not like, except myself. By now I hope everyone knows that there is no one Establishment in Jewish life. There are various Establishments, and I dare say that almost everyone here is a member of one of them. Like all human institutions, Establishments have their faults and even their sins—both acknowledged and unacknowledged. But, it has been my experience that the leadership of American Judaism is by and large open to all reasonable suggestions. Furthermore, the anti-Establishmentarians I have encountered don't seem to be much better than those whom they seek to replace. One is reminded of the definition of a liberal as a person who wishes to replace present evils with new ones.

I wish also to put in a word about fragmentation. I find it somewhat ironic that those who have spoken the loudest about Jewish unity, organic community, ecumenicity, and breaking down denominational lines are making their own *shabbos* (as the saying goes). Instead of having three groups here—as might have happened some two or three years ago—we now have five; and the newly added members have been the most vocal against fragmentation and most insistent upon community (the new candidate for the most O.K. word amongst those who are "with it").

There have been changes in the forms and even content of Jewish education over the centuries. The *yeshivot* in Babylonia were not the same as those in Lithuania. The Hasidic *yeshivot* were different than their Misnagdic counterparts—and the Sephardic academies distinct from their Ashkenazic fellows. But when the changes were instituted, they were not faddist in nature. They were responses to really new conditions—not novelty for novelty's sake. An old tradition is conservative (I refer to an attitude, not to a specific branch of Judaism); it changes slowly and deliberately. This might enrage the impatient—for a while. But when the shambles of the remains of the latest fads cover the landscape, the community is grateful that somewhere men stood loyal to that which they believed to be true. Frankly, there is too much talk in American Judaism—not enough learning, not enough doing, not enough self-improvement. The trouble is that we are not Jewish enough and therefore we believe that salvation will come from introducing new courses or playing around with psychedelic titillations.

What I am saying is that Jewish theological education is best when it is true to itself—when it is teaching Torah and attempting to produce personalities dedicated to and hopefully embodying Torah. The rabbinate, I believe, is the most important calling any young man can now undertake who is concerned about the future of Judaism. He will best prepare himself for this test by hard study, difficult training in reverence and piety, and patient efforts at self-improvement.

Hospitality to strangers is important; visiting the sick is a sign of compassion and concern; attending the dead to the grave is an expression of reverence for life. All these —even making peace between fellow men—are excelled by the study of Torah. This should be our slogan: *Talmud torah keneged kulam.*

CHARLES S. LIEBMAN

I guess somebody has to play the role of the devil's advocate; so I'm in the paradoxical position of defending rabbinical seminaries. In the light of what has been said here, they deserve to be defended.

First, a minor comment. I agree with Mr. Loeb that some aspects of Rabbi Silver's paper reflect particular problems of HUC-JIR rather than of JTS and Yeshiva University. I hope Rabbi Silver won't quote my article against me on that, but that was my feeling when I read his paper.

I would like to respond to some general attitudes I find expressed in Rabbi Silver's paper in the remarks that were made here, and in Rabbi Wolf's review of my paper in JUDAISM.

We can view the seminaries as institutions of Jewish religion, learning and culture. All of us have agreed that there is great room for improvement. In a way, this was the context in which my article was written—that there are problems within the institutions. There are problems with respect to the curriculum itself. There are problems with respect to teaching. There are problems resulting from the absence of faculty-interest in students. There is need for a greater student voice and student participation. We could sit around for days and condemn the rabbinical seminaries for their shortcomings in these respects, and rightfully so.

Much of this kind of discussion could cut across Orthodox, Conservative and Reform lines. I think it is interesting that nobody here has spoken about denominational or ideological differences between Orthodox, Conservative and Reform. In one respect, they are not relevant; but in a second respect, they are quite relevant, and we have been too quick to gloss over them. Much that has been said and written about rabbinical training has no resonance or meaning for me and does not include, I feel, the community or sub-community with which I am identified. Not only that, but I think there are certain implicit assumptions built into the papers that have been presented and into much that has been said that I find downright objectionable from my point of view.

It does not seem to me that we can meaningfully discuss rabbinical training or the role of the rabbi in the community, unless we have some agreement on the meaning and value of Judaism. One central aspect of Judaism is the primacy of the textual tradition and of Jewish text within Jewish life. This means that there is an insignificance —virtually an utter insignificance —in such courses as New Testament or psychotherapy or cultural anthropology or in sociology of the ghetto or in Buddhism or Hinduism. Certainly, such courses are utterly insignificant before the rabbinical student has a basic knowledge and understanding of the Jewish texts and of the Jewish tradition. It would be hypocritical of me if I said that I do not think people ought to know about or read about Hinduism and Buddhism and Islam and cultural anthropology and psychotherapy. Fine! But to introduce this into a rabbinical school curriculum? At the expense of what? Of a basic knowledge of Jewish sources? Someone who advocates this and I are on two different sides of the fence; we are simply

---

CHARLES LIEBMAN *will be teaching in the department of political studies at Bar-Ilan University in Israel, starting this fall. He is the author of the widely discussed essay "The Training of American Rabbis," published in the* American Jewish Year Book, 1968.

410 : *Judaism*

not talking the same language. Your whole notion of what Judaism is and what is built into Judaism and mine are so far apart that, at this point, I am not sure we really can talk meaningfully anymore.

Secondly, I do no tthink the seminaries—or, for that matter, Judaism—are open to just *any* kind of idea, or to *any* form of experimentation, or to a *total* variety of Jewish experiences. It also seems to me that if the price that Judaism and Jews have to pay for this today is the alienation of most intellectuals or of radical college youth, then let us pay the price. Having observed at first hand the behavior of Jewish intellectuals and radical college youth, I, for my part, am quite prepared to pay it. I think Judaism will be served, much better served if we create *mehitzot* (separations) between them and ourselves. I do believe that there is a context and an area of agreement in which at least Orthodox, Conservative and Reform can meaningfully talk, but if the non-Orthodox do not accept the context of Judaism as a textual tradition and insist that Judaism is open to any experimentation or exposure, I must retreat behind denominational lines.

The faults of American Judaism are not necessarily attributable to the seminaries. I do not think we can blame the state of American Judaism on the conditions within rabbinical seminaries. If the picture of American Judaism today is a very dismal one—and I believe it is—if the future of American Judaism looks very grim—and I think it does—that is in great part due to the fact that we live in an essentially hostile environment. Today, in 1969 in the United States of America, the American environment, the American culture at its best, not at its worst (I'm not talking about drugs and extreme Right or extreme Left), is hostile to Judaism and to basic Jewish values. Consequently, the most meaningful response that the seminary can make to this kind of environment is basically defensive. By and large for all their faults —and there is, as I repeat, much to criticize in the seminaries—this has been their response.

I do not think this was a thoughtful response. The seminaries were defensive at a time when, perhaps, they shouldn't have been defensive. They were defensive at a time when they and their graduates might have done much more for American Jews. But today, by happy coincidence, the seminaries are defensive about the environment, defensive about forces pressing on Judaism at precisely the time they ought to be. If one is going to remain in America (and I don't believe one ought to remain in America) this, it seems to me, is one's only option.

Another objection I have to the papers and discussions about the rabbi's role is a kind of implicit acceptance of the American *status quo* by supposed radicals. I have heard this opinion expressed: Let's turn out rabbis who may or may not be called rabbis to serve the Jews wherever they are and in whatever condition we may find them. In that case, why not send the rabbis into Unitarian churches? At some point, I would think, we have to say we stand for something; and unless you marginal Jews make a move there is nothing at all that we can do for you.

Discussion

DANIEL JEREMY SILVER: That my paper represents the particular existential realities of my community and my experience goes without saying. We can argue only from our own experience, though I think many of us felt this kind of meeting has provided us with one of the few chances to realize that we share some common problems. All of us had taken the broom and swept some institutional dirt under the carpet. There is much more that binds most of us than separates us. So I plead guilty to this kind of constructive bias. I don't think any human being can escape it.

But I frankly must state my vigorous disagreement with Prof. Liebman. I read his article at the same time that I was sent a long questionnaire by him, having to do with theological positions. I found I could not, in good conscience, answer his questionnaire. The whole assumption on which it was based was utterly foreign to me. I do not believe that if I turn the Torah over and turn it over again I'm going to find everything in it. I will find great things in it; I have found great things in it. But I don't believe that the rabbi is simply one who is an expounder and master of this traditional text. He must be that and he must be much more.

I do not believe that I am simply being relevant to the complaints of the uninterested and the unaffiliated. I believe I am being relevant to my own complaints, and when I speak, as I do, of the need to revise and radically to reform, I am speaking out of my own felt need, not out of a desperate attempt to have some carrot at the end of a stick to bring in those who are tangential to Jewish life. I don't like *mehitzot*. Our world is one, the Jewish people is one; and my belief is that Jewish values are one (though each of us will have his own understanding of that oneness), even as our God is one. I rather resent this attempt to build up those things which separate us, to build them higher now.

Rabbi Rackman said that the rabbi means so much, yet means so little. He was saying it in the sense of the traditional master of the Talmud. I think that one of the things that concerns many of us here is the fact that the rabbi does mean a great deal in the American Jewish community. People *do* come to us, they *do* seek answers, they *do* want the warmth of our personalities and the warmth of our learning. The tragedy is that often our learning is scant, our answers trite, and we turn them off because of what *we* are, not because of what Judaism is, and we turn them off from Judaism. The rabbinate means a great deal to me, and if one wants to argue that we ought to have a different term for *my* meaning of the rabbi and for the traditional *rav*, so be it. The word, as I understand it, is an accordion word which once had to do with relevance. I found in the sources an attempt to define the term "rabbi." "He who has disciples and whose disciples again have disciples is called 'rabbi.' When his disciples are forgotten, he is called *rabban*. And when the disciples of his disciples are also forgotten, he is simply called by his own name."

GERALD ZELIZER:* Assuming that not all laymen are those types who brush lint off rabbis' jackets, I think it would have been valuable in this type of symposium, or in any future symposium, to ask some of the educated and well-intentioned laymen to share their views as to what we rabbis are lacking and what, perhaps, could be implemented in our curriculum. I think that often the educated and committed layman does have valuable suggestions in this realm: to simply overlook them or ignore them is doing ourselves a great disservice.

Secondly, as a rabbi in the field, I strongly disagree with those who want to de-emphasize professionalism in the rabbinate. To me, professionalism means to move away from being the community *schlemiel*. If, in professionalizing the rabbi, we have lifted the

---

* Gerald Zelizer is rabbi of Temple Israel, Union, N.J.

standards and, perhaps unfortunately, have moved away from the religious image of the rabbi, yet the rabbi is not subjugated in terms of salary, in terms of standards, in terms of what he is expected to do, then, as a Conservative rabbi, I must say I am all for professionalism, and would disagree with some of my colleagues.

Lastly, I think that the greatest lack in my personal rabbinic training in the seminary, even though I personally came from a rabbinic family, was awareness of all the "political" nuances of synagogue life. I am not critical of the Jewish Theological Seminary where I studied. I think my courses were quite good in terms of teaching texts and in terms of preparing one for the rabbinate. The one lack I feel is that a man is not introduced by other rabbis to the nuances of synagogue life. Some rabbis who are experienced in the field do have very good insights and guidelines to deal with the obstreperous congregant. I think that in rabbinic training young men like myself could benefit by a formal introduction to this aspect of practical rabbinics.

EDWARD GERSHFELD:* I would only like to make a very brief comment, and perhaps put it in the form of a question to Prof. Liebman. It seems to me that there might be a parallel in the rabbinical schools to the situation that exists in the universities in this country—a tendency to polarize opinion. On the one side, some consider the university a place where abstract contemplation can go on; where total freedom of thought and philosophical or other speculation can be encouraged; where study, completely untrammeled by any other consideration, can go on; where research into the practical and the impractical can go ahead without any control and without any pressures. On the other hand, some see the university as a place where the young generation must be prepared to move out and fight the good fight, and where the university itself must be prepared to put its hand into all the problems, immediate and not so immediate, around it—social problems, political problems, and so on. I think this may be going on in our rabbinical schools. If we do make that distinction, perhaps we would see that such institutions as the *Chavurat Shalom* have much in common with the *yeshivas* of the Satmer Hasidim, in that both expect the mood of their institution to be one of introspection, study of their own religious life (of course in their own terms), without being concerned with the large masses of Jews, without being interested in creating religious activity outside their own institution. On the other hand, the larger seminaries are split internally on this issue. The older faculty, the European faculty, are more interested in the seminary as a place of research and contemplation, as a place of timelessness; the younger, activist faculty and students are interested in using the rabbinical school as a place for developing personal religious ideas, personal conduct, pietism, and, of course, extending it out into the broader community in order to radicalize the Jewish people.

I would like to ask Prof. Liebman: Is it true that this kind of polarization may be at work in our schools, perhaps not even completely noticed? And is it possible that in the throes of general American confusion on the role of higher education, we Jews and, especially, we professional rabbinical educators may be in the throes of confusion as to what exactly is the purpose of our seminaries? We may be trying to accomplish two contrary ends at the same time. Perhaps what we ought to do is try to devise a new method of accomplishing whatever it is we want to accomplish with new machinery which will create the kind of seminary (or

---

* Edward Gershfield is a member of the faculty, Jewish Theological Seminary of America.

LARRY KAPLAN:* It would seem to me that unless you want to take the attitude that Alvin Reines has taken, that Judaism is a polydoxy—like Paul, all things to all men—then Judaism must, of necessity, draw *meḥitzot* somewhere. While we try to reach as many as we can with our message, you can't dilute it in order to get everyone, because then you're going to be left with nothing.

I also think that the down-grading of professionalism carries the implicit assumption that there are no ready-made answers to anything. It would seem to me that there *are* ready-made answers to some problems, particularly in the area of Jewish law (*kashrut* for example), and that to down-grade answers because they are ready-made is a glorification of subjective intent, of mere meaningfulness at the expense of the objective deed which has always been of prime value in the Jewish tradition.

LEO DIAMOND:* I am neither a rabbi nor the son of a rabbi, but permit me nevertheless to comment on the subject of our discussion.

Having spent the last year or two engrossed in Jacob Neusner's study of the history of Jews in Babylonia, I have learned some very interesting things about the rabbinic role, which may have some contemporary relevance. Obviously, the rabbi of the present day cannot be altogether like his Babylonian predecessors, the Sages who were the fathers of the Talmud. However, I feel that a return to some of the more basic functions of the rabbinate might well be in order today. I was fascinated by the fact that the rabbis at that time had, as now, very little control over the personal compliance with various religious laws by the people in their households. However, in many instances, they were powers for real good in the civil and even political life of the community. I'm afraid that our rabbis today, in the main, are forced to become helpers in the ritual life of the community, forgetting their real functions as teachers and as judges. I think that a re-examination of those basic functions would, in large measure, give new life and meaning to the role of the rabbi in the American Jewish community.

ARNOLD JACOB WOLF: I regretfully express my moral revulsion at the statement of Prof. Liebman, and at the defense of the new seminary in Philadelphia by my friend, Ira Eisenstein. It seems to me that it is altogether too late for this kind of premature self-congratulation. How can it be that the seminaries are so good if men graduate, as Prof. Liebman himself has said, with less faith than they come in with? How can the seminaries be so good if what happens is that at the end of four or five or six years of study men still do not know the texts, men still do not know what the rabbinate is all about, and in some ways, as persons, they are less than they were when they came in? How can it be that the seminaries are doing such a wonderful job if the best men are leaving the rabbinate, either while still rabbinical students, or after their ordination, or after a few years of work in the active rabbinate? How can it be that the seminaries are doing so well if what we have in each one of the schools is something very like a revolt, if not a revolution? How can it be that the seminarians are so good if what we experience over and over and over again in our contacts with students from each of the schools —and we are ecumenical in our distress if in nothing else—is a malaise, an agony, and, at the end of the road,

---

* Larry Kaplan is a rabbinical student at Yeshiva University.
* Leo Diamond is a member of a Reform synagogue in New York.

414 : *Judaism*

something which approaches a disaster? And how is it possible that a seminary so new as the one in Philadelphia can already be so smug as to pretend that it has all these problems solved? Not only in Rabbi Eisenstein's eloquent defense of it today, but in the literature which it has already produced, how it is possible that already they can say that we have the answers in a new school, the old schools having clearly failed to give us any of these answers?

I am sympathetic with the call of Rabbi Green for a new kind of Judaism and a new kind of seminary. The problems which Rabbi Silver has set before us, which I do not think are Reform problems or Conservative problems or Orthodox problems, but Jewish or at least American-Jewish problems—these problems will not be solved in the present seminaries, even if they affiliate with Temple University and give Ph.D.'s. They will only be solved by a revolutionary approach to Judaism and to the instruction of the young teachers of Judaism. If you wish to reply to that, you are certainly welcome to, Ira.

IRA EISENSTEIN: I think the meeting is going to start getting interesting. If I have given the impression to my dear friend, Arnold Wolf, that I am smug, then I must have succeeded in doing something I haven't succeeded in doing in forty years. With all due respect to his judgment, I do not think I was being smug. I was simply trying to describe the program of a new school which is attempting to correct some of the errors of the old ones. And I measured them against what Rabbi Silver, in his paper, was calling for.

No, we haven't succeeded, but within a year we have certain intimations of accomplishment. Why didn't you invite one of our students? (That, too, is a rhetorical question.) We have involved students, for example, in the administration of the school. Rabbi Borowitz said that the students know best. Well, I do not think they know best, but I think they know something. They know what they want, they know what they need. Many of them have come to us inspired by rabbis, but determined never to follow in the footsteps of those rabbis. We've been trying to find out why, what is it about the life those rabbis have been leading which directed them away from the pulpit rabbinate, and we're trying to redirect them toward the synagogue, if possible. They have sat in on faculty meetings, they have helped to decide about grading, they have even sat in on the admissions committee. And so far we have no reason to regret any of these decisions.

We have also been aware of the fact that students come in with very good college records and very poor Hebrew background; so instead of some time in the future having them spend a year in Israel, we require that they take their first year in the Chaim Greenberg Institute in Jerusalem, and then come back and take their five years with us, so that they have at least a basic knowledge which will help them master the texts. I think that's a wise decision: we will know better a year from now whether to be "smug" or not.

We have reached out into the community. We live in Philadelphia in the heart of the black ghetto, and our students, even though they are sometimes a little troubled by the insecurity, welcome the opportunity to translate into activist terms what they are being taught. They are trying to act like *menschen*. And they have organized a rabbinical social-action group which has now grown larger than our own small student body.

When Rabbi Silver said that we've got to restructure the synagogue, he touched upon something which had been touched upon only tangentially by others. When you train men—and

I'm not sorry for using the word "train"—when you train men and prepare them to serve, you prepare them in a context. The present context of American Jewish life requires a series of types all well-trained. The training of the rabbi is not going to change the character of the community. Those of us who are in the community are going to have to see to it that the synagogue and the rest of our community are restructured. But for the time being we are trying to train people who will fit in to the situation as it exists.

May I also say a word in response to Prof. Liebman. I was really surprised to hear him talk this way—I was a little shocked because I know him quite well and it's the first time he's talked this way, at least to me! Let's try to make one thing clear—I say this to the young student at the Yeshiva—diversity within Jewish life does not mean dilution. It means enrichment. And as long as Jewish life is what it is —and we are living in the 20th and the beginning of the 21st century—we have to reckon with the fact that we are not going to achieve unanimity in theology or ritual or worship. We are going to be able to cooperate on many things, but we are going to have pluralism within Jewish life, and our pluralism will give some of us a chance to learn from others. If you want a monolithic Judaism, you're going to read an awful lot of us out, though perhaps you'll be satisfied to be left with a handful of Jews. Maybe God will be pleased with that, but it won't be my God. I believe this is a general confusion among our Orthodox brothers. The non-Orthodox have grown to understand that pluralism and diversity are here to stay, and that our real problem is to achieve a unity without sacrificing diversity.

CHARLES S. LIEBMAN: First, I'm glad I have a second chance to speak, because I may have been misunderstood in reference to Rabbi Silver's paper. What I said was that I felt it reflected primarily an HUC-JIR experience rather than that of JTS or YU. I did not mean that HUC-JIR were the only people that had problems, not by any stretch of the imagination. What I meant was that I felt that if I were writing the paper, these would not be the problems that I would be writing about. In other words, YU has *its* problems, JTS has *its* problems. Although there's much that cuts across all institutions, some of the things that caught my eye in Rabbi Silver's paper were particular problems of HUC-JIR.

Secondly, I really don't understand Rabbi Wolf's moral revulsion. I suggested this symposium years ago to the editors of JUDAISM, and for one reason or another the proposal was rejected then. I said that much was wrong with our seminaries that had to be brought into the open and discussed. When JUDAISM turned down the idea of the symposium, I went to the *American Jewish Year Book* and proposed the article. I am the last person in the world to feel there was anything to be smug about with respect to the seminaries.

Thirdly, I think I was misunderstood about *mehitzot*. I feel very strongly that there are sharp differences between Orthodox, Conservative and Reform. However, I did not mean to put up the *mehitzot* between Orthodoxy and everyone else. That is not what I had in mind. Let me introduce a very personal comment: as I visited the various seminaries for my *American Jewish Year Book* study, I felt that everybody at JTS spoke my language in my Jewish context. There are great disagreements between myself and friends of mine within the Conservative movement. But the kind of thing that I alluded to in my first remarks, where I said I felt that there had to be a basic level of agreement before we could go on to discuss rabbinical training, that agreement certainly existed at JTS. At HUC-JIR, I found a common language and a common tradition among some people but not all. With people like Prof. Borowitz, there's no question about a common language and a common tradition. I felt that *meḥitzot* exist somewhere in HUC-JIR. But on my side are a substantial proportion of people who are associated with Reform. I might add that they also tend to be those associated with JUDAISM.

I would agree with Rabbi Eisenstein that there's room for pluralism in Jewish life. I may deplore the fact that not all Jews are Orthodox, but I recognize that there is a place within Judaism for the non-Orthodox. There is a point, I would say, however, at which dissent reaches a limit. There is a point at which one has to set up certain boundaries which we don't cross. The *meḥitzah* always is open, but we don't go through the *meḥitzot* to you; you must come from outside the *meḥitzot* towards us. Some of the most distressing discussion that is taking place, some of the discussion here today, and some of the things that have been written in the last year or so about Judaism and rabbinical training, imply that we cannot afford to have any kinds of *meḥitzot*, that we must have an entirely open community. A reference was made earlier to Paul. This reminds us of a similar fight that we fought out two thousand years ago. I thought we won it then, but apparently we have to keep fighting it.

SHELDON ZIMMERMAN: First of all, regarding what Rabbi Eisenstein had to say regarding Prof. Borowitz's comments. I think Prof. Borowitz was misunderstood. We have HUC-JIR student representation in the faculty; we went to their curriculum meetings; students are everywhere involved; they are involved in social action. We are talking together about higher Hebrew standards, and we are eventually going to have a compulsory year in Israel. But those are not the answers. Students don't feel that that kind of involvement is the answer. We are looking for the *chevrah*, the community, the fellowship; we are looking for persons; we are not finding them.

Secondly, Rabbi Silver in his paper mentioned being isolated in mid-New York. He is absolutely right. I must express a personal grievance here. When the Jewish Theological Seminary students decided to get together with Christian denominations regarding Biafra, they did not ask the HUC-JIR in New York. We finally got together a year and a half ago to settle where we could meet. It had to be at the Seminary. But then, of course, we wouldn't go unless we had one of our men speaking. I think both sides should be condemned here. I think we have lived our lives isolated long enough, like Biafra and Nigeria. We have to get together. And you see, Rabbi Eisenstein, I don't think your religious naturalism is the answer for most of us any longer, because we're no longer naturalists. I am very concerned and have read as much as I could, as an instructor in philosophy at Hunter College, about the goals and aims of religious naturalists. But naturalism is not working. We're not happy. We're still searching, and we still have to make the schools a place to search.

Lastly, we can't draw *meḥitzot*. The question of prayer and *mikvah* should be a part of the curriculum at HUC, as it should be a part of the curriculum of any other school. There is nothing in Judaism which should be alien to any of the seminaries. The present answers just haven't been good enough. HUC is wonderful. In certain respects my eyes were opened there. But too much of my spirit was destroyed. There, too, the question has to be: Where do we find the sources for spirit to go on?

EUGENE WEINER: The number of problems that we've all heard this afternoon is very great. What really concerns me is: Where is the lever of action going to be located? Who is most intimately concerned with the present situation? Who feels most acutely the needs that will require and bring into being the necessary changes? My belief is that the person who is most concerned about this, and must ultimately be the lever for action here, is the rabbi himself. The professor in the seminaries can find his own personal solution to the disenchantment of his own students, and the disenchantment that he feels frequently in his own professional life, by retreating into a scholarship that shuts out many others around him. The student can beat the system by just surviving and going through the hoops. Maybe here and there will be a cry for change, but the student knows that he has the system beat just by lasting it out. And if he has a brain, he can do just that. The congregants have a way out of the terrible malaise in the rabbinate by just not coming to synagogue and by turning rabbis off. But the person who really has very much at stake in regard to this whole situation is the rabbi who stands before his congregation week after week spiritually dry, intellectually deadened by the routine of congregational responsibility, who is surfeited with all of the inconsequential tasks of the rabbinate, some of which are of great moment and consequence and do bring satisfaction, but whose gigantic weight, year after year, is tremendously debilitating spiritually and intellectually. The only group that can mobilize itself to take the necessary movement to change is the rabbis. But they are drugged into a soporific state by the sheer imensity of their own obligations.

When I suggested that we try to free a group of people to study the problem of rabbinic training, I wasn't opting for the type of study that the Episcopalian Church recently made in a bureaucratic framework. I mean that we, as a Jewish community, must take seriously this whole effort towards revitalizing rabbinic education, put men out into the field and free them of responsibilities so that they can take a long hard look at the whole development.

If the rabbis can't muster the necessary self-discipline to free themselves and to take that long hard look, then some of us must do this. But it is the rabbis who are in crisis. They know it; the drop-out rate reflects it; the papers they write about the rabbinate reflect it; their congregants know it; their students know it; the rabbinical students know it. Why on earth won't the rabbis take the necessary action?

ARTHUR GREEN: I stand somewhere between Dr. Liebman and Rabbi Silver, though I certainly share Rabbi Silver's distaste for *meḥitzot*. On the other hand, I am very worried about Rabbi Silver's suggestion—and Rabbi Eisenstein's practice—in equating seminary and university, in joining us to the academic community. I am very worried about this partly because I think the university is in crisis and is being criticized for good reason. If there is a religious call in this matter, it would generally place us on the side of those who criticize, while disagreeing with some of their tactics, rather than have us join that malaise.

More deeply, I think, we are talking, or we should be talking, about a qualitatively very different type of learning than what the university is talking about. I have been a graduate student in Judaic studies. I do not think that is "where it's at." I think those of us outside the Orthodox community have to rediscover for ourselves in our own way what religious learning means, which is something very different than academic study of religious texts. I am not saying I know, or that we in Cambridge have clearly defined what religious learning means. We do know that our kind of learning differs very seriously from anything that could happen at a university, even in its finest sense.

I'd want to say to Larry Kaplan that I have no clear answers to the religious questions that affect the Jewish community. There was a time when I envied those clear answers, but no longer. In this respect, those of us who represent Orthodoxy and those of us who are heterodox Jews do stand in rather different worlds, and our views of what rabbinic education should be are bound to be different. We should recognize this openly before we begin dialogue.

Finally, I don't consider myself an elitist, but only something of a pessimist, when I talk about the American Jewish community. I do not know that very much can be done for the American Jewish community in great numbers. It seems to me (again particularly outside the Orthodox community), that we should be talking about a meaningful *she'erit ha-pleita*. It seems to me that I, at least, do not know how to foster meaningful religious Jewish survival for the masses, and I don't think much is going to happen in this country. I do think that we should be particularly distressed, not by the quantity of those leaving Jewish life, but by their quality. If we don't have things to say in very intensive ways to very small groups of real religious seekers and those troubled by the spiritual dryness of our society, we may as well not say anything to anybody.

MARK LOEB: Some rabbinical students answered Dr. Liebman's question, "What do you need?" as follows: "We need a rabbi." When I entered the Jewish Theological Seminary I had three classmates who were among the most capable students the Seminary had ever accepted. Two of them since left to go on *aliya,* turned on to *aliya* by being turned off by the Seminary; the third went to the University of Pennsylvania to undertake studies in comparative religion. Now these symptoms are never discussed in only one part of the school, and that is the faculty, particularly the older faculty.

I think one of the problems has been that the faculty has answered our problems with stiffness. When we finally came to saying, "You know this text system is very nice except we're a little bit bored doing this all the time," someone responded, "Well, let's see if we can find an answer. Ah, here's the answer, you'll take a course in reading Yehezkel Kaufmann." "But we read Kaufmann last year, as well as three medieval Jewish philosophers, and it's all an endlessly repetitive series of stagnant answers." "Look, if you have spiritual questions, you should go to our wonderful Institute of Pastoral Psychiatry."

I think our problem has always been the staffing of the institution, which leads to the critical point I wish to make. Our school is led by a man who is well into his seventies, and I'm told that Drs. Glueck and Belkin, if they are not already in their seventies might as well be. As Milton Galamison said of the Board of Education of the New York City: "They have tenure? Hell, they have immortality." Now, these are the great men, wise men. I do not mean to deride them. But the only way any kind of change can come is by students participating in faculty selection. The faculty should be drawn in the future not only from professional rabbinical scholars, but from rabbis—like Rabbi Herschel Matt, for instance, who is here. It wouldn't be a criminal idea of men who are in the rabbinate, who are not all feisty, musty and dusty, who have much to contribute in the way of personal example, piety and some learning, would be allowed to teach at the Seminary. The rabbinical organizations do not pressure for this, and we, as students, have no power to insist on it. I think it is absolutely essential to infuse into the schools, and certainly into ours, an element of student selection on who is to be hired, because the kinds of people who are now being hired clearly are limited to their own interests, which in no way reflect ours, either our daily lives or our spiritual concerns.

Afterword

ARNOLD JACOB WOLF

It is clear from the statements included in this symposium that there is, indeed, a crisis in rabbinic education in America. Some of this is simply the crisis in American Jewish identity; theological dissolution, personal *anomie,* bureaucratic gigantism, generational split. But the seminaries have created as well as inherited some of the general disaster. Else why would we discover less conviction in their senior students than in freshmen? Why would the new schools, despite their poor facilities, their untested faculties, their doubtful placement-power have in a year attracted as many applicants as all the established theological schools? Why are the schools so indefensibly defensive about their results, considering all hard questions disloyal?

But the purpose of this symposium is not to blame but to counsel, to find not scapegoats but alternatives. Perhaps we have found a few:

1) The model of rabbinic training should not be a German university but a kind of *Lehrhaus.* The student should not be processed but inducted. The curriculum should not be crowded, monolithic and immutable, but innovative as well as resolutely demanding. Jewish learning is instruction of a person, not collection of material, though it remains true that the unsophisticated man is only apparently pious.

2) Some new personnel are required. One might ask why Lou Silberman or William Braude or Emil Fackenheim, Monford Harris, Richard Rubenstein, Zalman Schachter, Steven Schwarzschild or, for that matter, Aden Steinsaltz are not regular members of one of our seminary faculties. The present staff is inadequate both quantitatively and qualitatively to the task it has set for itself. It sorely needs an infusion of experienced rabbinic and theological talent to offset its dangerous inbreeding. Incredibly, many present faculty members have remained in the very same institution—even in the same building—since they were twenty. With the end of European immigration, we immediately require an internal *aliya* to keep us honest.

3) Ecumenical needs call for joint action. In every major city graduates of the seminaries are working together, despite differences that are often greater within denominations than between them. But the seminaries will not come together for libraries, social action, professional cross-criticism or joint fund-raising. Except for one course at the Jewish Theological Seminary, there is no opportunity for students to hear rabbis and teachers from other groupings. Our new schools prove that new students care less about labels than about learning to teach the congregation of Israel. But the seminaries persevere in denominationalism!

4) The problem of our world will have to find their place in our curricula. If Judaism has nothing to say about Vietnam, poverty, Israel, radical tension, then it has nothing to say. But it *has* something to say, and good teaching requires that its teaching be educed from its sources. Such education is sharply different from Bible 400 and Codes 456, but not because it takes Bible or Codes less seriously. Rather, it has the *hutzpah* to affirm that it is not our religion which is irrelevant but only its fearful interpreters.

420 : *Judaism*

5) Priorities require reconsideration. Since the Reconstructionist College began to offer a first year in Israel and doctorates along with *semikha*, the President of the Hebrew College has come to see a merit in these proposals he could not find in similar earlier recommendations. Soon, all the seminaries may find it possible to give more financial help to rabbinical candidates than to Christian fellows, and give faculties time to think before they teach. These needs surely come before buildings, "institutes" whose only value is public relations, or elaborate journals of only remote antiquarian relevance. And about journals—why do our schools publish in history, text-analysis, bibliography—but not in theology? Why must it be left to the American Jewish Congress to sponsor Judaism as well as JUDAISM.

6) Relationships with existing congregations and rabbis are totally inadequate. It is the business of the seminaries to speak directly to rabbis' loneliness and frustration, to young people's restless self-criticism, to the vapidity and vulgarity of what passes for education or religion in most of our congregations. The *yeshiva* that hides behind its own walls betrays Yitzhak Elchanan as well as Stephen Wise. Jewish scholarship must interpenetrate the practical even to be scholarship, but surely to be instructively Jewish.

Times are rapidly changing. The end of this decade will see almost twice as many students in almost twice as many rabbinical schools as did the beginning. The next decade will see new heads of all our schools. The proliferation of Judaica programs in many major universities, the death of whole urban Jewish communities, the importance of Israel in our religious and communal perspectives—all these have changed the setting for rabbinic education suddenly, unexpectedly and utterly.

But there may not be much time to respond. Almost half of last year's freshmen did not come back to at least one rabbinical school this term. If we do not believe they were recklessly admitted, we must conclude the school failed many of them. Even the new seminaries are already in danger of perpetuating policies that the new kind of *yeshiva bahur* cannot in self-respect permit.

We need not panic, but it would be worse to sit tight. Our learned symposiasts have given us warning and all of us Jews must try to hear and obey.

The Conservative Rabbinate—In Quest of Professionalism

VIVIANA A. ZELIZER
GERALD L. ZELIZER

A RESOLUTION PASSED AT THE 1970 CONVENTION of The Rabbinical Assembly formalized what had been, for several years, a latent feeling among Conservative rabbis:

> Be it resolved that the president of the Rabbinical Assembly be redirected to establish a commission to execute a thorough restructuring of our self-defined function as an assembly, devising procedures whereby the Rabbinical Assembly shall become a strong agent to negotiate with a congregation on behalf of its member rabbis.

Such words obviously reflect a feeling among Conservative rabbis that what they conceive of as professional status is not yet theirs. Similar cries have been heard from the rabbinate of the Orthodox and Reform movements. It is crucial to identify the feelings and frustrations which were the basis for this formal expression, but more important is an understanding of exactly what is meant by "professional," as well as a diagnosis to find which aspects of professionalism are already the rabbi's, and which aspects still delude him. Above all, is the expressed desire of the Conservative rabbi to attain professional status a reasonable goal or a pipedream?

The very emergence of rabbis who seek professional status is a step beyond other typologies which have in the past been ascribed to them. The first attempt to delineate categories of rabbis divided the Orthodox into traditional, free-lance and modern, but confessed that, among Conservative rabbis, "role differentiation was not extensive enough to warrant more than a single category."[1]

It was Arthur Hertzberg who first established categories of Conservative rabbis. One group were either themselves foreign born or first-generation, lower-middle-class Americans, and their immediate spiritual and cultural roots were implanted in East European Jewry.[2] The main function of these rabbis was, in Marshall Sklare's terms, to "stem the tide of indifference," and to that end they developed a battery of "protestantized" functions such as preaching, teaching, pastoral duties, and relationship with the non-Jewish community. On the other hand, Hertz-

---

1. Jerome E. Carlin and Saul H. Mendlovitz, "The American Rabbi: A Religion Specialist Responds to Loss of Authority," in Marshall Sklare, *The Jews* (Illinois: The Free Press, 1958), p. 382.
2. Ibid., p. 331.

VIVIANA A. ZELIZER *is a Ph.D. candidate in Sociology at Columbia University.*
GERALD L. ZELIZER *is Rabbi of Temple Neve Shalom, Metuchen, N.J.*

berg identified a second group of Conservative rabbis who were American born, as were at least one of their parents, and who came from a Conservative family of much higher socio-economic status than did the older category.

As far back as 1960, Eli Ginsberg urged the Conservative rabbis to professionalize the rabbinate.[3] But his recommendation fell on deaf ears because it did not elicit, even among them, unanimity of opinion. The voices in opposition beckoned the rabbis to a calling which somehow precluded professional status. "The rabbinate is not merely a profession but . . . for most of us a vocation." "I am not sure that you can apply the same standards that one applies to other professions and unions . . . we have some messiahs and it is hard for us to think of a union of messiahs."[4] But with the 1970 resolution we see the attempt to give birth to yet a new type of Conservative rabbi, the professional. What is still undetermined is whether we will see birth or stillbirth.

The best studies of work indicate that four characteristics are necessary, if not always sufficient, for an occupation to be rated as a profession:

1. *expertise*—the technical competence and specialized knowledge that legitimizes one's work.

2. *specialized training*—this same competence and knowledge stems from education or apprenticeship.

3. *service*—the work one does is regarded, not solely as a means of income but, rather, as a life-long commitment of dedication.

4. *autonomy*—the professional enjoys maximum personal responsibility and initiative, but minimum supervision.

To what extent are each of these qualifications already present, or at least reasonable, goals for the Conservative rabbinate?

It is because of the nature of the American-Jewish society which he serves that the Conservative rabbi has developed clear and special expertise. Ironically, the kind of professional expertise which is his leaves him personally frustrated.

In the Eastern European *shtibel* the rabbi's main function was the study of Jewish texts. He was the highest legal, religious and scholastic representative of the Jewish community. Pastoral duties, such as visiting the sick, comforting the bereaved and even preaching were eagerly carried out by laymen. What has made the rabbi the possessor of expertise in so many areas is the abdication, by laymen in this country, of the kinds of pastoral functions which are jocularly summarized as "hatching, matching, and dispatching" (birth, weddings, and funerals). The rabbi is expert in so many areas because no one else wants to do them.

It was Salo Baron who pointed out that in an age of specialization

---

3. *Rabbinical Assembly Proceedings, 1960*, p. 137.
4. Ibid., p. 102.

492 : Judaism

it is the rabbi who has, paradoxically, despecialized. A comprehensive study of the Conservative Rabbinate in 1971, by the Martin Segal Company, found that no less than seventeen separate and distinct functions are carried out by the Conservative rabbi.[5] Whereas the psychiatrist might be capable of counseling more expertly, the professor of teaching more clearly, and the speechwriter of writing more interesting orations, none of these is in the unique position of the rabbi who executes all these functions together. He is an expert in despecialization, and, in this sense, a professional.

This expertise has been called many "dirty" names. Hertzberg, himself a rabbi, has identified the American Conservative rabbi somewhat disdainfully as an "institutional executive." Salo Baron calls him the "financial manager of his congregation."[6] Eli Ginsberg most poignantly denies any value whatsoever to rabbinical expertise which is "wasteful of a serious person's time . . . this performance as a jack of all trades makes no sense today."[7] It is pulpit rabbis, themselves, who voice the greatest frustration with this strange kind of expertise which has been foisted upon them. Their complaint is that they spend the greatest amount of time in matters which they regard as least important. While teaching is considered most crucial for many of them, they spend only eight out of a median fifty-four weekly hours in that activity.[8] The kind of mastery which they idealize is that of religious text, but sheer survival requires that they be masters of everything from warmth of personality to manipulation of persons. Thus we see that, even though the Conservative rabbis enjoy professional expertise, that expertise leaves them personally frustrated.

This expertise is a direct result of the rabbi's fulfillment of the second quality of professionalism—specialized training. Ironically, here, too, professional and personal fulfillment are not synonymous.

Louis Finkelstein, retired Chancellor of The Jewish Theological Seminary, conceives of the ideal rabbi as a person with sufficient knowledge of Talmud to decide questions of religious law. The curriculum which he shaped in quest of this image concentrated on Talmud and *halakhah* (Jewish law) in an attempt at recreating "19th century Eastern European Jewish life."[9] Unfortunately, the realities of Jewish life in Fargo, North Dakota, or even in Metuchen, New Jersey, do not require thorough knowledge of Jewish law. As a matter of fact, to the ex-

---

5. Martin E. Segal Company (Consultants and Actuaries), *The Conservative Rabbi: An Economic and Professional Profile* (New York: 1971), p. 55.
6. Salo W. Baron, *Steeled By Adversity* (Philadelphia: Jewish Publication Society of America, 1971), p. 149.
7. *Rabbinical Assembly Proceedings, 1960*, p. 27.
8. Martin E. Segal, *Op. cit.*, p. 55.
9. Charles S. Liebman, "The Training of American Rabbis," *American Jewish Yearbook*, 1968 (New York: The American Jewish Committee and JPS, 1968), p. 108.

tent that the Conservative rabbi spends his time acquiring this specialized knowledge, thus, necessarily, precluding involvement in the manifold duties which are required of him, he may suffer dire consequences. This same disparity between the specialized training of the Seminaries and the needs of the actual ministry is not limited to the rabbinate, but extends to all American religious denominations.[10] Here, too, what the Conservative rabbi gains professionally he loses personally.

Service orientation, the third prerequisite of professionalism, is already a part of the rabbi's portfolio. The rabbinate is work which is not regarded solely as a means of income, but a life-long commitment. Typically,, his service orientation, too, is fraught with all kinds of personal disappointments. In no other profession is there an inherent contradiction between service to others and personal remuneration. But from the very beginning of his education, the rabbi is encouraged to suspect an incompatibility between the two. Dr. Finkelstein's own attitude, imparted to Seminary students, is that "when you begin to be a rabbi, the salary you will receive the first year is one million dollars, plus what the congregation will give you."[11] That some rabbis themselves have internalized this view is indicated in the very statement by one rabbi that "it would be unseemly to say that the rabbi works on the Sabbath."[12] Of course, regardless of the spiritual quality of the rabbi's Sabbath duties, what he does is, indeed, expenditure of great energy, while the supermarket will not accept Dr. Finkelstein's mythical million dollars.

Rabbis share this dichotomy between service and salary with their non-Jewish counterparts. In a study of altruistic professions, by T. Parsons, clergymen, in general, are depicted as being among the most altruistic. In another study, Protestant ministers noted their financial insecurity as their main complaint, yet at the same time they feel too guilty to demand larger salaries for fear of being overconcerned with money.[14] Who does not suspect even the most dedicated clergyman who drives a Cadillac, although there is certainly no suspicion of the service orientation of a hardworking doctor who drives up in a Mercedes-Benz.

Yet studies show that motivations for entering the ministry are frequently no different from those which draw people to other occupations. The writer of a doctoral thesis which compared two generations of Seminary graduates concludes that the choice of the ministry was not the result of a special "call" but, rather, a deliberate choice of distinct pro-

---

10. Ivan A. Vallier, "Religious Specialists," *IESS* (New York: Macmillan Co.), vol. XIII, pp. 444–453.
11. *Rabbinical Assembly Proceedings, 1970,* p. 157.
12. Martin E. Segal, *Op. cit.,* p. 57.
13. T. Parsons, *The Professions and Social Structure: Essays in Sociological Theory* (Illinois: The Free Press, 1954), pp. 34–49.
14. Linda S. Elfenbein, *Career Change in the Ministry* (M. A. Thesis, Political Science Dept., Columbia University, 1970), p. 15.

fessional advantage: opportunity for study, relationship to people rather than to things, and a certain degree of status.[15] Parsons has clearly shown that there is little difference of altruistic motivation between the businessman and the professional.[16] Certainly, then, the emerging, "professional type" rabbi is no exception. How can the dichotomy between rabbinic service and rabbinic remuneration not be distressing to him?

It is argued, of course, that what the clergyman loses in income he gains in prestige. It might be comforting to the financially struggling clergyman that answers to the question, "Which one of these groups do you feel is doing the most for the country at the present time?" placed religious leaders third in 1942 and first in 1947.[17] Perhaps it is scarcity of personnel in a given occupation which brings increased functional importance and high prestige. Whatever the reason, even so critical an observer as C. Liebman concludes that "the rabbi is the most important figure in American Jewish life today."[18] Prestige replaces pennies.

Unfortunately, the clergyman is not encouraged to believe this. It is significant that "most Conservative parents rank other professions far ahead of the rabbinate."[19] It is equally true that at least the emerging professional rabbi is beginning to question the incongruence between salary and service. Precipitating the 1970 resolution at the Rabbinical Convention was an address by one of the younger men urging that rabbis "must seek adequate livelihood and concern with their personal welfare . . . idealism alone cannot provide food and clothing for a rabbi's family." That this change in attitude has already permeated future rabbis now "in training" was indicated in the Charles Liebman study which found that Jewish Theological Seminary students who are close to ordination tended to expect greater financial rewards from the rabbinate than did first year students.[20]

Nevertheless, it remains to be seen if this self-image will be aborted. Not all rabbis have resolved in their own minds the alleged contradiction between salary and service. The Jewish Digest of April 1971 reported about a rabbi who was so irritated when a congregant asked him how much he charged for a wedding that he published a sarcastic bulletin article containing a mock scale of prices. More than embarrassment, this kind of overreaction indicates that some rabbis have not yet reconciled, even to themselves, the projected higher income of real professionalism with the altruistic service which they allegedly render.

---

15. Maynard L. Cassady, *A Comparative Study of Two Generations of Theological Graduates* (Ph.D. Thesis, Columbia University, 1934), p. 161.
14. Parsons, *Op. cit.*, pp. 34–49.
17. Elmo Roper, quoted in Will Herberg, *Catholic, Protestant and Jew* (New York: Anchor Books, 1960), p. 58.
18. Liebman, *Op. cit.*, p. 5.
19. Marshall Sklare, *Conservative Judaism* (Illinois: The Free Press, 1955), p. 196.
20. Liebman, *Op. cit.*, p. 88.

The Conservative rabbi does, then, possess three prerequisites of professional status: expertise, specialized training, and service orientation, in spite of the personal frustration and inconsistencies which the very fulfillment of these requirements creates. But it is really the fourth condition of professionalism which the Conservative rabbinate does not at all possess, and until it is achieved, those who aspire to rabbinic professionalism are deluding themselves. That qualification is autonomy.

It was Marshall Sklare who most clearly documented how, historically, the Conservative Movement has been lay-oriented. Laymen fashioned rabbis in their own image. They initiated whatever changes they wanted in synagogue life and chose rabbis who preached, educated, and reinforced those changes. The personal result, for the rabbi, was that he had the worst of both worlds. Normally, a professional man accepts a salaried position when he wants to exchange income for greater security, whereas a self-employed professional prefers the greater income and will take the risk of less security. It is the rabbi, alone, among professionals, who must suffer longer hours, less security, and lower income. His job combines the worst aspects of the free and salaried professionals while enjoying none of the advantages. The backdrop for that 1970 resolution was a demand by Rabbi William Lebeau that "the necessity for many (rabbis) to curry the favor of his *ba'alei batim* in hopeful anticipation of improving his financial position is to many of us distateful and potentially destructive."[21] The Martin Segal study which resulted from that resolution revealed that high on the list of rabbinic complaints was the feeling of being a "hired hand." A joke now popular tells of a rabbi who, when asked if the eventuality of his winning the state lottery would cause him to retire from the rabbinate, responds, "No, but my sermons would surely be a lot different." Insecurity in their jobs is the most felt hindrance to preaching and teaching in the rabbinate. Autonomy, the prized possession of real professions, is not at all the property of the rabbi, and blocks whatever aspirations to total professionalism which he might have.

This lack of autonomy cuts across religious lines. The prime reason, besides low salaries, for Episcopalian ministers to leave their profession is dependence on parishioners. Conversely, those clergy belonging to strong denominational organizations have a lower rate of turnover than those controlled by lay parishioners.[22]

It is easier to diagnose the problem than to find a solution for the lack of rabbinic professionalism. One suggestion has been to strengthen the Rabbinical Assembly as a professional organization, with the ex-

---

21. William Lebeau, "The Rabbinical Assembly, A Look Toward the Future," *Rabbinical Assembly Proceedings, 1970*, pp. 96–108.
22. Elliot A. Krause, *The Sociology of Occupations* (Boston: Little, Brown and Company, 1971), p. 183.

pressed purpose of protecting its member rabbis against the abuses of "congregationalism." One of the frequent criticisms of The Rabbinical Assembly, as uncovered in the Martin Segal study, has been this lack "of moral support of colleagues in dealing with the congregation." Eli Ginsberg recommended, as far back as 1960, that rabbis organize themselves into a more effective "trade association." Interestingly, much of the resistance to this kind of solution comes from those more powerful rabbis who are really in a position to effect a change. Wolfe Kelman, executive director of The Rabbinical Assembly, has expressed his own feelings that he ". . . is not sure there isn't something to be said for the more free-wheeling and more elastic situation that exists here."[23] Of course, it is more free-wheeling for only the strongest of rabbis, whereas in the average situation the elastic stretches in the direction of congregational power and away from rabbinic autonomy. Kelman's view is unacceptable in the face of studies by sociologists like Peter Blau who have concluded that employment security is an absolute prerequisite for people to assume responsibility for innovation.[24]

More radical solutions have included the socialization of rabbinic salaries and the actual unionization of the rabbinate, perhaps even affiliation with the AFL-CIO. But the achievement of autonomy need not come through such extreme measures. Minor but vigorous adjustments would be sufficient. The Martin Segal study discouraged an episcopal type organization in favor of minimum salary standards guidelines, with the individual rabbi and congregation free to negotiate beyond that point. The mere insistence on some kind of salary standards by the parent organization would automatically bestow on a rabbi greater autonomy and, hence, a greater measure of professionalism. The Rabbinical Assembly recently took an important first step in providing its members with model contracts to be utilized, with the help with attorneys, when negotiating with congregations. But total autonomy and, therefore, total professionalization will come about only when The Rabbinical Asseembly itself provides the moral and legal backing for what is negotiated. That will finally happen when the all-important function of rabbinate placement is withheld from those congregations which do not live up to minimum standards and minimum conditions of model contracts. This kind of power has not yet been utilized, nor is there any plan to do so. With power will come autonomy. In spite of his fulfilling the other three requirements of professionalism, it is when, and only when, the Conservative rabbi achieves autonomy that he can be truly called a professional in the fullest sense of the word.

---

23. *Rabbinical Assembly Proceedings, 1960*, p. 72.
24. Peter Blau, *Bureaucracy in Modern Society* (New York: Random House, 1956), p. 61.

Acknowledgements

Bloom, Jack H. "Inner Dynamics of the Rabbinate." *Proceedings of the Rabbinical Assembly 42 (1981)*: 132–37. Reprinted with the permission of the Rabbinical Assembly. Courtesy of the Rabbinical Assembly.

Cohen, Arthur. "The Seminary and the Modern Rabbi." Conservative Judaism 13 (1959): 1–12. Reprinted with the permission of the Rabbinical Assembly. Courtesy of Yale University Divinity Library.

Glazer, Nathan. "The Function of the Rabbi." *Central Conference of American Rabbis, Yearbook* (1967): 130–142. Reprinted with the permission of CCAR Press. Courtesy of the Rabbinical Assembly.

Gordis, Robert. "The Role of the Rabbi Today." *Conservative Judaism* 3 (1947): 14–22. Reprinted with the permission of the Rabbinical Assembly. Courtesy of Yale University Divinity Library.

Greenberg, Ephraim. "The Rabbinate—A Restless Body of Men." *Conservative Judaism* 14 (1960): 17–28. Reprinted with the permission of the Rabbinical Assembly. Courtesy of Yale University Divinity Library.

Greenberg, Simon. "The Rabbinate and the Jewish Community Structure." *Conservative Judaism* 23 (1969): 52–59. Reprinted with the permission of the Rabbinical Assembly. Courtesy of Yale University Divinity Library.

Hertzberg, Arthur. "The Changing American Rabbinate." *Midstream* 12 (1966): 16–29. Reprinted with the permission of the Theodor Herzl Foundation, Inc. Courtesy of Yale University Sterling Memorial Library.

Himmelfarb, Milton. "The Intellectual and the Rabbi." *Proceedings of the Rabbinical Assembly* 27 (1963): 118–32. Reprinted with the permission of the Rabbinical Assembly. Courtesy of the Rabbinical Assembly.

Kelman, Wolfe. "The Synagogue in America." In David Sidorsky, ed., *The Future of the Jewish Community in America* (New York: Basic Books, Inc., Publishers,

1973): 155–75. Reprinted with the permission of the American Jewish Congress. Courtesy of Yale University Social Science Library.

Lenn, Theodore I. "The End Is Where We Start From...." In Theodore I. Lenn, ed., *Rabbi and Synagogue in Reform Judaism* (New York: Central Conference of American Rabbis, 1972): 384–407. Reprinted with the permission of Central Conference of American Rabbis Press. Courtesy of Yale University Sterling Memorial Library.

Rabinowitz, Stanley. "The Changing Rabbinate: A Search for Definition." *Proceedings of the Rabbinical Assembly* 37 (1975): 51–60; Arthur Hertzberg. "The Changing Rabbinate." *Ibid.*: 61–70. Reprinted with the permission of the Rabbinical Assembly. Courtesy of the Rabbinical Assembly.

Reichert, Victor E., Marcus Kramer and Ephraim F. Einhorn. "The Inner Life of the Rabbi." *Central Conference of American Rabbis, Yearbook* 69 (1960): 177–82. Reprinted with the permission of CCAR Press. Courtesy of Yale University Sterling Memorial Library.

Routtenberg, Max J. "The American Rabbi in Transition." *Proceedings of the Rabbinical Assembly* 30 (1966): 1–12. Reprinted with the permission of the Rabbinical Assembly. Courtesy of the Rabbinical Assembly.

Rubenstein, Richard L. "A Rabbi Dies." In Jacob Neusner, ed., *American Judaism: Adventure in Modernity* (Englewood Cliffs, NJ: Prentice-Hall, Inc., 1972): 46–59. Reprinted with the permission of the author. Courtesy of Yale University Sterling Memorial Library.

Rubenstein, Richard. "Studying at Hebrew Union College, 1942–1945." *Midstream* 20 (1974): 68–74. Reprinted with the permission of the Theodor Herzl Foundation, Inc. Courtesy of Yale University Sterling Memorial Library.

A Symposium: Arnold Jacob Wolf, Daniel Jeremy Silver, Sheldon Zimmerman, Mark Loeb, Ira Eisenstein, Emanuel Rackman, Eugene Weiner, Eugene B. Borowitz, Arthur Green, Seymour Siegel, Charles S. Liebman. "The Future of Rabbinic Training in America." *JUDAISM* 18 (1969): 387–420. Reprinted with the permission of *JUDAISM*. Courtesy of Yale University Sterling Memorial Library.

Zelizer, Viviana A. and Gerald L. Zelizer. "The Conservative Rabbinate—In Quest of Professionalism." *JUDAISM* 22 (1973): 490–96. Reprinted with the permission of *JUDAISM*. Courtesy of Yale University Sterling Memorial Library.